CHESTER HIMES

CHESTER HIMES

A Critical Appraisal

Stephen F. Milliken

University of Missouri Press
Columbia, 1976

Copyright © 1976 by The Curators of the University of Missouri
University of Missouri, Columbia, Missouri 65201
Library of Congress Catalog Card Number 75-44081
Printed and bound in the United States of America
All rights reserved

Library of Congress Cataloging in Publication Data

Milliken, Stephen F
    Chester Himes.

    Bibliography: p. 309
    1. Himes, Chester B., 1909–   Criticism and interpretation.
PS3515.1713Z7   813'.5'4   75-44081
ISBN 0-8262-0190-3

Permission for the quotations from Chester Himes's novels has been
given by Roslyn Targ Literary Agency, Inc., 250 West 57th Street, New
York, New York 10017: *The Real Cool Killers*, copyright © Chester Himes
1969; *The Crazy Kill*, copyright © Chester Himes 1959; *All Shot Up*,
copyright © by Chester Himes 1960; *The Heat's On*, copyright © 1966
by Chester Himes; *For Love of Imabelle*, copyright © 1965 by Chester
Himes; *Pinktoes*, copyright © 1961, 1965 by Chester Himes; *Cotton Comes
to Harlem*, copyright © 1965 by Chester Himes; *Blind Man with a Pistol*,
copyright © 1969 by Chester Himes; *If He Hollers Let Him Go*, copyright
© 1945 by Chester B. Himes; *Cast the First Stone*, copyright 1952 by
Chester Himes; *The Third Generation*, copyright 1954 by Chester Himes;
The Primitive, copyright 1955 by Chester Himes; *Lonely Crusade*, copyright
1947 by Chester Himes, copyright 1975 by Chester Himes.
    Quotations from *The Quality of Hurt*, copyright © 1971, 1972 by Chester
Himes, and *Black on Black*, copyright © 1973 by Chester Himes, reprinted
by permission of Doubleday & Company, Inc.
    Quotations from "My Man Himes: An Interview with Chester Himes,"
by John A. Williams, copyright © 1970, in *Amistad I*, edited by John A.
Williams and Charles F. Harris, reprinted by permission of Random
House, Inc.

Preface

Chester Himes was born in Jefferson City, Missouri, on July 29, 1909. He is the author of many books, including *If He Hollers Let Him Go, Lonely Crusade, Cast the First Stone, The Third Generation, The Primitive, Run Man Run, Cotton Comes to Harlem, Blind Man with a Pistol, Pinktoes, The Quality of Hurt,* and *Black on Black.* He is a black American.

My purpose in this work is to present my personal impressions of his novels, novellas, and short stories and to argue my conviction that he is one of the great writers of our time.

One goal that every critic who discusses black American literature should set himself, I feel, is to write in such a manner that no reader will be able to determine with any certainty whether the critic himself is black or white. If he does not, his comments will trigger automatic reactions of prejudice—some negative, some positive—that will almost certainly bar his opinions from whatever serious consideration they might merit. I doubt that I have succeeded in reaching this goal, but I do hope that I may have slightly confused at least a few readers, on this one point only.

Chronology

1909—Chester Bomar Himes born in Jefferson City, Missouri, July 29.

1926—Suffers serious back injuries in a fall down a hotel elevator shaft. Drops out of Ohio State University at Columbus in his second quarter.

1928—Sentenced to twenty years in the Ohio State Penitentiary for armed robbery.

1932—Publishes first stories in black magazines.

1934—Publishes first story in *Esquire*.

1936—Released on parole from Ohio State Penitentiary.

1945—Publication of his first novel, *If He Hollers Let Him Go*.

1947—*Lonely Crusade*.

1952—*Cast the First Stone*.

1953—Leaves the United States to reside permanently in Europe.

1954—*The Third Generation*.

1955—*The Primitive*.

1957–1969—Publishes Harlem detective novellas in France and the United States.

1961—*Pinktoes*.

1972—*The Quality of Hurt*.

1973—*Black on Black*.

Contents

1

Introduction

Himes in Focus

I The Critic and Chester Himes

The central critical problem presented by the great body of fiction published by the American novelist Chester Bomar Himes is easy to state, difficult to resolve. His work has obvious power. It moves the reader enormously, involves him completely. Yet at all points in every part of Himes's work, weaknesses of the most obvious kind are evident. The author seems continually to be opting for the worst of two possible routes, to be choosing, for example, the more striking effect for its impact value alone, or to be choosing the most tired cliché available in full and triumphant knowledge of its falsity and tawdriness. He can in fact be embarrassingly bad, and yet the apparent weaknesses in Himes's work seem somehow to be essential to the strengths. Himes is a writer who is frequently thrilling and often exasperating. His work cannot be approached apologetically—it is too obviously strong for that—but neither is it a suitable subject for conventional encomiums. The critic who discusses Himes's work has to accept the uncomfortable stance of the self-contradictor. He may very well find himself discussing a particular passage in terms alternately condemnatory and adulatory. In spite of his best efforts at clarity, he will at times appear to be attacking work he admires or to be praising aspects of it that he deplores. Himes's work succeeds, but it does so in violation of some of the most fundamental rules the critic can prescribe for literary success.

Chester Himes has always been above all else a man who does not take advice. His work is totally innocent of the smooth, professional polish of the writer who has been told ad nauseam, to the point of final belief, in dozens of creative-writing classes and workshops, that you simply cannot do everything at once, that art involves choice, that final solutions have been found to many writing problems, that models that work do exist, and that in the end every writer must submit himself to the exigencies and expectancies of the typical cultivated reader. Chester Himes never even entertained the notion that his writing could be more effective if it were motivated by anything other than pure Himesian impulse and instinct. His work is ferociously idiosyncratic. It is a completely personal chaos, but one that does communicate. It does somehow capture the ever-elusive reader, often in defiance of logic.

The critic must concede much more than the apparent irrelevance of many of his own strictures, however, when considering the special qualities of Himes's work. He must also apply with extraordinary caution whatever Aristotelian, or neo-Aristotelian, categories he is personally committed to. Few writers resist classification as persistently as Himes. He is, very nearly, sui generis.

Himes is a black American, and inevitably—in spite of his own very different ambitions—the role of spokesman for the race was thrust upon him as a writer. Few categories could have suited him less, yet he could not put pen to paper without telling the story of his people, and, from the beginning, critics insisted on judging his writing, to his own immense disgust, solely on its value as "protest." In addition to its special provinces, Himes's work treats—and this is true too of all the important modern black American writers—every aspect of the human condition, the complete plight of twentieth-century man. The harsh issues of race and racism in Himes's work are immensely important, but they are very far from being the only issues treated. Every fully committed writer is of one time and one people, but also of all times and all people, and there can be no question as to the completeness of Himes's commitment.

To attempt to single out one set of concerns in an artist's work as more important than others is much like trying to decide which of the vital organs of the human body is the most vital. Himes, like every true writer, has given up his entire life to the effort to articulate his experience, to reduce it to literary form—all of it, and not just one selected segment. His writing is totally honest, brutally and even viciously honest. He acknowledges no limitations on what he can or will tell. He has told his own story, and that of the people he knew, Americans, both black and white, in a time of disintegrating cultures and agonizing clashes. He has told it as he has lived it, with passion, bias, and anger, and a compulsive integrity that pierces beyond everything else.

He is black and a writer, both to a supreme degree, but the category "black writer" cannot contain him. Like all labels, it explains much and conceals more and must be regarded with suspicion as well as respect.

There is, quite obviously, on the other hand, no way that the critic of Himes's work can escape dealing with the label "black writer." An essential component of the task of understanding and describing Himes's work is in grasping to what extent this term does apply, and the ways in which it applies. The label must be closely challenged, but it cannot by any means be discarded without hopelessly distorting any attempt at a discussion of Himes's writing.

Every black American brings special credentials to his work, which cannot be ignored. The black writer, alone among American writers, fully understands the phenomenon of racism, which is at the same time one of the most basic and one of the least understood aspects of American life. Only the black man knows—and lives with the knowledge—that no single individual among us, black or white, has completely escaped this crippling disease of the spirit. He alone understands, with the special insight of the chosen victim, how futile, how empty, are the subterfuges that most Americans resort to to persuade themselves that they are free of this degrading sentiment.

Racism is a process of inflicting pain through a thousand subtle ways of indicating rejection, refusal of brotherhood, and only the black man has actually felt that pain in its most extreme forms. The black writer has supplied the cry of rage before the universality of this evil that was so long lacking in our literature.

But the black writer's uncomfortable secret knowledge, purchased through pain, is also one that is supremely difficult to communicate. Every one of us has firm convictions, basically inflexible views, on the American racial question, and few care to have these views disturbed by writers possessed of deeper and clearer insights. Edmund Dantès, the fictitious Count of Monte Cristo—the creation of an earlier writer of partially African ancestry—scraped away stubbornly through endless days at the stone walls of his dungeon with the fragments of a broken jug and a saucepan, hoping desperately to make contact with another human being. The situation of the modern black writer is scarcely less difficult.

In addition to "black," there exists a series of other labels that conveniently categorize writing—*serious, satire, naturalism, protest, humor, realism, allegory*—which must also be approached by the Himes critic with strong misgivings and which he cannot in any way avoid. They pertain, in ways seemingly inevitably paradoxical, to the shape and circumstances of Chester Himes's literary career and achievement.

At about the halfway point in his career, Himes abandoned the "serious" novels he had labored at so long to write a series of detective novellas, but he remained one of the most deadly serious writers of his time within the forms and traditions of this apparently frivolous "popular" genre.

The bitter laugh of the dedicated satirist runs through much of Himes's work, but nowhere is there to be found the limpid moral certainty of the greatest satirists. And Himes's laughter is jubilant and gay as often as it is bitter.

His favorite subject was pain, and it screams in naked release on almost every page he has written, but justice, easily the most turgid and pompous of literary subjects, is invoked only slightly less often.

In his youth Himes served a long term in prison, and at times his writing has the glacial hardness that tends to characterize much of the work of those writers, from Dostoevski to Dalton Trumbo, who have been purged in that particular scale model of hell. Moreover, disturbing shadows of sadism flicker through many of Himes's lovingly detailed descriptions of violence. Yet it is always with the victim that this writer identifies, even when the victim is white and the assailant black. And he can be guilty of the most egregious sentimentalism wherever young lovers are involved.

John A. Williams has written: "Himes is perhaps the single greatest naturalistic American writer living today. Of course, no one in the literary establishment is going to admit that; they haven't and they won't."[1] The label "naturalistic" is a particularly attractive one, suggesting as it does the extraordinary fidelity of Himes's fiction to his actual experience, but this label too needs to be challenged. Himes is preeminently a writer who is fully aware of the gap that separates art from life, of the permanent incapacity of art to capture fully the complexity of life itself. His style can veer sharply from soberly conventional naturalism to the most radical extremes of surrealism. He is forever seeking the form that will fit, and he never denies to his characters the full range of contradictions that he finds in himself.

Himes's work is social, personal, symbolic, and frankly commercial. It is bleak tragedy, sophisticated parody, hearty folk humor, and storytelling for the sheer excitement of story itself. It operates on many levels, unleashing echoes from abysmal psychic depths, and the raffish charm of the huckster out to capture a popular audience, on his own terms.

The critic who discusses Himes's work may hope to find the key to a synthesis, the secret of the harmony that must bind together all of the elements in the seeming chaos of art, but he must be aware at all times that the greatest danger he affronts is that of oversimplifying an authentically complex figure.

II Himes and Black American Literature

The closely autobiographical novel *The Primitive* (1955) contains some of Himes's sharpest and clearest statements on the situation of the black writer in America. The protagonist, Jesse Robinson, is a struggling black writer who is in many important respects indistinguishable from Himes himself. Even physically,

1. John A. Williams, "My Man Himes: An Interview with Chester Himes," in John A. Williams and Charles F. Harris, eds., *Amistad I*, pp. 76, 77.

with his "trim, muscular body, the color of Manila paper, with the broad-shouldered proportions of a pugilist,"[2] Jesse Robinson is twin to Chester Himes.

In one short scene of this novel Himes brings Jesse face to face with the full range of prejudices and preconceptions he felt the black writer encountered in the plush offices of the publishing world, personified in a pontificating "liberal" white editor named, not unexpectedly, Pope:

> Pope's face resumed its customary expression of shame and guilt, like that of a man who's murdered his mother and thrown her body in the well, to be forever afterwards haunted by her sweet smiling face.
>
> "I'm afraid I have bad news for you."
>
> Jesse just looked at him, thinking, "Whatever bad news you got for me—as if I didn't know—you're going to have to say it without me helping you. I'm one of those ungracious niggers."
>
> "We're given your book six readings and Mr. Hobson has decided to drop the option."
>
> Jesse had been prepared for this from the moment he'd read Pope's letter and now, before the reaction had set in, he just felt argumentative. "I thought you were going to cut it."
>
> Pope reddened slightly. "That was my opinion. I like the book. I fought for it all the way. I think all it needs is cutting. But Hobson thinks it reads like fictional autobiography. And he doesn't like the title."
>
> "I Was Looking for a Street," Jesse quoted, turning it over in his mind. "I was looking for a street that I could understand," he thought, and for a moment he was lost in memory of the search.
>
> "He said it sounds like a visiting fireman looking for a prostitute's address," Pope said with his apologetic smile.
>
> Jesse laughed, "That ought to make it sell."
>
> Pope again assumed his look of guilt and shame. "The truth is, fiction is doing very poorly. We're having our worst year for fiction."
>
> "Why not publish it as autobiography then?"
>
> "It would be the same. Hobson thinks the public is fed up

2. Himes, The Primitive, p. 25.

with protest novels. And I must say, on consideration, I agree with him."

"What's protest about this book?" Jesse argued. "If anything, it's tragedy. But no protest."

"The consensus of the readers was that it's too sordid. It's pretty strong—almost vulgar, some of it."

"Then what about Rabelais? The education of Gargantua? What's more vulgar than that?"

Pope blinked at him in disbelief. "But surely you realize that was satire? Rabelais was satirizing the humanist Renaissance—and certainly some of the best satire ever written ... this—" tapping the manuscript neatly wrapped in brown paper on his desk—"is protest. It's vivid enough, but it's humorless. And there is too much bitterness and not enough just plain animal fun—"

"I wasn't writing about animals. . . ."

"The reader is gripped in a vise of despair and bitterness from start to finish. . . ."

"I thought some of it was funny."

"Funny!" Pope stared at him incredulously.

"That part where the parents wear evening clothes to the older son's funeral," Jesse said, watching Pope's expression and thinking, "What could be more funny than some niggers in evening clothes? I bet you laugh like hell at Amos and Andy on television."

Pope looked as if he had suddenly been confronted by a snake, but was too much of a gentleman to enquire of the snake if it were poisonous.

"All right, maybe you don't think that's funny. . . ."

"That made me cry," Pope accused solemnly.

"I suppose you think I didn't cry when I wrote it," Jesse thought, but aloud he continued, "But how do you make out that it's protest?"

Looking suddenly lost, Pope said, "You killed one son and destroyed the other, killed the father and ruined the mother . . ." and Jesse thought, "So you find some streets too that you don't understand," and then, "Yes, that makes it protest, all right. Negroes must always live happily and never die."

Aloud he argued, "What about Hamlet? Shakespeare destroyed everybody and killed everybody in that one."

Pope shrugged, "Shakespeare."

Jesse shrugged. "Jesus Christ. It's a good thing he isn't living now. His friends would never get a book published about him."

Pope laughed. "You're a hell of a good writer, Jesse. Why don't you write a Negro success novel? An inspirational story? The public is tired of the plight of the poor down-trodden Negro."

"I don't have that much imagination." (*The Primitive*, 93–94)

Like Jesse Robinson, Himes is determinedly "ungracious." If his humor does not always make his readers cry, it at least never fails to make them acutely uncomfortable, and he does routinely supply, for their further discomfort, "a vise of despair and bitterness." More important, he too rejected the narrow limitations he felt publishers tried to impose on the black writer, and their low horizon of expectations where black writers were concerned implied in their special use of the term *protest*. Like the stubbornly argumentative Jesse, Himes possessed the massive ego of the consciously talented and aspired to comparison with the greatest figures of Western literature. He wanted to be judged on his merits as an individual and not as a member of a group, however sympathetic he might find the group. He confidently believed—not entirely without reason—that his not infrequent excursions into vulgarity were Rabelaisian and that his characteristic unchecked exuberance was Shakespearian.

Nevertheless, among the mass of sterile preconceptions haltingly suggested by the professionally apologetic Pope, there exists a certain amount of solid substance. In this passage Himes deliberately confronts a type of criticism he despised but could not dismiss. He allows Pope, who can see and speak only in terms of stereotypes, to accurately delineate traits of his own work that are at the same time traits of the work of black writers in general. The game is that of devil's advocate, and, though Himes's devil is obviously an ass, he is allowed to kick with both force and precision. The passage is Himes's characterization of the kind of black writer he typified, seen from the standpoint of the literary establishment. In this passage he subjects himself to a kind of trial, a searching and resolutely hostile self-examination that must have been extraordinarily painful. Jesse, who has little of his creator's toughness, emerges from his interview with Pope irreparably damaged.

Pope quickly pinpoints, with implacable complacency, two of the most evident distinguishing characteristics of the work of the leading black American writers, including Chester Himes: first, a degree of complexity in the humor that makes it extremely difficult to grasp; second, an excessive subjectivism, a compulsive preoccupation with self verging on narcissism, recognizable in a marked reluctance ever to get very far from straight autobiography. Black writers, Pope implies, are capable of little beyond the heavy-handed presentation of their private litanies of woe. And any humor they may attempt is certain to bog down in self-indulgent eccentricity.

These traits are, of course, also to be found in the work of many other modern writers, most notably James Joyce, the most elusively introspective and deviously humorous of writers. In addition, Joyce was the unwilling spokesman of an embattled colonial people, and, much like such prominent black American writers as Richard Wright, Chester Himes, and James Baldwin, he found it expedient to pass a major part of his writing career in voluntary exile in Europe in order to preserve intact the inner certainties and private memories that were to be his literary material. But the complex humor and compulsive egocentrism of James Joyce differ markedly in quality from those of Wright, Himes, and Baldwin; his were the products of less brutal pressures, less stringent limitations. Joyce was in rebellion against and in flight from vulgarity, ugly banality, and the nagging distractions of present and, therefore, insistent reality. What the black American writers sought was, quite simply, a refuge from the constant threat of physical and psychological violence. And violence is a singularly effective psychological marker, in a class all by itself as a literary influence.

In *Lonely Crusade* (1947), Himes limned the portrait of the typical black intellectual, in the murky thoughts and blunt words of a "Negro hustler and criminal," his horrendous Luther Mc-Gregor:

The way he figured it, such a Negro should be smarter than any white man who ever breathed, having gotten the white folks' education and know-how from the white folks, their own damn selves, on top of all the nigger wisdom that had been kicked up his black ass.[3]

For most of the protagonists of Himes's early novels, black intellectuals all—and in large part impressionistic portraits of Himes himself—the "kicking" that Luther mentions is a very literal process. For Bob Jones of *If He Hollers Let Him Go* (1945), life holds little else:

A guy leaned over the hole and swung at my head with a ball-peen hammer. I was going down forward with my hands on the railings and saw the hammer coming. It didn't look like a hard blow; it looked as though it floated into me. I saw the guy's face, not particularly malevolent, just disfigured, a white man hitting at a nigger running by. But I couldn't do a thing; I couldn't let go the railing to get my hands up; couldn't even duck. I didn't feel the blow; just the explosion starting at a point underneath my skull and filling my head with a great flaming roar.[4]

The experience of the black man in America unquestionably represents a totally unique episode in human history. Citizen of a nation that offered unprecedentedly rich ideological and material opportunities, the black American found himself, at the same time, confronted by impassable barriers that existed for him alone, barriers maintained by violence, and by law. The contrast between the bright and the dark is duplicated in the experience of no other people. No other people was promised so much and given so little. Not even the extraordinary men who become great writers can be expected to pass unmarked through conditions that are special to such a degree. The black American experience left indelible marks on all who survived it.

An intense preoccupation with self is natural and inevitable in a man who has been confronted from childhood with a pious establishment's insistent denial of his full humanity. And the dom-

3. Himes, *Lonely Crusade*, p. 325.
4. Himes, *If He Hollers Let Him Go*, pp. 170–71.

inance of the autobiographical element in black American writing extends even into the purest abstractions of the allegory of protest. Richard Wright's insistence on personally playing the role of Bigger Thomas in the film version of *Native Son* is a notable case in point. However crudely stereotyped the violent and lumpish Bigger might have seemed to many of that novel's critics, to Richard Wright, Bigger was first of all an image of himself. The black writer's fiction is always uncomfortably close to lived experience. The anger that Chester Himes's characters express is his own anger, and more often than not, it is aimed directly at the reader. Power, the shocking immediacy of personal confession, is purchased at the expense of aesthetic distance.

The black writer's "difficult" humor is also rooted directly in his special experience. This humor that merges in perfect harmony with the harshest and most despairing views of human life is closely related to a gut-level existentialism that the black man has no need to formulate in intellectual terms, an unshakable conviction that the world is indeed absurd based on a lifetime of absurd experience. The black man's greatest pride is in what he believes to be his total freedom from comforting illusions, the special toughness he possesses that enables him to gaze without flinching on the grim realities of his life. This mordant pride is the dominant note in the laughing–crying blues lyrics and in the coldly raucous humor of the great black comedians, humor that is curiously akin to horror and sorrow—and this pride in the toughness to be free is also the existential stance of "authenticity" in its purest form. It is thus not at all surprising that when black American writers like Wright, Himes, and Baldwin turned up in the intellectual circles of Paris in the early fifties they met with instant acceptance as fully established initiates. As black men they had from the beginning of their lives no choice but to live by the existentialist attitude; agonizing, total awareness of the absurdity of modern Western experience had been thrust upon them. Richard Wright's friendship with Jean-Paul Sartre was emblematic of this special rapport that exists between the black experience in America and European existentialist theory. The traumas of war had momentarily freed French intellectuals from the characteristic Western optimism that still blinded white

America. They easily perceived the greatness of these black American writers. It was in Paris, working with a French translator, that Chester Himes found for the first time an open market for his writing, and an editor for whom he was simply a writer whose work should sell.

Although the black author's humor is difficult to grasp, and has evident links with the unfunny existentialist "absurd," this humor is still distinctly funny. It is in part a scream of anger before the iniquities of our society, yet it excites laughter that is much deeper than mere nervous titters. Himes's Jesse answers his impenetrably indifferent editor's bland insistence that his novel is "protest" with the paradoxical assertions that it is both "tragedy" and "funny." Significantly, in their classical origins comedy and tragedy were recognized as kindred genres, both forms implying the most complete confidence in the fundamental worth and dignity of every facet of the human phenomenon. And this affirmation of the value of life itself, this much lamented "lost" dimension of ancient literature, is inescapably present everywhere in black American folklore, in the lyrics of the blues, in the humor of the black comedians, and in the literature nourished by these sources.

In an article first published in 1966 in John A. Williams's anthology *Beyond the Angry Black*, Himes wrote:

> There is an indomitable quality within the human spirit that can not be destroyed; a face deep within the human personality that is impregnable to all assaults. . . . we would be drooling idiots, dangerous maniacs, raving beasts—if it were not for that quality and force within all humans that cries "I will live."[5]

Himes's confidence in the existence and universality of this mysterious central core of humanness justifies—or at least explains —much of the easy ranging from tone to tone that characterizes his work. Confronted with so basic a unity all differences must seem transient illusions. Laughter can blend into frustration and pain, and a man may be gaily bitter or passionately "cool." The

---

5. Abraham Chapman, ed., *New Black Voices* (New York: New American Library, A Mentor Book, 1972), p. 400.

only error would be to present drooling idiots instead of men, men simultaneously happy and tormented. Himes is a very angry writer but a substantial part of his total work is nevertheless devoted to the elaborate development of consciously comic situations. At times, in the most serious novels, the action is unexpectedly held up for a page or more to allow him to insert a joke that is convulsing him at the moment. He is, among many other things, a very funny writer, one of the great masters of gallows humor in our fiction.

There is, however, one item in the barrage of solemn accusations that Pope levels at Jesse, Himes, and black writers in general that is allowed to pass unchallenged—the absence of "just plain animal fun." Jesse has instant and effective rebuttals for charges of flat humorlessness and autobiographical hang-ups, but to the charge that his work lacks spontaneity and gusto and a full awareness of the importance of the senses, he can only answer lamely, "I wasn't writing about animals." The stricture does have, within narrow limits, some justification, particularly for the novel of Himes that most closely fits the descriptions given of Jesse's manuscript, his starkly tragic The Third Generation (1954). There is, too, a characteristic dourness in most of the work of Himes's generation of black writers, the pivotal generation dominated by Richard Wright whose emergence marked a dramatic turning away from the paths of the earliest figures, from Dunbar and Chesnutt through Cullen, with their full acceptance of the forms of the white literary establishments —and even, on occasion, of white concepts of black men—and their heavy emphasis on entertainment values, faintly punctuated by dim echoes of muted protest. The brief, brilliant episode of the Harlem Renaissance dignified the trend without reversing it. Richard Wright's new note was one of angry, strident protest, undisguised fury, and for a time he carried all new black literature with him. When the vogue for Wrightian protest had passed, however, a new group of black writers of greater depth and wider range came into prominence. Himes was both one of those that first followed Wright, and one of those that remained to exploit the richer possibilities that Wright's unprecedented success had opened up.

The "protest" genre involved deliberate limitations that Himes was quick to perceive and to repudiate. "Just plain animal fun" was perhaps the most conspicuous desideratum in his work in the first stage of his career, but it was soon to become one of its most prominent features. Mr. Pope was in part a vehicle for the expression of Himes's own self-doubts, his harshest criticisms of his own work and that of his contemporaries. And, in Himes's case, the capacity for doubt held the promise of growth.

In *Nobody Knows My Name* James Baldwin—who remembered "the tough and loyal figure of Chester Himes" as a witness to some of his own famous confrontations with Richard Wright in Paris—was one of the first to see in Himes a breaker of boundaries, an explorer of new territories: "In most of the novels written by Negroes until today (with the exception of Chester Himes's *If He Hollers Let Him Go*) there is a great space where sex ought to be; and what usually fills this space is violence."[6] In the foreword to *Black on Black* (1973), a very miscellaneous collection of his shorter pieces, Himes himself gave sex an important place in his oddly assorted range of literary concerns: "These writings are admittedly chauvinistic. You will conclude if you read them that BLACK PROTEST and BLACK HETEROSEXUALITY are my two chief obsessions."[7] Sex appears in his pages, though, less as an obsession—few writers are more truly at ease with the subject—than a delightful mystery, an elusive quality of magic he never tires of pursuing. Ishmael Reed, a notable connoisseur of the more subtle nuances of the black "soul" mystique, dedicated his anthology *19 Necromancers from Now* (1970) to Chester Himes, "The Great Mojo Bojo" (master of occult knowledge), suggesting in that one phrase the fascination of Himes's more delicate probings into the puzzles of human personality more accurately than has Himes himself in all of his own trenchant and ruthlessly unapologetic self-criticisms.[8] The magician is not always the best judge of the effects he produces.

6. James Baldwin, *Nobody Knows My Name* (New York: Dell Publishing Co., Inc., 1963), pp. 151, 167.

7. Himes, *Black on Black*, p. 7.

8. Ishmael Reed, ed., *19 Necromancers from Now* (Garden City: Doubleday Anchor Books, 1970), p. x.

Himes's relation to the brotherhood of black writers has been both that of maverick and of leader, though in recent years, as his popularity and influence among the younger black writers have steadily and rapidly increased, his role as leader has become more and more prominent. In a freewheeling interview with John A. Williams at Himes's home in Spain, published in Williams's *Amistad I* in 1970, Himes suggested some of the peculiar difficulties that beset the writer who must belong both to himself and to a struggling people:

"What is he [any black writer] saying about the conditions of the black people in America?" Well, most black writers have something to say about this because most black writers from America—what else can they say, what else can they write about, what else do they think about? So that is why it becomes an absolute part of their writing, because it's part of their thinking. But I don't think it's all done deliberately— just to sit down and make a statement; it's subconscious. . . . to sit down and deliberately do so, results in a tract which often gets away from the author.[9]

He assured Williams that he had arrived at a new level of optimism in his thinking, grimly explaining that he now believed that black people had at last found the solution to racism: "organized violence to the saturation point."[10] Something more similar to ordinary optimism is evident in his comfortable assumption that it is possible for a writer to have the best of both possible worlds, leaving all questions of both personal integrity

9. Williams, "My Man Himes," pp. 76, 77. On May 15, 1969, during the same week that Williams conducted his interview sessions with Himes, Himes was also interviewed by Hoyt Fuller. Fuller's interview appeared in the March 1972 issue of *Black World*, an issue devoted to Himes's work, career, and opinions. The Fuller interview is almost completely unedited, without attention to transitions, continuity, or clarification and seems to have been intended primarily for readers who were already thoroughly familiar with the Williams interview. It covers the same topics and elicits the same opinions, often in almost the same words. Several important points of fact, however, which will be noted below, are stated much more explicitly by Himes in the Hoyt Fuller interview. Hoyt Fuller, "Traveler on the Long, Rough, Lonely Old Road: An Interview with Chester Himes," pp. 4–22, 87–98.

10. Williams, "My Man Himes," p. 60.

and ideological fidelity to the trusty subconscious. Black writing, he suggested to Williams, could find its triumphant future in a generation of writers who were completely true to themselves, freed of all inhibitions, social, esthetic, or psychological:

> And it is conceivable, since black people are creative people, that they might form on the strength of these creations an entirely new literature that will be more valuable than the output of the white community. . . .
> . . . Well, I would like to see produced a novel that just drains a person's subconscious of all his attitudes and reactions to everything. Because, obviously, if one person has a number of thoughts concerning anything, there is a cohesion. There has to be because they belong to one man. Just let it come out as the words generate in the mind, let it come out in the phrasing of the subconscious and let it become a novel in that form. . . . Since the black American is subject to having millions of thoughts concerning everything, millions of reactions, and his reactions and thoughts will obviously be different from that of the white community, this should create an entirely different structure of the novel.[11]

This was not so much a program for the future for other writers as as account of Himes's own practice through the years.

One result of the complete creative freedom he allowed himself was a work greater in sheer extent than that of most of his contemporaries—"Well," Williams remarked, "you know the younger black writers back home always say that Chester Himes has given away more books than most people have ever written."[12] Himes's creative energies, in a lifetime filled with a staggering assortment of personal disasters, have proved equal to the creation of an *oeuvre*: a body of published work large enough to expose the full range of his thought and sensitivity. He has continually pursued one particular set of themes, but he has never quite repeated himself. Each work adds something essential to the whole. It is in the completeness of his work above all that he is unique among modern black writers. He alone has succeeded in

---

11. Ibid., pp. 69–73; cf. Fuller, "Interview with Chester Himes," pp. 15, 97.

12. Williams, "My Man Himes," p. 33.

traveling the full route and in closing the circle. For some forty years, through all his frustrations and personal defeats, he was stubbornly true to his vocation as a writer. Even after he had published some of his most widely reviewed novels, Chester Himes was obliged to accept the most menial jobs to earn his living: porter, doorman, butler, typist, handyman. Jesse Robinson, of *The Primitive*, whose situation was precisely similar, vainly sought consolation in the motley relics of his trade:

> Inside the cabinet, behind the closed doors, were his stacks of unpublished manuscripts, carbon copies, old papers, and letters which he always kept nearby, carting them from place to place, hanging on to them year after year, to remind himself that—no matter what he did for a living—he was a writer by profession. (*The Primitive*, 24)

Himes's own identification with writing was far more determined:

> No matter what I did, or where I was, or how I lived, I had considered myself a writer ever since I'd published my first story in *Esquire* when I was still in prison in 1934. Foremost a writer. Above all else a writer. It was my salvation, and is. The world can deny me all other employment, and stone me as an ex-convict, as a nigger, as a disagreeable and unpleasant person. But as long as I write, whether it is published or not, I'm a writer, and no one can take that away. "A fighter fights, a writer writes," so I must have done my writing.[13]

Though he was sometimes accused of betraying or maligning the race, the very existence of his *oeuvre* is proof that in his own highly personal and perhaps self-indulgent way, he fulfilled the promise of his talent and delivered his full testimony as witness and artist.

13. Himes, *The Quality of Hurt: The Autobiography of Chester Himes*, Volume I, p. 117; cf., Himes, *The Primitive*, p. 100, and Williams, "My Man Himes," p. 44, for the line, "A fighter fights, a writer writes."

2

Take a Giant Step

Himes's Beginnings as a Writer

I One Snowy Night

The night of Sunday, November 25, 1928, was freezing cold with snow flurries and driving westerly winds in Cleveland, Ohio, and for Samuel Miller and his wife, residents of an exclusive section of the Cleveland Heights suburb, it was to be a terrifying night. They returned to their home on Fairmount Boulevard very late, very tired, and suddenly found themselves confronted with an almost hysterical young black gunman, who had forced his way into their home to rob them. The man with the gun was Chester Bomar Himes, nineteen years old, very handsome, very intelligent and sensitive, and completely desperate, but all that mattered to the Millers was the enormous pistol he waved at their heads with murderous intensity.

Himes has described that night many times. In one of his earliest stories, the novella "Prison Mass" serialized in the black magazine *Abbott's Monthly* in 1933 while Himes was still serving his prison term, the events concerning his intrusion into the Millers' home are retraced in precise detail, in the reveries of one of the central characters, nicknamed Brightlights, a young black convict who is attempting to become a writer. Brightlights cannot wrench his mind from the events that brought him to prison: "He could picture again the enacting of that little drama with a vividness that stung him. It seemed, sometimes, as if he had witnessed the whole thing in a theatre and not acted it in life."[1] In Brightlights's vision of the crime, cast in self-consciously

1. "Prison Mass," *Abbott's Monthly*, VI (March, April, May, 1933), p. 51 (April installment).

"hard-boiled" prison jargon—for instance *heat* for *pistol*—there is disturbingly little remorse. There is apparent, in fact, a suggestion of hatred for the victims, and even a touch of gloating as Brightlights recalls their anguish:

> He had had his long blue heat in his hand. And the other two people in the room had stood out in the floor, white-faced, their hands reaching ceilingward. He had felt like God then, all powerful, he confessed to himself with a little self-pity in his heart. . . . He had thought condescendingly of Jesse James—such a cheap, two-bit chiseler compared with himself. ("Prison Mass," 51 [April])

In an earlier story, "His Last Day," published in *Abbott's Monthly* in 1932, hatred—this time in the mind of a character called Spats, a condemned killer on death row whose name had been "a byword in police headquarters for crimes of unusual viciousness"[2]—is an overt emotion:

> His mouth crooked in a mocking grin as he thought of the wide, frightened eyes of the little Jew when he commanded him to get 'em up. Why, the little sucker trembled so that he could hardly hold his arms above his shoulders, and just because a guy had a heat in his face. ("His Last Day," 33)

In Himes's long prison novel *Cast the First Stone* (1952), the protagonist's memory is similarly haunted, by the same crime, its details ever the same: "And then a queer, rushing kaleidoscope of faces and places and things came out of the past as to a drowning man. . . . I was saying, 'Stick 'em up!' and the man's face was turning suddenly, desperately white. . . ."[3] Although remorse exists in this late work, it is presented as a weakness in the convict's pitiless world:

> It spewed up from those years of being half scared of everything and trying not to show it; half scared of someone thinking I was a girl-boy, half scared of someone running

---

2. Himes, "His Last Day," *Abbott's Monthly*, V:5 (November 1932), 61.
3. Himes, *Cast the First Stone*, p. 211.

over me or taking advantage of me, half scared that I might feel remorseful for my crime, or sorry for my mother, or sorry for anything I had ever done. (*Cast the First Stone*, 205)

Even in Himes's autobiography *The Quality of Hurt* (1972), his attitude toward the Millers is not of the type that parole boards piously and scrupulously exact from their clients:

One night . . . I listened to a chauffer bragging about the large sums of money his boss always kept in his house. . . . I have forgotten the chauffer's name but I recall that he was a somewhat vain and handsome mulatto man in his forties. Like many blacks still possessed of a slave mentality, he boasted of his employer's possessions as though they were his own, or as though he at least had a vested interest in them. His boss was named Miller. He boasted of Mr. Miller's platinum watch and diamond-studded watch chain, of the stacks of hundred-dollar bills Mr. Miller kept in his wall safe. . . . I both envied and resented their wealth and their life.[4]

A certain epic quality pervades the long account of the crime in Himes's autobiography. Even his ancient pistol is distinctly Homeric: "a huge, old-fashioned .44 Colt frontier revolver that looked like a hand cannon and would shoot hard enough to kill a stone" (p. 47). The Millers' terror is less a real emotion than a quaint datum in a faintly preposterous old tale, and the tone is jovially philosophical: " 'Stick your hands up,' I said. Their heads wheeled about; their eyes stretched; and they turned as white as the outside snow. There was no doubt of their race then—they were white" (p. 51).

Himes forced the Millers to open their safe, stole what money and jewelry he could, and fled in one of their two cars, just as the police, alerted earlier by the Millers' black maid, arrived on the scene. In "Prison Mass" the flight is no more than a minor highlight in Brightlights's regretful gloating: "He could still experience a thrill as he recalled that midnight ride" ("Prison Mass,"

4. Himes, *The Quality of Hurt*, pp. 47–48.

51 [April]), but in the autobiography it is one of Himes's most imaginative passages:

> So I just stepped on the gas and drove the Cadillac in a straight line down the snow-covered street. I remember it being exceedingly pleasant in the softly purring car moving swiftly through the virgin blanket of snow and the white translucent falling curtain. Soon the sound of shooting died away and the sight of the pursuing car disappeared in the snowscape in the rear-view mirror, and I was moving swiftly through the completely deserted, almost silent night. There was not a sign of life in sight. Falling snow refracted the headlights and shortened the perimeter of visibility and I had the illusion of hurtling silently through an endless cloud. (*The Quality of Hurt*, 52)

Even the technical seriousness of the crime, the precise amount of money and jewelry stolen, is enhanced and amplified in the autobiography, though this seems quite natural, since by this time the metamorphosis from actual to literary event was substantially complete. In this final telling, the wildest exaggerations of the Millers' garrulous black chauffeur prove true: "It [the Millers' safe] contained five or six stacks of hundred and twenty dollar bills still wrapped in the bank bands" (p. 51). In Himes's account of the robbery in *The Quality of Hurt*, the sum was substantial: "The total insurance for the jewelry amounted to twenty-eight thousand dollars, and there was a little over twenty thousand in cash" (p. 57). But for Brightlights the rewards were as slim as the crime was sordid: "And there had only been a few hundred dollars in it [the safe] after all" ("Prison Mass," 51 [April]). In the official records of Chester Himes's trial, he is charged with stealing only a single ring valued at $1,500 and $200 in cash.[5]

Two days after the robbery in the Millers' home, on Tuesday, November 27, 1928, Chester Himes was arrested in Chicago. The robbery had been a complex and confusing event in Himes's

---

5. Criminal Files, Court of Common Pleas, Cuyahoga County, State of Ohio, No. 35051, Vol. 1398, p. 584.

emotional life. It was self-destructive and violently antisocial, but at the same time it had demanded a certain amount of determination and dash, and might easily be romanticized in the American tradition of frontier bandits like Jesse James. But the aftermaths of the robbery, the events surrounding his arrest and sentencing, were devoid of all ambiguity. They were horribly clear. There are few variations in the different accounts. He had fled by train to Chicago immediately after the robbery and arrived Monday afternoon; on Tuesday, November 27, 1928, he was arrested in a pawnshop where he had tried to sell Mrs. Miller's ring for five hundred dollars to the owner, who he had been told was "a notorious fence called Jew Sam" (*The Quality of Hurt*, 56), but who had immediately called the police. The humiliating ease of his capture, and the mysterious paralysis of will that accompanied it—"it must have seemed to others that I was bent on self-destruction" (p. 60)—remained irreducible puzzles to the writer, even more than forty years years: "I suspected he was calling the police. I should have let him keep the ring and escaped. But I couldn't run; I never could run. I have always been afraid that that one stupid mental block is going to get me killed" (p. 56). The inability to run that can affect a threatened man, the absolute refusal to collaborate in any way, to acknowledge the existence of the threat even in avoiding it, was to remain one of his distinctive literary themes.

Himes was badly beaten at the police station in Chicago, and as a result he signed a confession. For the protagonist of *Cast the First Stone* (1952) this was the most tormenting, unthinkable, ultimately unacceptable memory:

> I tried to go to sleep but I couldn't. All that stuff that happened in Chicago kept coming back. . . .
> I could feel the cops hitting me in the mouth, hanging me by my handcuffed feet upside down over a door, beating my ribs with their gun butts. I could feel the blood running down my legs from where the handcuffs pinched them on the anklebone. . . .
> I had never confessed anything in my life before. Since I was old enough to remember, the beatings I'd gotten from

mother and father had taught me one lesson: *Never confess.* No matter what you ever did, always say you didn't do it. Let 'em prove it. But still deny it. That had been the one rigid rule in my code of existence. *Never confess.* Then there would always be a doubt, if not a chance.

But I had confessed. Now it was too new to stand thinking about. I felt like vomiting whenever I thought about it. (*Cast the First Stone,* 19–20)

In *The Quality of Hurt* Himes recounted the same facts, rapidly and concisely, without emotion: "I wanted to faint but I remained conscious. There was too much pain and not enough hurt. Finally, I mumbled that I would confess" (p. 56). It is an experience that few American writers have shared, part of the special dues Chester Himes paid for his profession.

But for nineteen-year-old Chester Himes the culminating blow was not the brute force experienced in a Chicago police station. It was his sentencing by Judge Walter McMahon on December 27, 1928. For Brightlights, created only a few brief years later, the memory had the impact of a branding iron: "He wrenched his mind away from the searing moment with difficulty" ("Prison Mass," 51 [April]). Even later, however, the emotions of that moment are still white hot:

> The judge was named MacMahon; he was an old man with flinty gray eyes and a merciless expression. There were no spectators, I am certain.
> I had never really hoped to be put on probation; I was already on probation. But when Judge MacMahon sentenced me—"I sentence you to twenty to twenty-five years of hard labor in the Ohio State Penitentiary, because you have taken ten years from the lives of each of your victims"—I was shocked. At that instant I suddenly knew that this mother-fucking bastard had hurt me as much as I could ever be hurt if I lived a hundred thousand years; he had hurt me in a way I would never get over, I thought. (*The Quality of Hurt,* 59)

Even for the casual researcher reading the official records in full foreknowledge of their essential contents almost half a century later, the wording of the sentence comes as a distinct shock:

"Plea of guilty of robbery (Sec. 12432—C.C.), hard labor, no part of said time to be kept in solitary confinement, for a period of not less than twenty years."[6]

It had been a difficult year for Judge Walter McMahon. In the court term that ended in December, 1928, he and his assistants had "handled" 671 criminal cases, according to a contemporary newspaper account, and had meted out 135 penitentiary sentences, as well as 172 to the reformatory and 138 to the workhouse, with only 37 acquittals.[7] Chester Himes could appear as only one more dim face in a crowded calendar, and the records clearly indicated that he was an extremely dangerous youth. The Cleveland newspapers had given some attention to the Miller robbery, though not with the "banner headlines" mentioned in *The Quality of Hurt* (p. 58), and they were uniformily hostile. A story in *The Cleveland Press* on the day of Himes's arrest in Chicago caustically reviewed Himes's "record":

> Six weeks ago Chester Himes, 20, was released by Cleveland police after he was given a suspended fine as a "suspicious person."
>
> Tuesday Cleveland and Cleveland Heights police were seeking a way of getting Himes from Chicago to face a $15,000 robbery charge.
>
> Himes, according to Chicago dispatches, admitted he took $10,000 in jewels, $200 in cash and a $4,000 automobile from Mr. & Mrs. Samuel Miller when he surprised them at their home, 2685 Fairmount Boulevard early Sunday.
>
> Himes was released by federal officials and Cleveland police after he had been linked with theft of five automatic pistols from the Ohio National Guard armory, 7511 Cedar Avenue, on Sept. 27.
>
> Himes was arrested in Warren, O., on Oct. 4 with Cornalee Thatch 21, and Benny Barnett, 21.[8]

He was "on probation" at the time of the Miller robbery for passing bad checks in Columbus, Ohio, with a stolen student I.D. card. He had been paroled to the custody of his father with

6. Ibid.
7. *The Cleveland News,* December 27, 1928.
8. *The Cleveland Press,* November 27, 1928.

a two-year suspended sentence by an understanding judge, but now he had entered a private home with a loaded gun in his hand. The sentence he received from Judge McMahon was harsh but not surprising, given the circumstances, and within the logic of the time and place. In his autobiography Himes himself clearly acknowledges how truly dangerous he was at this time:

> I discovered that I had become very violent. I saw a glimmer of fear and caution in the eyes of most people I encountered. . . . I had heard that people were saying, "Little Katzi [his nickname] will kill you." I can't say what I might have done. (*The Quality of Hurt*, 47)

He was for the moment literally a desperado, a man who had completely exhausted all his stores of hope, the most dangerous of men.

His first nineteen years of life had buried him under a flood of troubles that neither he nor anyone else could have coped with. For years his family had been violently torn by internal racial tensions; an open war—deadly hate mixed with hopeless love—raged endlessly between his almost-white mother and his very black father, with the three "brownskin" sons caught helplessly in the middle. His parents had completely demolished their own lives with their desperate quarreling, reduced one another in the course of a relatively short marriage to the verge of madness and shattered, premature old age. The father, Joseph Sandy Himes, sank from positions as professor of metal trades and black history in Negro "A.&M." colleges in the South, to menial odd jobs in Ohio cities, defeated by his wife's open contempt for his colleagues and associates, for everything and everybody black, and by her insidious talent for provoking dangerous racial incidents. And—to judge by the numerous portraits of her that appear in Himes's writing—the mother, Estelle Bomar Himes, prey to a peculiarly racial psychosis, came to the very edge of permanent insanity before the divorce. Of the three sons, only Chester, the youngest, was damaged to a similar degree. The oldest son, Eddie, a decade older than Chester and coolly independent, became a waiter and detached himself completely from the family at an early age. The second son, Joseph, only one year older than Chester and linked to him almost as a twin, was almost totally blinded in an accident in his early teens—an accident for which Chester considered himself partly responsible—and had as a result his own special protective insulation, and in the dark world of the partially blind he made his way through a brilliant academic career to national recognition as a sociologist. But, for Chester Himes it would take a lifetime of groping effort—including three closely autobiographical novels and one official autobiography—to disengage himself completely fom the last scalding traces of the tangled loves and hates of his tormented parents, and the flood of related troubles that surged around him in his youth. He too suffered a crippling accident in his teens. In 1926, sixteen years old, he fell down an open elevator shaft in the Cleveland hotel where he was working as a bus boy and fractured three vertebrae in his spine, his lower jaw, and two of the bones in his left arm. For the next ten years he would need braces for his back, and he was paid a pension for total disability by the Ohio State Industrial Commission. His hopes for an early romantic marriage were blasted by his fears that his mother—whose will he could never resist for long—would object to the girl's too-dark skin. His one attempt to obtain a college education, at Ohio State University in Columbus, was a humiliating and definitive fiasco. He had been precociously successful in black schools in the South, but, at seventeen, recently crippled, he was totally unable to adjust emotionally to the traditional patterns of racial segregation on a Northern university campus. He pledged an all-black fraternity, Alpha Phi Alpha, bought a coonskin coat and a Model T roadster with his pension money, failed all of his courses the first quarter, and was "allowed to withdraw" by the dean over a disciplinary matter before the end of his second quarter.

Thus, at seventeen, dropped from college, trapped again in the private hell maintained by his family, he began to slip inexorably into a typical pattern of incorrigible delinquency. "I passed the spring in a daze," he remarks laconically in *The Quality of Hurt*, "But when summer came I got up and out" (p. 31). He became a habitué of the blackjack table in a gambling club frequented by the sporting element among Cleveland's most solid black citizens. The club's flashy and highly successful proprietor was first his personal hero and then "something of a father figure" (p. 38). Flush with reserves of pension money, and then incidental winnings as his gambling skills sharpened, he began to dress more lavishly in imitation of the cool, hard-faced black gamblers he so admired but with a style all his own, "I got to know the expensive men's stores where blacks rarely ventured" (p. 36). As the thrills of gambling began to pall, he became increasingly familiar with the most sordid section of Cleveland's black ghetto, Scovil Avenue, "the Bucket of Blood," and he took brief jobs involving both the sale of illegal whiskey and the promotion of prostitution. With a few friends of similar tastes, and drives, he experimented progressively with drugs, the thrills of petty thievery, and finally a full-scale burglary (the affair of the armory pistols), with a brief gambit into passing bad checks on his own. During all this time relations between his parents steadily worsened; their violent and vindictive spats furnished a sinister backdrop for his own ever-widening spiral of delinquency and vice:

> It was an unusual period of my life. I seemed to be in a trance. I think it was the result of so many emotional shocks. My parents' quarreling had entered its final stages; sometimes my father would strike my mother and she struck back. I would separate them when I was at home. (*The Quality of Hurt*, 37–38)

His parents finally divorced, sold their house in Cleveland, and each moved into rented rooms in the city as far apart as possible. His brother Joe chose to live with his mother, but Chester, since he had been officially paroled into his father's custody after his bizarre check-cashing spree, had no choice but to move in with his father. This was his period of final desperation. He began to wander the streets at all hours—"Anything to keep away from that room that stank of my father's fear and defeat" (p. 47)—and at last, on one cold and snowy night, as the official record reads, he "upon one Samuel Miller with force and arms did make an assault." Instead of receiving the amount of money he wanted, to take him very far away, he went to prison.

Incarceration in an overcrowded state prison is neither isolation nor escape nor a choice refuge for a battered psyche, but it did provide Chester Himes with a wholly new identity in a wholly new context, and this was what he needed. For seven and one-half years, until he was released in May, 1936, twenty-six years old, he was relatively detached from the unbearable tensions that plagued his family. Prison left him freedom enough to discover that he was a writer, possessed of a unique gift that could give him a degree of mastery over even the most painful experience, even the almost unendurable.

Nothing in his vast range of autobiographical writings makes precisely clear how he came to discover his vocation, when or how he first decided that he could write publishable material, stories that publishers would buy. In *Cast the First Stone* a friendly murderer interests the novel's protagonist in a writing course as "something to do," when you are lost at the bottom of an ocean of dead time (p. 124), and in *The Quality of Hurt* Himes simply says, "I began writing in prison." It was the most radical transformation imaginable, from apprentice hoodlum to apprentice artist, the biggest single step he ever took, and the most positive. Yet, it is one personal mystery that he did not choose to explore publicly in any depth. In the reveries of Brightlights in "Prison Mass" there is a brief suggestion of a tangle of motivations, with vanity and loneliness somewhere at the center:

But within his heart of hearts he could still feel the passionate longing for the bright lights, for the limelight, for adulation; but now in a different way. . . . He lived for one thing—for the adulation of the mob—everything he did, everything he said. But he no longer wanted to be known as a good spender, a fast gambler, a scion of the bright lights. He wanted to do something worthwhile, but it had to be something that would bring him fame. That was the secret reason he had taken up writing, he admitted to himself. He had wanted the renown more than the money; wanted to see his name on the pages of popular magazines, wanted others to see his name. "I shall pass beneath this earth no common shade." That was his motto now—I shall be no *forgotten man*. What was important in life? From his burning thoughts came the answer—ambition, achievement, fame. A smile curved the corners of his lips, and for the moment, a dull, red glow suffused his eyes.

He would succeed, he told himself; would succeed in spite of hell, high water or damnation. Then his eyes became expressionless once more; the determination receded from his smile leaving it a mirthless grimace. ("Prison Mass," 61 [May])

Whatever might be the precise nature of the great changes that occurred within him in prison, the transformations proved permanent. He left prison a professional writer, no longer a confused and dangerous youth, the kind that might easily kill you. He had already published a handful of stories, not only in black magazines, but in *Esquire* as well, then at the very peak of its brief period of prestige as an open forum for the world's greatest writers.

For a short time following his release from prison, Himes seemed to be slipping back into the old patterns. His mother was living in Columbus, keeping house for his brother Joe, who was a graduate student at the university, and he was paroled into her custody. At twenty-six, with a wider range of experience than most men twice his age, he docilely accepted a pattern of childlike dependency, building into it elements of equally childlike rebelliousness, "For some reason, perhaps the effect of freedom of movement, I became more hysterical than I had ever been before" (*The Quality of Hurt*, 66). He frantically sampled every vice available in the city's black ghetto, from prostitution to drugs. His mother continually threatened to have him returned to prison, and his parole officer soon decided to transfer him to the custody of his father in Cleveland. This apparent disaster proved his salvation. His emotional ties to his father were far less explosive, and, with genuine independence, he began to rebuild completely his long neglected personal life. On August 13, 1937, he married Jean Johnson, whom he had loved in the years before his prison term. In the autobiography he describes her as "the most beautiful brownskin girl I had ever seen," and even stoops, briefly and apologetically, to frank sentimentality, in his otherwise crisp and casually cool account of these years: "What there was about me that attracted her so I never knew, but she fell desperately in love with my immortal soul. I know that sounds puerile and exaggerated" (*The Quality of Hurt*, 39).

His disability pension had been stopped shortly before his release from prison, and he took whatever odd jobs he could find to support himself and his wife, and he continued to write, though the returns were slender. As a working man with a family he began for the first time to feel enormous weight of the burdens of the black man in America. In the end, after fourteen years with Jean, his inability to accept gracefully the humiliations, the petty defeats, and the ever-present economic handicaps imposed on him by a society openly tolerant of racism would destroy his marriage. But in the beginning the marriage was strong, and he found new and undreamed-of sources of personal strength in the quiet and unpretentious courage of his wife. And there were even a few people who recognized his potential and encouraged him to write. He found a job in the Cleveland Public Library preparing vocational bulletins, which quickly led to a position with the WPA Ohio Writers' Project, helping to research and write a massive guidebook and history of Cleveland that was never to be finished. N. R. Howard, editor of the *Cleveland News*, accepted a few short pieces by Himes for his editorial page and contributed some sound advice: "... it was Mr. Howard who said to me, 'Chester, you have paid the penalty for your crime against society, now forget about it'" (pp. 71–72). The novelist Louis Bromfield—who was, according to Himes, the model for Louis Foster, one of the most unpleasant characters in his *Lonely Crusade* (p. 98)—was interested in Himes by the directors of the Karamu settlement house and theater in Cleveland, and he tried, without success, to help him find a publisher for an early version of his prison novel, then entitled *Black Sheep*, and even gave him a job on his celebrated Malabar Farm. And, most important, magazines continued to accept and publish his stories.

Even after seven and one-half years of prison he was still surprisingly youthful in appearance. Pearl Moody, who was his supervisor during the time he worked at the Cleveland Public Library, remembered him as a "remarkably attractive young man," "very, very young and determined," though "nervous, restless, not at all settled in his ways," whose work was always "very satisfactory."[9] Though he was, as always, laboring under great difficulties at this period, the thrust was forward.

II   Giant Steps: Chester Himes's Short Stories

Almost all of Chester Himes's writing is in the form of novels, and only a very small section is in short stories. A collection of all the short stories he has published could be fitted easily into a single volume, while a collection of his novels would fill a full shelf in anyone's library. The short stories are, nevertheless, a very important segment of his total production, important out of all proportion to their bulk.

Himes wrote short stories exclusively for the first third of his career, and for many years it was the only form through which he could reach the general public. He was in his early twenties when he published his first short story and well into his middle thirties before his first novel was accepted by a publisher. But though he was to abandon the short story almost completely once he began to market his novels, he cultivated the form with a zeal and an assiduity that were anything but perfunctory.

Himes's stories come in an amazing variety of shapes and colors. In fact, they display a wider range of themes and styles than the novels. He wrote the greater part of the stories while he was still trying to find out exactly what kind of a writer Chester Himes was, and this partly explains their bewildering variety, but he also found the medium surprisingly pliable. Within the limits of this genre he could isolate and pinpoint themes so subtle and ephemeral that they would be lost completely in the more complex texture of the novel. There were, too, myriad styles and themes, some quite foreign to his major concerns, that he wanted to try his hand at, at least once, and the relatively modest demands of the short story, in terms of time and effort, made it a convenient key to fit many doors. However, even his very earliest and clum-

9. Telephone conversation with Mrs. Pearl Moody, in Cleveland, Ohio, June 6, 1973.

siest efforts cannot be dismissed as merely beginner's botches
or unproductive experiments. From the start Himes produced
valuable work, and his voice is recognizable even in the most
atypical of his early products. His first stories are in some ways
very crude indeed—like many a young writer he was at times in-
fatuated with certain worn but still glamorous clichés of popular
fiction that he had temporarily mistaken for reality—but he very
quickly eliminated his more obvious mistakes, and even in the
crudest of these early stories he displays an impressive degree of
control over the medium. The stories are truly giant steps, in the
sense that they represent an amazingly rapid progress toward professional competence. But their variety is equally noteworthy.
Widely scattered over so broad a spectrum of types and forms,
they display aspects of Himes's talent and sensitivity that sur-
faced very rarely, faces of Himes that were seldom seen.

The story "His Last Day," which he published in *Abbott's
Monthly* in November of 1932, is typical of Himes's first efforts,
both in its massive weaknesses and its saving strengths. It is over-
written, overdetailed, overexplained, and finally unforgettable.
It is a five-page account of the last few hours of a man on his way
to die in the electric chair, but it has a plotline long enough for
a short novel. The author seems determined to leave no detail of
his hero's tumultuous past history unmentioned. Flashbacks
crowd in on top of flashbacks, and while the dossier fills to overflowing, detail by detail, the story dissolves into a murky confusion that not even repeated rereadings can remedy. Even the style
is hectic and muddy. Abundant concrete details, in staccato bursts
of pungent vernacular, do not always create easily visualized
images—"And a few minutes later he had taken hot lead in the
guts from a Tommy gun wielded by a squad of coppers" ("His
Last Day," 62)—and, too often, what is called to mind is less
recognizable reality than familiar scenes from the kind of movie
Thurber was satirizing with Walter Mitty:

> He said a few words to the deputy warden in a snarling whis-
> per through the corner of his mouth. He gave a snort of
> harsh, mirthless laughter once. And on his lips he wore a
> frozen, sneering, mocking smile. But in his eyes there was
> the subtle hint of utter fear. ("His Last Day," 63)

There is a remarkable penetration, however, in the coldly precise detailing of the symptoms of fear. The story is literally bathed in fear, saturated with the actual smells of it:

> ... he wouldn't be doing this tomorrow. He would be dead— burnt to death in the chair—and crammed into one of those small wooden coffins that fundless executed men were buried in. A stifling sensation came in his chest and his breath whistled through his mouth. His fingers turned to thumbs and he found it impossible to button his shirt. ("His Last Day," 33)

It is an extraordinary effort of the imagination, in which the convict Himes displayed the imaginative power to project himself through those silent and threatening walls of the prison death house and into the most terrifying cell of all:

> He began to fight for control. . . . The smoke tasted like burning straw in his mouth but after a while it created a sort of dullness in his mind. He threw the cigaret from him and rolled and lit another one. ("His Last Day," 62)

The second piece Himes published in *Abbott's Monthly*, "Prison Mass," is also heavy in plot, but this time he had greatly extended the story length, to that of a novella, almost a short novel, and it runs through three issues of the magazine, March, April, and May of 1933. Though there is still some impression of crowding, great density of detail, there is no confusion, no lack of clarity, and the story even manages to flow easily and smoothly at times. This time, however, Himes insisted on imposing a rigid structure, an overall organization, with heavy use of repetition, repeated phrases, even poetic refrains to define and identify the blocklike segments of its loose and convoluted ground plan. By a curious coincidence, the story's structure is very similar to that of James Baldwin's *Go Tell It on the Mountain*, with the main characters gathered in church on a particular day, each one recalling past events from his own very personal point of view as the service proceeds. Himes's setting is the Roman Catholic chapel of a large American prison on Christmas Day. The characters are three black convicts, Brightlights, Signifier, and the Kid. Their characters are sharply distinct, very much in the same manner as those of

Dostoevski's three Karamazov brothers, a neatly triangular pattern of oppositions made up of one ironically detached intellectual, one sensuous man of action, and one mystic believer. Brightlights, the aspiring prison author, is the central figure, the unifying link, a close friend of the other two, who cordially detest one another. Himes seems to have invented nothing that he put into this characterization. Detail for detail, Brightlights is a resolutely objective self-portrait. But Himes also used factual details from his own past in constructing Signifier and the Kid. Signifier has Himes's curious inability to run when running is the only sane course, and he assigned to the Kid's past his own agonizingly close relationship with his brother Joe. He had already discovered the frustration involved in any effort to construct an assemblage of words that can approximate the bottomless complexity of self.

Like that of all his stories of this period, the prose of "Prison Mass" has moments of beauty, lines that pulse with the rhythms of art:

> A tiny flake of vagrant snow fluttered in through an open window, appearing eerily from the translucent gray of the early morning like a frightened ghost seeking the brilliant cheer of the lighted chapel, and quickly melted on the back of a convict's hand. ("Prison Mass," 36 [March])

There are, too, however, more than a few passages in which bombast parades as lyricism:

> Men from the four corners of the world. Some were from the gutters of New York, some were from the wharves of Shanghai, some from the underworld of Chicago, some from the decadent cities of Europe, some from the scum of the border, some from the cages of stately banks, some from the ornate drawing rooms of a forgotten past, some from the very seats of government. ("Prison Mass," 36 [March])

Himes had not yet acquired his flair for sketching in vivid backgrounds.

The story's strength lies almost entirely in its characterizations, which rescue it from the pulpy clichés that he used to describe the prison itself. Brightlights is perhaps a bit too photographically precise and exhaustively detailed to be entirely convincing or interesting. His endless philosophizing, à la Ivan Karamazov, has more weight than substance:

> Of course there was a God, some kind of Supreme Power or Infinite Being. No one could dispute that. Such a belief was an integral part of every human mind. . . . Anyway, why should God judge a man according to how well he lived up to the prescriptions of a specified doctrine if He was a just God? . . . He recalled a line from an essay by Theodore Roosevelt: "Religion is necessary for the average man." . . . But then, on the other hand, Holbach said that: "Ignorance and fear created the Gods. . . . weakness worships them." . . . And was religion really for the craven and belief for the credulous? He didn't know, he didn't know. ("Prison Mass," 50 [April])

Signifier, the man whose reality is sensual rather than intellectual and who is in church only to borrow money from Brightlights, is a more casual, and a more captivating study. He is a smalltime "grifter," in prison on a minor charge, "guilty of being broke, and dull, and uninteresting" (p. 48 [April]). He is, as his nickname implies, a coolly imperturbable troublemaker. "He jeered at God, the President of the United States, the leaders of his race, and his fellow convicts indiscriminately. If a fellow broke his leg, Signifier laughed" (pp. 60–61 [March]). Signifier's reveries are confined to the many women in his life, with whom "he had always had a way" (p. 61 [May]), and when the spell of the central religious service briefly captures his attention he hurriedly shakes himself loose: " 'I must be going nuts,' he muttered to himself, 'getting emotional as some old sister in the amen corner' " (p. 49 [April]). But Signifier's deepest thoughts have a bleak lucidity, an absolute freedom from cant, and the characterization has at this level, both substance and solidity. More often than even his sullenly resentful cellmates, Signifier himself feels the sting of his own acid scepticism: "Then suddenly it came to him that there was something wrong with that thought. It didn't sound right even to him and he knew it wouldn't sound right to anyone else" (p. 20 [April]).

Some of Himes's best characters—and Signifier is an early sketch of the type—are like shellfish, all hard, gleaming symmetries on the outside, but inside, where the life really is, a blob-like quivering mass of fears and desires. What redeems them is the singular honesty, the refreshing shamelessness, of their private thoughts. The blob freely acknowledges itself, making no claim whatever to the jewellike sinuosities of the shell. They are hustlers, actors, public deceivers, compulsive performers, but their introspections are innocent of hypocrisy. They have no serious problems with the subconscious because they make no attempt to barricade its entrances and exits. Himes was fascinated by the intricate interplay between the specious surface images projected by such men and their surprisingly complete inner integrity. Unlike Ralph Ellison, one of his closest friends, he admired the Rineharts of the world, not only the grand masters but the marginally competent as well; he never tired of their inexhaustible variety. Signifier, at the story's end, is even permitted to say a few warm words to his friends, slight but gratifying evidence that his seemingly rocklike heart might have in it some faint traces of gold: "Brightlights smiled. There was a warm glow of admiration in his heart, admiration for his friends. He knew that old Signifier would come through. He was really a pretty good guy, just had a criminal mind, a petty criminal mind" (p. 62 [May]).

The Kid, the third convict of "Prison Mass," is Himes's only major effort to understand a much rarer human phenomenon: the saint. The Kid is twenty-six years old, and he has been in prison since he was seventeen, serving a life sentence for a murder his brother had actually committed. Everything about him is unusual. He is black, but blond and blue-eyed. In Himes's youthfully strenuous attempts to singularize his descriptions of the Kid's vaguely Lincolnesque appearance, he delicately picked his way, with a few fumbles, through the sleazy vocabulary of racial stereotyping created by several generations of white writers:

> His complexion was the peculiar whiteness of Swiss Cheese. . . . an Eagle face, wide and sullen in repose, singularly eager and appealing when he smiled. There was just the suggestion of bluntness about his features that pointed to his Negro origin. . . . There was the subtle hint of plow handles in his long, bony hands, and the faint suggestion of the rural in his over-sized feet and loosely hanging clothes

that bespoke of years spent on the farm. ("Prison Mass," 62 [March])

The Kid had once attempted to escape by tunneling his way out of his cell. Like Monte Cristo he had spent twelve months "digging upward in hard concrete, with nothing but a dull chisel and a padded shoe heel for a mallet" (p. 54 [April]), only to turn back and surrender at the very moment of success, shocked in his soul by the crime involved in his bid for freedom, the defiance of legitimate authority. The Kid's world is an appealing but nebulous fantasy that Himes struggles to understand: "he lived in a land of dreams and ideals where faith and love and hope were tangible things" (p. 55 [April]). Strangest of all for Himes, in this period when he himself was "matriculating in the university of hell" (p. 52 [April]), the Kid is happy:

> He felt immensely relieved, cheered. It was as if God had washed all the doubt and anxiety from his heart and in its stead put peace and happiness. Yes, happiness. He thought of a line from a song he had composed—"I'm for the sunshine, don't like the rain; but if it rains, then the sun will shine again." *Happiness Coming*, that was the title of his song. . . . It was hope that took the sting out of prison walls; hope that alleviated the pain of life with the promise of joy in the future. ("Prison Mass," 37 [May])

The Kid's fate is even grimmer than Himes's own, but he has found extraordinary strength in a weapon very uncharacteristic of Himes: totally unqualified resignation, surrendering even his longing for death: "he had found out that people don't die from sorrow and despair and heartache, not when they are young and have strong, healthy bodies" (p. 63 [March]). The Kid, nevertheless, at scattered moments, bears more than a slight resemblance to Himes himself, or at least a potentially possible Himes. The Kid's serenity is a difficult trick, a product of will, needing to be reconstructed from moment to moment, forever at odds with a childlike moodiness that surges beneath his quiet surface in violent waves:

> He was an idealist by nature, enthusiastic, impulsive, trustful, therefore easily hurt. He had a simple faith in the good-

ness and truthfulness of all mankind, when things were going right. And when things were going wrong, he hated and mistrusted almost everyone. ("Prison Mass," 62 [March])

In 1970 John A. Williams described Himes in terms curiously similar to those Himes had used for his tormented but saintly convict:

One remembers his [Chester Himes's] eyes mostly; they sit in that incredible face upon which ravages show—but which they have been unable to destroy—and at certain angles the long-lashed eyes are soft, *soft*, as though clinging to some teen-aged dream of love and goodness and justice.[10]

For the Brightlights of "Prison Mass," possibly the most completely autobiographical of any of Himes's characters, the Kid's faith is almost hypnotically attractive, but also obviously and forbiddingly dangerous:

Suddenly he experienced an odd desire to believe as the Kid believed. He smiled a little wistfully, thinking what a simple solution for all his problems that would be. But then, on the other hand, that would make life important, make it significant; and he didn't want his life to become as that. ("Prison Mass," 55 [April])

Nevertheless, Himes ended "Prison Mass," that searching inventory of available life styles, mental, physical, and spiritual, with a line the Kid himself might have written, and Himes's narrator is allowed an open religiosity that never appears in his other works: "And Christ in heaven looked down on this day in commemoration of His earthly birth, eyes bright with immortal pity, over the lot of man" (p. 62 [May]).

For Himes's short stories, 1933 was a year for radical ploys and rash gambits, both profitable and unprofitable. After "Prison Mass" he tried his hand at a typical "women's story," "Her Whole Existence, A Story of True Love," an earnestly saccharine little fable with a plot strongly reminiscent of Dashiell Hammett's *The Glass Key* (1931). A black society girl, daughter of an ambitious

10. John A. Williams, "My Man Himes: An Interview with Chester Himes," in *Amistad I*, eds. John A. Williams and Charles F. Harris, pp. 26–27.

"reform" politician, falls madly in love with the powerful and dashing black gangster whose support is essential to her father's election—"His kisses were brutal, crushing, but she gloried in the pain."[11] The story's dialogue would have proved a severe trial a few years later, but Himes had his sense of humor under very firm control at this stage of his career: "Lord, you're beautfiul, Mabel. . . . the golden bronze of your complexion and the moonbeams playing hide-and-seek in your midnight hair" (p. 25). In October, with "I Don't Want to Die," Himes achieved the ultimately lugubrious tearjerker. A sick convict expires in the prison hospital with visions of God's love, a tiny cottage home in the country, and lawful marriage to a pure woman, thronging through his fevered brain: "The dream of his little paradise lingered in his mind even through death. And perhaps he will find the paradise of his dreams out there, somewhere. Who knows?"[12] Then, with an abrupt and clanking shift of gears, he ground out a starkly realistic crime story, "He Knew," published in December 1933. "He Knew" offers what is almost a preview of the two fictional black detectives, Coffin Ed Johnson and Grave Digger Jones, that Himes made famous in the long series of detective novels that he wrote in the last phase of his career, some twenty-five years later.

The central characters of this early story are two black plain-clothes policemen whose resemblance to the celebrated detectives of the later novels includes even the name "Jones": "Detectives John Jones and Henry Walls tramped their dreary beat, heads pulled down into the upturned collars of their overcoats like the heads of startled turtles, hats slanted forward against the cold December drizzle."[13] This Officer Jones, however, with a "harsh black face" and a "short, solid body," also calls to mind, more immediately, descriptions of Himes's own father in his autobiographical novels. The patrolling policeman John Jones is primarily an authority figure, tough and unsympathetic, more than a bit

11. Chester Himes, "Her Whole Existence, A Story of True Love," *Abbott's Monthly* (July 1933), 54.

12. Chester Himes, "I Don't Want to Die," *Abbott's Monthly and Illustrated News* (October 1933), 21.

13. Chester Himes, "He Knew," *Abbott's Weekly and Illustrated News* (December 1933), 15.

self-righteous, almost all-knowing, forever fretting grumpily over the ingratitude and unruliness of his two teen-aged sons as he doggedly stomps his beat, and, in the story's morbidly ironic ending, the two burglars he and his partner ruthlessly gun down in a dark warehouse turn out to be his own sons. In spite of the story's trick ending and its bitter autobiographical echoes, the character John Jones possesses a sturdy reality all his own: "He experienced a sudden distaste for his job—shooting men down in the darkness, like rats, rats! . . . His thoughts whirled chaotically" (p. 15).

The next year, 1934, marked a major breakthrough in Himes's career as a short-story writer: the crucial move from publication only in black magazines and newspapers, whose audience was limited largely to the nation's black ghettoes, to acceptance by an important national magazine. In *The Quality of Hurt*, which is not exactly a chronicle of triumphs, Himes records the event with undisguised pride: "I sold my first short story, *Crazy in the Stir*, to *Esquire* magazine in 1934. . . . After that, until I was released [from prison] in May 1936, I was published only by *Esquire*" (p. 64). In addition to Chester Himes, in 1934 *Esquire* published works by Hemingway, Fitzgerald, Dos Passos, Ring Lardner, Ben Hecht, Conrad Aiken, Thorne Smith, Bertrand Russell, Emil Ludwig, Luigi Pirandello, Theodore Dreiser, and Langston Hughes— exhilarating company for a young convict in an Ohio prison. He was at last, beyond all question, a writer, and for a time he tried to lose himself completely in this new identity.

He had no ambitions to be a leader of his race, a role heavy with dull responsibilities, and heavier still with the inevitability of unbearable frustrations. And, like many black writers—most notably Frank Yerby and Willard Motley—he attempted briefly to separate his blackness and his writing. The central characters in his first *Esquire* stories are white, and it was not until 1936 that the magazine gave its readers any indication at all that he was black. His stories were prison sketches, and the magazine's editors laid heavy stress on the fact that their author was himself a convict—"a long-term prisoner in a state penitentiary tells an authentic story about life on the 'inside' "[14]—and the editors may well have thought this was for the moment a sufficient strain to lay

14. *Esquire* (August 1934), 28.

on their readers' prejudices. Himes was not long in discovering, however, that for him writing was simply a natural function like breathing, that could not be separated and controlled, and that he could not live or write or breathe in a vacuum, cut off from the most vital part of his experience. In September 1936, *Esquire* published, in its opening profiles of authors, a pen-and-ink drawing of Chester Himes that made it clear, to any readers who might be interested, that his face was handsome, hard, defiant, slightly sarcastic in expression, and definitely black.[15] And in January 1937, *Esquire* published Himes's "The Night's for Cryin'," his first story for the magazine that was not primarily a prison sketch but a sketch of life in the black ghetto. This is the only one of his *Esquire* stories that he chose to reprint in *Black on Black* (1973), his own highly selective anthology of his stories and articles.

The editors of *Esquire* described one of the prison sketches contributed by the author "known as No. 59623 . . . in the Ohio State Penitentiary"[16] as "a swell story."[17] It is a glib and easy judgment, but quite accurate. Himes's *Esquire* stories are far from novice work, though he had yet to reach the level of his full powers. The central characters are types *Esquire* readers might be expected to admire: white, mildly bigoted, tough and uncomplicated, rapidly drawn in crisp, authoritative strokes on the two levels, surface and immediately below, that were by now already distinctive features of Himes's style. A solidly competent command of background is the most striking new feature of these stories. Himes had at last achieved a kind of objectivity about the prison and could begin to bring to bear one of his most important talents, his ability to see and record the details of an ambiance with a degree of accuracy that few writers have equaled. He was beginning to be a master of descriptive prose, able in a few short sentences to suggest not only the look, but the feel, the very atmosphere of a setting, to give something very much like recognizability to locales that for most of his readers were both alien and bizarre. The *Esquire* stories are also, however, narrowly and

15. "Backstage with *Esquire*," *Esquire* (September 1936), p. 28.
16. *Esquire* (October 1934), 16.
17. "Backstage with *Esquire*," p. 28.

overtly didactic. They are units in a lightning fast correspondence course on prison lore for squares, and Himes's new command of background is put to use only as the most convenient device available to point the lesson of the day. The destructive impact of the prison environment upon even the most insensitive personality is his subject here.

The first two stories in the set, "Crazy in the Stir" and "To What Red Hell," were accepted together by *Esquire* in 1934 and appeared in the August and October issues. These two stories closely parallel Chapters 14 and 21 of Himes's prison novel *Cast the First Stone* (1952); but, though these chapters retain many phrases and even sentences from the stories, the differences are more striking than the similarities, so complete was the rewriting involved. In *Cast the First Stone* Himes was also primarily concerned with the effects of prison on his central character—who is depicted as white to eliminate all purely racial problems from the paradigm—but in the novel both the prison and the central character are explored in depth, both depicted with degrees of complexity that verge on the inordinate. There are no simple and obvious lessons for today in the novel.

"Crazy in the Stir" is a study of hysteria produced by the most basic deprivation of all, the freedom to be alone, all alone and perfectly quiet, if only for a few moments, whenever the company of others begins to seem more burden than comfort. The setting is a prison dormitory, "a steady hum of noise . . . air thick with the odor of tobacco fumes and unwashed bodies . . . rows of bunks,"[18] in which one hundred convicts seem to be confined permanently, without work, much like the "cripple company" Himes was assigned to through most of his stay in prison because of his injured back, though no special circumstances of this type are alluded to in the story. The story's protagonist, Red, is a formidable figure, feared by the other convicts, a veteran both of trench warfare in World War I and Marine campaigns in Nicaragua and China. He is in prison because he killed a man in a fit of anger, over a verbal insult, "a name that a man couldn't take" (p. 114). As the story opens he has been playing poker for ten hours, when he suddenly becomes aware that his nerves are play-

18. Himes, "Crazy in the Stir," *Esquire* (August 1934), 28.

ing strange tricks on him: "... his hickory-striped shirt felt moldy; his long prison underwear crawled on his skin; his prison-fit trousers chafed him. Even his shoes felt slimy to his feet" (p. 28). He stalks belligerently through the dormitory, torn by violent impulses, though he is always restrained at the last moment by his inner machinery, his prison conditioning, "that queer docility common to prisoners" (p. 28). He finally seeks refuge in the one nearly quiet place available, the dormitory's latrine:

> He moved down to the other end of the latrine, took three rapid drags from his cigaret. He could feel the smoke way down in the bottom of his lungs. His skin was tight on his face.
> But it was quiet down here. He tried to relax. And then sound creeped into his mind. A broken commode leaked with a monotonous gurgle. The skin crawled on his face like the skin of a snake's belly. ("Crazy in the Stir," 117)

There is no conclusion, just a portrait of a swaggering tough who has been completely unmanned by the most banal pressures, repeated *ad nauseam*. In *Cast the First Stone* the hero's similar attack of "jitters" ends in a suicide attempt, bizarrely interrupted by the flashing of the dormitory lights, the signal to go to bed, which he is powerless to resist even in the depths of hysteria, and he climbs down from the wall from which he had meant to jump and goes to bed, seething with frustration and impotent fury (p. 214). The incident marks the point at which the novel's hero has at last become peculiarly susceptible to homosexual overtures, an aspect of prison life that is only vaguely hinted at in "Crazy in the Stir." There is also a much sharper insistence in the novel on the pathological nature of the hero's emotional crisis (which in the short story seems less a debilitating sickness than an appallingly severe temper tantrum):

> I started back to my bunk. I felt if I could just get back to my bunk and lie down I'd be all right. It was as if I had hurt myself in some kind of way and was trying to get home. If I could just get home I'd be all right. But it seemed like miles back to my bunk. I seemed to be walking all right but I didn't feel as if I was moving. I began getting scared

I wouldn't be able to make it to my bunk. (*Cast the First Stone*, 212)

The story "To What Red Hell" deals with Himes's most horrifying prison experience, the disastrous fire that swept through the Columbus penitentiary on April 21, 1930, Easter Monday, burning 317 convicts to death in their cells within less than an hour, and setting off a chain of riots that continued for nine days. The massive flash fire would have been a colossal nightmare anywhere. Set amid the strangling tensions of the primitive and crowded prison of Himes's stories (and memories), it is a turn of the screw of demonic proportions. The short story's central figure is again rocklike and elemental, a man to fear in any normal circumstances. He is a former war hero and a prizefighter who had reached the top ranks of his division, but prison discipline has so diminished him that he is totally incapable of functioning in the overwhelming crisis of the prison fire:

> He heard a voice say: "Get a blanket and give a hand here." His lips twitched slightly as a nausea swept over him. He said: "No can do," in a low choky whisper. . . . Didn't know what the hell was the matter with him. . . . He really wanted to go up in that smoking inferno. . . . But he couldn't, just couldn't, that's all.[19]

He wanders aimlessly through the confusion, wonders briefly if he should try to rescue his tan shoes, but decides it might be too dangerous. He manages only one brief spurt of activity, one tiny break in his paralyzing lethargy, when he sees a black convict robbing one of the corpses that have been laid out in long rows in the prison yard:

> . . . [he] swung a hard, wild haymaker at the shiny, black face. He missed and went sprawling across the corpse. He felt the soft, mushy form beneath him. He got up, started shaking his hands and feet with quick, jerky movements like a cat walking in molasses. He didn't see the black boy any more, but he saw other guys, white guys, stripping the shoes from the dead men's feet. . . . Well, what did he have to do with it anyhow? he asked himself.

19. Chester Himes, "To What Red Hell," *Esquire* (October 1934), 100.

Suddenly he felt an insane desire to laugh. Something sticky was crawling about in his mind. He felt for a moment that he was going crazy. He started moving fast, trying to get away from the dense crop of corpses. ("To What Red Hell," 101)

In the chapter devoted to the prison fire in *Cast the First Stone*, the novel's hero, far from remaining uniformly passive, runs through an incredible gamut of extreme and excessive emotions, bounding to heroic heights and then diving down to squalid depths, in a frenetic and erratic but continuously evolving pattern. The descriptions of the actual fire are similarly heightened, unveiling levels of horror that the short story had only suggested, as though the passage of years had eroded in the writer's mind the psyche's resistance to the full enormity of the horror, or added details from a hundred nightmares to the blurred memory of the actual, lived trauma. It was an experience that prose could reach only through frank exaggeration, seeking emotional rather than statistical truth, and the naturalistic style maintained in the story gives way to unabashed surrealism in the novel's parallel passages:

I swung at his shiny black face. I missed him and went sprawling over a corpse. The soft, mushy form gave beneath me. I jumped up, shook my hands as if I had fallen into a puddle of filth. Then the centipede began crawling about in my head. It was mashed in the middle and it crawled slowly through my brain just underneath the skull, dragging its mashed middle. I could feel its legs all gooey with the slimy green stuff that had been mashed out of it.

And then I was running again. I was running blindly over the stiffs, stepping in their guts, their faces. I could feel the soft squashy give of their bellies, the roll of muscles over bones. I put my face down behind my left hand, bowed my head and plowed forward.

A moment later I found myself standing in front of the entrance to the Catholic chapel. I felt a queer desire to laugh. (*Cast the First Stone*, 137)

The stories "The Visiting Hour" and "Every Opportunity," published in *Esquire* after Himes's release in 1936, completed the prison sequence. They are grimly ironic little tales of the convict's difficult relations with the outside world. In "The Visiting Hour" a convict spends the few fleeting moments of his wife's visit struggling futilely to make her understand exactly how he feels about his eight years in prison, without ever quite recognizing that he too has failed, just as drastically, to understand her feelings. Both of the story's characters are groping slowly toward a realization, amid shrinking sensations of guilt, that at some unnoticed point in their long mutual ordeal their love had turned to hate: "Emotions crawled in him, squirmy, dirty, smeary emotions. . . . Patting her hands and wanting to hurt her."[20] The irony of "Every Opportunity" is of a much heavier variety, mordant and bitterly sardonic. It takes a convict from the moment of his release on parole, from the chief parole officer's overripe and treacly speech about full opportunities, support, assistance, encouragement, through a series of jobs—laborer in a laundry at fourteen dollars a week, dishwasher at eight dollars a week—to his inevitable return to prison as a penalty for his failure to remain fully employed and morally upright in the nightmare world of the Great Depression.[21]

The story "The Night's for Cryin' " is closely related to Himes's prison stories, but it is also very different, and much more complex. It is, on the one hand—since the central character finally does wind up in a death-row cell in the Columbus penitentiary—a sketch of a prison grotesque, very similar in kind to those that make up much of Dostoevski's *The House of the Dead*. It is one of Himes's many attempts to understand and depict one of the more violent types among the horde of strange and dangerous men he came to know well during his years in prison, men for whom monstrous acts were normal.

On the other hand, the background of "The Night's for Cryin' " —however deep its roots may be in Himes's prison experience— is not painted in the grim prison grays of the earlier *Esquire* stories but in the lurid, splashy rainbow of colors that characterized the night life and the night people of Cleveland's black ghetto. Black Boy, the story's monstrous central figure, is black— and his blackness, the blackness that isolates him in the ghetto,

20. Himes, "The Visiting Hour," *Esquire* (September 1936), 143.
21. Himes, "Every Opportunity," *Esquire* (May 1937), 99, 129, 130.

is the essential key to the deformity of his soul. Himes told John A. Williams that one major motivation behind all of his writing was the desire to force white Americans to grasp fully the violent potential of the closed world of the ghetto, closed in as much by white indifference as by white hatred: "White people in America, it seems to me, are titillated by the problem of the black people, more than taking it seriously. I want to see them take it seriously, good and goddamn seriously."[22] A means to this end, employed by many black writers, was to incarnate the violence of the ghetto in a single character. The almost innocently murderous Bigger Thomas of Richard Wright's *Native Son* is the most notable example. Himes contributed many studies of this type to the nation's literature, endowing them with an authenticity that was peculiarly his own, and Black Boy, the lovelorn, knife-wielding protagonist of "The Night's for Cryin'," is not only one of the first but also one of the most successful of these grotesque and demonic characterizations (though he is also clearly an early sketch of the Luther McGregor of *Lonely Crusade* [1947]). The editors of *Esquire* supplied, by way of "illustration" for the story, a pen-and-ink drawing of a very ugly, very confused, and very funny black man, in classic comic-book style, but Himes's Black Boy is not really a very funny character.[23] The mildly humorous, bemused-raconteur tone of the physical descriptions given of Black Boy in the story, however, might easily have misled even an illustrator who was not at all of a mind to be titillated by the monstrous forms spawned out of the ghetto's violence:

> His red tongue slid twice across his thick, red lips, and his slack, plate-shaped face took on a popeyed expression, as startlingly unreal beneath the white of his precariously perched Panama as an eight ball with suddenly sprouted features. The puffed, bluish scar on his left cheek, memento of a pick-axe duel on a chain gang, seemed to swell into an embossed reproduction of a shell explosion, ridges pronging off from it in spokes. . . .
> Standing, his body was big, his six foot height losing im-

22. Williams, "My Man Himes," p. 63.
23. *Esquire* (January 1937), 64.

pressiveness in slanting shoulders and long arms like an ape's.[24]

Black Boy is pure violence, uncomplicated by intellect, the sort of man who can flourish only in areas where civilization's restraints have been permanently abolished. His reaction to seeing his girl with another man is to stab the man to death and pound the woman senseless:

> He never said a word, he just reached around from behind and smacked her in the face with the open palm of his right hand. She drew up short against the blow. Then he hit her under her right breast with a short left jab and chopped three rights into her face when she turned around with the edge of his fist like he was driving nails. (*Black on Black*, 142)

He is brought to "justice" by the white police cast in his own fearsome image, products of the same social order.

> The cops took him down to the station and beat his head into an open, bloody wound from his bulging eyes clear around to the base of his skull—"You'd bring your nigger cuttings down on Euclid Avenue, would you, you black—" (*Black on Black*, 143)[25]

Smith, the protagonist of the story "Pork Chop Paradise," written in 1938 and published in Himes's *Black on Black* (1973), is another variation on the basic Black Boy–Luther McGregor type —an extravagantly monstrous, violent black man—depicted this time with an unexpectedly playful admixture of fantasy. With Smith, Himes pushed Black Boy's bestial physical attributes one

24. Chester Himes, "The Night's for Cryin'," in *Black on Black*, p. 140. (Originally appeared in *Esquire* [January 1937], 64.)

25. Himes's later *Esquire* stories are: "Marihuana and a Pistol" (March 1940), 58 (brief and vivid portrait of a world perceived without causal links, in which even murder is incidental); "Money Don't Spend in the Stir" (April 1944), 75, 174, 175 ("comic" tale of a convict who inherits $5,000 and tries to buy his way out of prison, only to find that every official he approaches is honest); "The Something in a Colored Man" (January 1946), 120, 158 (a hipster is so stimulated by the excitement generated throughout the ghetto by the murder he committed the night before that he turns himself in to share in the notoriety); "The Snake" (October 1959), 147–49 (a little girl and an old man look at life in a lonely mountain house full of poisonous snakes, incest, and murder; good snake-fighting scenes).

wild step farther, to the edge of the inhuman, and perhaps a bit beyond, and added to them a rare complication of moral turpitude:

> His body was thick and muscular, with the suggestion of a paunch to come in later years when his appetite could be sated, and his shoulders sloped like an ape's. He had huge, muscle-roped arms and weird, long-fingered hands of enormous size and grotesque shape, a strangler's hands. He could scratch the calf of either leg without stooping. Flat, splayed, fantastic feet, which could not be comfortably encased in any shoe smaller than a size 16, grew from abnormally small legs as straight as sticks.
>
> His eyes squinted and his gold teeth gleamed in his black face when he grinned. While in prison he always grinned for white people, be they convicts or guards, no matter what they said or did to him (*Black on Black*, 161)

Smith is a fairy-tale ogre, a black gargoyle compounded out of the stuff of imbecilic and vicious racial caricatures, gleefully exaggerated, and "Pork Chop Paradise," though told in a soberly documentary style, resembles nothing else so much as a fable out of Uncle Remus, a fable about an ugly, black toadlike creature who has the strange gift of a voice that people cannot listen to without believing what it says. Smith is a convicted rapist, called "fink" and "degenerate" by the other convicts (accurately, so the narrator informs us), who has discovered the power of religion while in prison. Endowed with a magnificent and strangely compelling voice, Smith prays his way out of prison and straight into a career as ghetto evangelist as lucrative as those of Father Divine or Sweet Daddy Grace:

> Out of this grotesque black man who looked half frog and half ape there came a voice that transcended all human qualities. It was perhaps one of the greatest speaking voices ever to be heard on this earth. . . . If one can imagine the voice of God speaking from the burning bush of biblical legend one can imagine the voice of Smith. (*Black on Black*, 162)

Not having to settle for any halfway measures, with a voice so irresistibly mesmeric, Smith adopts the name of Fathah and per-suades his followers to accept him, not as a mere prophet, but as God in person. The rapist lives on within the evangelist, however, and Himes's characters can flourish in hypocrisy only so long as they remain completely lucid, fully and cynically aware of their mendacity at every moment. Fathah comes to believe that he really is God, and a black street woman proves his undoing, quickly setting him on the way back to prison:

> Then he leveled his grotesque, thrice-ringed finger at her and thundered, "Wipe dat paint frum yo' face!"
> "Whaffaw?" she asked, unabashed.
> He looked startled. After a long moment he asked her, "Does yawl know who Ah is?" There was a note of bewilderment in his voice.
> "Naw, who is you?" she asked, taking a stick of gum from her pocket and unwrapping it, dropping the wrappers on the floor and sticking the gum in her mouth.
> "Ah is God!" he pronounced in imperious accents.
> She looked at him and chewed her gum. "Is you?" she asked at last. "You looks like a big black nigger to me."
> His face contorted in a sudden spasm of emotion. Her remark had sparked, not anger, but a sudden uncontrollable lust in him. . . .
> Fathah lost his head. Lost his head over a half-drunk chippy. He sprang at her like a wild beast, gibbering undistinguishable sounds and drooling slobber from the mouth. He threw her to the floor and assaulted her. (*Black on Black*, 174–75)

Himes's interest in the monsters of prison and ghetto was not limited to the simpler brutes, creatures of rudimentary violence; it included the con men as well, violators of more subtle sanctuaries, assaulters of truth itself, and belief and trust. It was the variety of forms that the con men's menace could assume that fascinated him. In later stories he would complete the spectrum with equally perceptive studies of the victims of violence and deception, virtuosos of suffering whose passivity presented as wide and ingenious a range of deformity as their more aggressive brethren. The basic conditions of overcrowding and hopelessness subjected the people caught in both of Himes's special environments, prison and ghetto, to pressures inconceivable to the outsider and threw their myriad human eccentricities into harder and bolder relief, as though they were under a sharper and clearer light that could be found nowhere else. Had Carl Van Vechten or Marc Connelly written "Pork Chop Paradise," its power to offend would be formidable. But Himes's story is not an amusing sketch of quaint black folk mores. It is a parable about religious hypocrisy, a comment on the ambiguous sexuality and the longing for self-deception that can be involved in the seductive ecstasies of religiosity. Himes did not write as an outsider. He himself had lived under the special pressures of prison and ghetto, had observed himself, long and fully, under their pitiless lights. The reader is not invited to look at "them," and guffaw; he is compelled to look into himself, and squirm. In the final analysis, the black monsters of Himes's stories are simply ordinary human beings, distorted by incredible pressures—though they are none the less terrifying for that.

There are other monsters in Himes's stories, however, for whom circumstances do not provide any justification. Evil, in an almost Manichaean sense, is one of the realities of his fictional world. It manifests itself as violence that is unprovoked, unmotivated, in no way a response to the pressures imposed by a rejecting society. The monsters who deal in such purely gratuitous violence are not black but white, and their violence seems to be called into existence largely by the availability of victims, a whole defenseless black world. In many ways they may be highly complicated human beings, but their reactions to black people are monstrously and monotonously simple. The mere presence of a black man seems sufficient to provoke them to acts of extreme and studied cruelty. Confronted with the black world, their one unvarying impulse is to hurt, to add something of their own, however small, to the burden of pain already carried by some black man or woman. Their presence is one of the most constant features of Himes's work. They are, after all, one of the givens of a society structured along racist lines. The type is already represented, and rather fully defined, in "His Last Day," in a white prison guard who gleefully tells a black man about to die in the electric chair that he should not worry about the rain falling in the prison yard because he will be a better electrical conductor if he is wet (p. 60).

In spite of their repugnant and basically absurd cruelty, however, characters of this type are almost always depicted by Himes with pity, and sometimes with curiosity, but their dominant central urge, a panicky and aggressive affirmation of their "whiteness" does not allow for a great deal of complexity in their personalities. In some of Himes's later novels, most notably *If He Hollers Let Him Go* and *Run Man Run*, characters of this type, white monsters, are assigned key roles in elaborate plot structures, and various aspects of their personalities are studied in great depth, but they never lose their absolute and terrifying predictability in any situation involving confrontations with a black man. Whatever else they may be, they become pathetic and dangerous emotional cripples, obsessed psychotics, whenever their racist impulses are triggered.

In "A Nigger," written in 1937 and published in *Black on Black*, Himes explored the thesis that the effectiveness of obsessively sadistic racists of this type, their power to hurt, must be to some extent a function of the black man's acceptance, or even tacit collaboration. The story's monster is an aging and very rich and conservative white businessman who pays regular visits to a black mistress he maintains in an apartment in the Cleveland ghetto. This relationship does not imply virility, amatory passion, or a sense of the brotherhood of man, the narrator explains, but precisely contrary qualities, characteristic of white men who are both impotent and affluent:

> Turning to Negro women because in them they saw only the black image of flesh, the organ itself, like beautiful bronze statues endowed with motion, flesh and blood, instinct and passion, but possessing no mind to condemn, no soul to be outraged, most of all no power to judge or accuse, before whom the spirit of exhausted sex could creep and crawl and expose its ugly nakedness without embarrassment or restraint. (*Black on Black*, 129)

In addition to the spirit of exhausted sex, this aging tycoon carries a complete set of prejudices involving the "lower classes" in general, and he devotes a large part of his visits to sputtery tirades against F.D.R.'s welfare and relief programs, sounding very much like a doggedly uninspired editorial out of some yellowed, ancient rightest newspaper: " 'By God, if I had my way, I'd make them work for what they get like people used to do in America. . . . 'If the rest of the colored people are as sensible as you, dear, we might get rid of him this time. By God, we'll put enough money behind Landon to get him there' " (p. 127). But his mistress, Fay, also has a black lover, Joe, a "broke, ragged lunger who claimed he was some kind of writer or poet or something" (p. 125), and one day when Fay's "rich white John out of Shaker Heights" arrives unexpectedly, Joe is forced to hide in the bedroom closet throughout his visit. He listens to all that passes with mounting confusion, fully aware that the white man is a fool, but also fully aware that he has been buying his food with part of the money this man pays for the privilege of "using" Fay as though she were something slightly less than a human being: "*If I can only get it funny,* he thought. *It is funny! Funny as hell! Goddamn, we're some simple people*" (p. 129). But beneath his fatuous and mildly preposterous surface image, Faye's white "benefactor" conceals a capacity for malice that is both subtle and deep. Just before he leaves he opens the closet door and, pretending he has not seen Joe, immediately closes it. It is a simple but devastating gesture, and it drives Joe into a despairing frenzy when he finally grasps its import:

> "He couldn't have seen you, darling," Fay was saying. "He gave me the two hundred dollars—see!" She waved a wad of bills at him. "He even kissed me goodbye," she added.
> Joe stood there looking at her without hearing, hardly seeing her. *Why, he had not only refused to recognize him as a rival, not even as an intruder; why, the son of a bitch looked at him as if he was another garment he had bought for her.* It was the first time he had ever felt the absolute refusal of recognition. (*Black on Black,* 131)

He beats Fay savagely with his fists, but to no avail; it is much too late to restore his shattered sense of manhood:

> . . . his shame. The fact was he had kept standing there, taking it, even after he could no longer tell himself that it was a joke, a trim on a sucker, just so he could keep on eat-

ing off the bitch. . . . Uncle Tomism, acceptance, toadying—
all there in its most rugged form. One way to be a nigger.
Other Negroes did it other ways—he did it the hard way.
The same result—*a nigger*. (*Black on Black*, 132)

Not all of Himes's early stories involving encounters with
sadistic whites, and their formidable expertise in inflicting pain
and enforcing humiliations, are this pessimistic, however. In
"Headwaiter," written a year later, in 1938, he presents a sharply
detailed, many-sided portrait of a black man who has learned how
to play the white man's deadly little games and win, learned how
to make refusal pass for acceptance, and a highly sophisticated
form of "shuckin' n' jivin' " seem to be nothing less than blatant
Uncle Tomism to the undiscerning eye. The headwaiter Dick
Small, the story's authentically heroic central figure, is in fact a
very great man, bringing to his not very grand job—an extremely
difficult executive position that is nevertheless close to the bottom
of the social ladder—abilities and qualities of character that would
grace a statesman of the first rank. He runs the dining room of a
large hotel with consummate skill, creating by the subtle impo-
sition of his powerful will an atmosphere of grace and gentility
out of a highly unpromising combination of sullen bus boys,
clumsy waiters, boorish patrons, and gaudy decor. His professional equipment includes a "creased, careful smile" (p. 144),
which he never abandons, and his aplomb is equal to seven-year-
old diners who call him "Dick," and men who jocularly remark,
"That's a good-looking tux, boy. . . . Steal it?" (p. 153). Beneath
the perfect sham of his obsequiousness, however, there is no
real humility at all. He has the lofty arrogance of a man who has
never encountered a situation he could not control, and he demonstrates his uncanny ability to reduce large waves to small ripples
a dozen times in the course of the story. "He was as the captain of
a ship, he reflected, the master of this dining room and solely
responsible" (p. 151). His arrogance is fully visible in his
dealings with waiters and bus boys, but so is a truly enormous
capacity for feeling. He can fire a drunken waiter without a moment's hesitation, but not without feeling the man's distress, and
showing it:

He said, "Accidents will happen, son. Yours just cost you your job. If there's anything I can ever do for you, anything in reason, let me know. And even if it isn't in reason, come and let me say so." He stood still for a moment. His face showed extreme weariness.

Then he shook it all from his mind. It required a special effort. He blinked his eyes clear of the picture of a dejected black face, donned his creased, careful smile and pushed through the service hall into the dining room. His head was cocked to one side as though he were deferentially listening. (*Black on Black*, 160)

Within his limited sphere Dick Small is a man of power, and he is not afraid to use it, even to risking his own job in hiring a black ex-convict he thinks will make a good waiter. He represents one of Himes's first real attempts to understand the kind of man his own father had once been, men who accept roles of leadership in oppressed communities, even at the price of apparent collaboration with the oppressor. Dick Small's redeeming feature is his perfect lucidity. He is a flawless player in a highly artificial game of manners, and he never forgets where the boundaries are that separate the real from the false. His world is largely absurd and he follows all of its rules punctiliously, but he never fails to see, and feel, the absurdity. There is no trace of satire in Himes's portrait of this black man of power. The story is a tribute to "soul," black soul, in a very unexpected setting, a tribute to a life style that Himes could never follow but to which he always gave ungrudging respect. Years later, in a few passages of Chapter 20 of the autobiographical novel *The Third Generation* (1954), the character Dick Small briefly reappeared for a second time in Himes's work, without any noticeable alterations.

The end of the decade of the 1930s marked a turning point both in Himes's still-budding career as a writer of stories and in his personal life. With the support of his parole officer he successfully petitioned the governor of Ohio for the termination of his parole and the return of his citizenship, and shortly thereafter he and his wife Jean left Ohio on a bus bound for California, where newly booming defense industries offered the promise of plentiful jobs and better wages. And there was good reason to hope that Himes might be able to find work in Hollywood as a writer. His last Ohio employer, Louis Bromfield, had gone to Hollywood in the fall of 1939 to work on the script of the film *Brigham Young*, taking a copy of Himes's unpublished prison novel with him to show to producers. But Himes's attempts at a career as a film writer ended abruptly after a few brief and abortive starts. He walked out of one story conference in a rage at what he considered racist attitudes on the part of the other writers, and, he told John A. Williams, he was promptly fired from a trial job at Warner Brothers when Jack Warner heard about him and said, "I don't want no niggers on this lot."[26] The promise of defense jobs proved equally illusory. Workers from all over the country had been drawn to California by the boom, including explosively high percentages of Southern whites and Northern blacks, and racial tensions were high in the new industries. And Chester Himes was not a man to tread softly in troubled times. Before he finally gave up and left for New York City, he had run through some twenty-three jobs in three years in wartime California, almost all as an unskilled laborer at low wages, despite the wide variety of "essential" skills he had acquired through the years, from typist to turret lathe operator (*The Quality of Hurt*, 75).

But, during these same years, the early 1940s, as the golden doors of economic opportunity were being repeatedly slammed in his face, a whole new range of interests and literary opportunities was opening up for him. A full citizen for the first time in his life, free to function politically, and to vote, he began to follow with keen interest every new development in black politics and the long-frustrated civil rights movement. His brother Joseph Sandy Himes had completed his Ph.D. at Ohio State University in 1938 and was already becoming well known as a sociologist, publishing many articles in professional journals and civil rights magazines like the National Urban League's *Opportunity* and the NAACP's *The Crisis*. Soon a long series of stories by Chester Himes, as well as fiery political articles, appeared in these same

26. Williams, "My Man Himes," pp. 59–60.

civil rights journals and related publications. He contributed almost a dozen pieces to *The Crisis* alone during the 1940s.

A few of the stories he published in these journals were almost identical to some of his earlier work. For example, "The Things You Do," published in *Opportunity* in May 1941, is an account of a prison visit that is cast in precisely the same patterns as "The Visiting Hour." The story in *Opportunity*, however—which also appears, only slightly rewritten, as Chapter 6 of *Cast the First Stone* (1952)—is a much stronger piece of writing. In a few pages Himes captures the immense despair of a young convict, already nerve-wracked, taut with the beginnings of prison hysteria, who suddenly perceives, as he studies his mother's haggard and defeated face across a prison table, the appalling scope of the hurts he has inflicted on all those he had left behind him in the outside world. An effect of total suffocation is achieved through the slow, methodical piling up of minute detail: the boy's nagging fear that his prison hat, which he has altered to make it more attractive, will be confiscated by a guard, his inability to eat the food his mother has brought, and the empty banality of everything they say in their efforts to bridge a gap that both recognize to be as wide as that which separates the living from the dead.[27] Himes had come a very long way in his struggle to develop a technique that would permit him to convert his prison experiences into art.

A number of the stories he published during the 1940s, however, show less concern for the problems of art than for those of propaganda and political persuasion. "Two Soldiers," published in *The Crisis* in 1943, is a noisy little epic that offers a vision of battle in the Sahara that could only have come from a Grade-B war movie: ". . . the Nazi tanks, specking the desert terrain for miles, darting about like vicious, fire-spitting bugs. . . . the Stukas, coming down one at a time in their crazy intricate dives with Spitfires on their tails and F.W. 190's trying to fight them off."[28] In addition to being literally "loaded with action," the

27. Chester Himes, "The Things You Do," *Opportunity*, XIX:5 (May 1941), 141–43.
28. Chester Himes, "Two Soldiers," *The Crisis*, 50:1 (January 1943), 13.

story is heavy with a message that it quickly delivers with splash-
ily sentimental impact, a comforting message about the inevitable
triumph of the brotherhood of man in the midst of the holocaust
of a war to end racism. Pvt. Joshua Crabtree, a rough and vindictive white soldier from Georgia and a crack shot, deliberately
holds his fire at a crucial moment, hoping that George, the black
soldier he is supposed to be "covering," will be killed, but George
fires his gun at a diving Nazi Stuka at the very moment he is
mortally wounded, saving Crabtree's life. From that moment
Crabtree is a changed man. He dashes onto the field and grabs
George up in his arms, frantically trying to save the life he had
deliberately endangered, heroically persisting in the face of
enemy fire and the dying man's own gentle remonstrances: " 'Set
me down, white brother, and save yo'self,' George whispered
through blood-flecked lips. 'Ah hear de chariot comin' ' " (p. 29).

The propaganda of uplift was evidently a new field for Himes,
but his efforts were not always this clumsy. "So Softly Smiling,"
which was also published in *The Crisis* in 1943, carries the same
message as "Two Soldiers," but it is also one of his very best
stories, though not by virtue of verbal restraint. The central
character, Roy Squires, is a black army officer spending a month's
leave from the North African battlefront in a picturesque, snow-
covered Harlem. The horrors of war are suggested only through
their effects on his badly battered nervous system, an area in
which Himes needed no help at all from the movies—". . . jerking
his reflexes and keeping his eyes constantly on the alert. . . . His
nerves were sticking out like wires. . . . too filled with something,
too much like just lying down and crying like a baby"[29]—and the
story's message comes through, quietly and unobtrusively, in
the central character's efforts to understand his role in the war,
to think his way through to some kind of reasonably clear perspective on just exactly what he is fighting for. He feels above all,
however, a desperate need to love, and his efforts to rationalize
the war are temporarily sidetracked when he meets, and immediately marries, a celebrated black poetess whose mere appearance is enough to lift his wildest romantic fancies into the

29. Chester Himes, "So Softly Smiling," *The Crisis*, 15:10 (October
1943), 302.

realm of reality: ". . . a tawny skin like an African veld at sunset, so smooth you forever wanted to touch it, crowned by blue-black hair that rolled up from her forehead in great curling billows like low storm clouds. That mouth, wide enough for a man to really kiss, and the color of crushed rosebuds" (p. 302). After an idyllic honeymoon in the country, and a few friendly spats, however, Roy Squires finally does arrive at some edifying answers:

> "I read where someone said, perhaps it was Walter White or Randolph, that America belonged to the Negro as much as it did to anyone. And I got a funny feeling, maybe it was pride, or ownership—I don't know. Anyway I enlisted. . . . I got to feeling that I was fighting for the Four Freedoms. . . . a bigger fight than just to keep the same old thing we've always had. . . . more like building, well, building security and peace and freedom for everyone." ("So Softly Smiling," 315)

In a third story published in *The Crisis* in 1943, "Heaven Has Changed," Himes tried his hand at straight allegory as a vehicle for his resolutely upbeat messages. A black soldier is killed on the battlefield and immediately awakens in heaven, where he finds in force the same rigid patterns of segregation he has lived under all his life. The black people's section of heaven is in the form of an antebellum cotton plantation, presided over by a very minor deity, who is black, and his trusty assistant, Old Jim Crow, a "tall, thin, sour-faced white man," who loves to say no.[30] But, as the soldier watches, the young black people of heaven cheerfully and good-naturedly try out a few elementary techniques of organized protest, and the Big White God soon decides to make some radical changes, sending Old Jim Crow to hell as a first step. Allegory is a medium that favors, and even demands, drastic resolutions to the problems that are posed.

In an early story from *The Crisis*, "Lunching at the Ritzmore," a pungently satiric and whimsical local-color sketch, the demise of Old Jim Crow was also celebrated, but in a somewhat less confident and definite manner. A white college student, arguing with a drifter in Los Angeles's Pershing Square, loudly claims that

---

30. Chester Himes, "Heaven Has Changed," in *Black on Black*, pp. 189–90. (Originally appeared in *The Crisis*, 50:3 [March 1943], 78, 83.)

there is no racial discrimination in Los Angeles, that it is in fact no more than a fiction of communist propaganda, and a crowd of onlookers slowly collects around the arguing pair until they are standing in the center of a mob numbering in the thousands. When the student finally decides to actually put his thesis to the test, by persuading a passing black youth to march with him into the swankiest hotel dining room on the square and demand service, the hotel's management is completely overawed by the enormous crowd surging through the square and into the lobby, and everyone is served without question. The student has triumphantly proved his point about the absence of discrimination in Los Angeles, the narrator wryly notes, but his joy is cut short when he finds he will have to pay the restaurant bill.[31]

On the whole, judged today solely in terms of their power to persuade, Himes's earliest wartime propaganda stories are not overwhelmingly successful. The handful of articles he published during those same years, however, between 1942 and 1945, leave no doubt at all as to the completeness of his own commitment at that time to a social philosophy that was frankly idealistic and totally optimistic. This was doubtless in part a response to the extraordinary conditions of the times. Wars routinely produce unpredictable aberrations in the thinking processes and mental sets of entire nations. Throughout America in the first years of World War II there was an unprecedented outpouring of idealism in its highest and purest forms. The hackneyed slogans dear to the hearts of Fourth of July orators were mouthed everywhere in tones of absolute conviction as practical programs for the immediate future. To Chester Himes this phenomenon was immensely exhilarating. He believed fervently and without reservations, and he was ready to shout his belief to anyone who would listen. He gave to each of his articles a rigidly logical framework, but he wrote them all in states of intense excitement, and they are less coolly compelling arguments than whirlpools of pure emotion.

In the article "Now Is the Time! Here Is the Place!," published

31. Chester Himes, "Lunching at the Ritzmore," in *Black on Black*, pp. 176–82. (Originally appeared in *The Crisis*, 49:10 [October 1942], 314, 315, 331.)

in *Opportunity* in 1942, he proclaimed his burning conviction that the black people of America could best support the national war effort by giving themselves wholeheartedly to the nation's vital and saving wave of rampant idealism and by applying it to their own ancient struggle for justice within America itself. By strengthening themselves by throwing off their crippling psychological bonds, black Americans would strengthen the nation itself. They must somehow accept the paradox that the nation's fight to preserve the *status quo* and their own fight to end the *status quo* were in fact the same fight.

No matter how we feel about it, no matter what emotional upheaval churns in our breasts, what protests gnaw at our minds, what abuses are heaped upon our persons, what degradations our spirits must wear for garments; . . . no matter the awful despair seeping into our souls, the oft-denied feeling of inferiority which in time comes to all oppressed—*we must enter full-bodied and wholehearted into this great war waged by the United Nations to stamp out nazism, fascism, and imperialism for all time to come.*

But how can we participate in this great war without giving the same effort to our home fight aginst our native enemies? . . .

In the broader view, the Negro Americans' fight for freedom is more than racial. It is a fight for justice, for an ideal, for a form of government in which people will be bound together, neither by race, nor creed, nor descent, but by common objectives and aims for the benefit of all. . . . No American of any race, true to the ideals of Americanism, can refuse to participate in the Negro Americans' fight and on their side.[32]

In the article "Negro Martyrs Are Needed," published in *The Crisis* in May 1944, he called upon the black middle classes to precipitate a peaceful "revolution," force the implementation of the spirit of the American Constitution, by the simple expedient of exposing themselves freely to every possibility of injustice that threatens the black man in America, thereby thrusting the hidden

32. Chester Himes, "Now Is the Time! Here Is the Place!," in *Black on Black*, pp. 215–18. (Originally appeared in *Opportunity*, XX:9 [September 1942], 272, 273, 284.)

machinery of social injustice into the healing light of full national publicity. After perfunctorily dismissing some ponderous Marxist pronouncements on the subject, he suggested that social revolution need be no more complicated than the simple act of saying "no":

> The martyr must make the stand and refuse to yield. The Negro middle class must come to his assistance, also refusing to yield, and must influence the Negro lower classes to follow.
>
> What is of utmost importance is the stand. And after we have made it, we must not give on any point.[33]

In "Democracy is for the Unafraid," published in *Common Ground* and in Bucklin Moon's anthology *Primer for White Folks*, he called more pointedly on white Americans to join the struggle by demonstrating once and for all that they were "not afraid to accept the fundamental fact of mankind's equality."[34]

The war years unleashed in America, however, not only a great upsurge of ideological faith but also some very primitive and brutal emotions. Along with the rallies and parades, there were race riots, mass outbreaks of white violence against black, Mexican, and Japanese Americans. Chester Himes's faith in the bright promises that flowed so freely on every side had to coexist with his growing fear that a national impulse toward hellish violence, which he could dimly perceive in spurts here and there, might be the more solid reality. In 1943 he published in *The Crisis* an indignant eyewitness account of a race riot in Los Angeles in which groups of white servicemen savagely assaulted Mexican American youths in the streets with complete impunity.

> This we know: That during the first two nights of the rioting, no policemen were in evidence until the gangs of sailors, outnumbering the pachuos two-three-four to one, had sapped up on the pachuos with belt buckles and knotted ropes. When the sailors departed in their cars, trucks, and

33. Chester Himes, "Negro Martyrs Are Needed," in *Black on Black*, p. 235. (Originally appeared in *The Crisis*, 51:5 [May 1944], 174.)

34. Chester Himes, "Democracy is for the Unafraid," *Primer for White Folks*, ed. Bucklin Moon (New York: Doubleday, Doran and Co., Inc., 1945), p. 481.

taxi-cabs, furnished them no doubt by the nazi-minded citizenry, the police appeared as if they had been waiting around the corner and arrested the Mexican youths who had been knocked out, stunned, or too frightened to run.[35]

Himes's wartime propaganda efforts also included a set of stories in which he embodied nightmarish visions of a present and future for the black man in America that would be darker and even more violent and bloody than the worst of the past had been. These are his ugliest stories, but they are also among the most powerful. The central action is always the total destruction of a black protagonist by an act of white violence that is completely unmotivated, perfectly mindless. In these stories he affronted for the first time the technical problems involved in depicting violence in writing—problems that were to be among his major concerns in the last phases of his career. What is involved primarily are strategies of attack against reader resistance that is both involuntary and almost impenetrable. The reality of violence, like the reality of death, is a fact that the human mind is conditioned to resist. Whenever normal people witness an actual act of violence they experience intense physical shock, nausea stemming from the violation of the mind's protective devices, but these same people can read minutely detailed accounts of acts of violence with no reaction whatsoever. The goal of every writer who seriously attempts to describe violence must be to generate a level of literary emotion that is in some way equivalent to the sick horror automatically generated by every real act of violence. In the stories he devoted entirely to depicting the violence of whites against blacks, Himes experimented with a number of approaches. In "Christmas Gift" (1944) he used a sentimental frame, a young and lovely black mother and her infant daughter alone in a Mississippi cottage on Christmas Eve, awaiting the return of Johnny, husband and father, from the war. And Johnny does return that night, in a splendid uniform covered with medals, and he is set upon and beaten to death by two white deputy sheriffs as he crosses the dark railroad yard:

35. Chester Himes, "Zoot Riots Are Race Riots," in *Black on Black*, p. 224. (Originally appeared in *The Crisis*, 50:7 [July 1943], 201.)

Slobby flashed a light in Johnny's face. "W'y, by God, it's the Stevens nigger!" He kept the light on Johnny, running it up and down. "Lookit them things this nigger got stuck on him—stripes and medals. W'ut you get them fur, Johnny, cleanin' out latrines?" He suddenly broke out laughing.[36]

In "One More Way to Die," published in *Negro Story* in 1946, Himes used first-person narration, with the hapless protagonist finally recounting his own murder at the hands of two California policemen, in an insidiously tricky finale:

I was begging 'em over and over again, "Cap'n, please don't kill me. Please, cap'n. I swear I'll never hit another white woman as long as I live, not even by mistake." I knew my lips were moving, but I couldn't even hear my own voice.

I heard the first cop say, "Let's get it over with."

Then I heard the sound of the shot and felt the bullet go right through my chest.[37]

In "All He Needs Is Feet," published in *The Crisis*, he fell back, not too ingeniously, on every reader's innate aversion to stories of mutilation:

But the people didn't want to lynch him. . . . all they wanted to do was teach him a lesson. A man with a C card furnished some gasoline and they soaked his feet, tied his arms behind him, set his feet on fire, and turned him aloose.[38]

These stories do generate shock waves, though they may never hit the reader quite as hard as Himes wanted them to. He had identified a number of essential ingredients that could be relied upon to heighten and intensify an atmosphere of terror: victims who are imperturbably good-natured and appealingly helpless; a balanced Kafkaesque mixture of absurdity and casual inevitability in the injustices described; the involvement of constituted authority, the police themselves, in obscene and irrational acts of violence.

36. Himes, "Christmas Gift," in *Black on Black*, p. 250.
37. Himes, "One More Way to Die," in *Black on Black*, p. 262.
38. Himes, "All He Needs Is Feet," in *Black on Black*, p. 253 (dated here as 1945). (Originally appeared in *The Crisis*, 50:11 [November 1943], 332.)

But even during this most narrowed and specialized phase of his career, while he was briefly trying out the role of Himes the haranguer in the cause of social improvement, Himes never ceased to be a man of many moods, many faces. He was, as always, a creature of extremes, and one set of preoccupations or one particular orientation never seemed to exclude another, even the most apparently incompatible. He continued to explore the almost inexhaustible variety of forms the short story could assume, and sometimes his strength registered only as awkwardness, and sometimes he produced a literary gem.

In "All God's Chillun Got Pride," which appeared in *Crisis* in 1944 and much of which was later incorporated into his novel *Lonely Crusade* (1947), he achieved a new intensity of self-revelation in an autobiographical fragment, almost psychoanalytical depth, in a study of a personality slowly disintegrating under the constant, grinding pressure of insecurity, groping endlessly through a whole deadly cloud of vague, nagging fears, whose very vagueness intensifies their power to undermine. With the inexorable neurotic persistence of a bad dream the story probes at the dark sides of the few bright episodes in Himes's past, including his job as research assistant in the Cleveland library:

> Scared of just being black—that was it. One of the ancient librarians who avoided him as if he were diseased, who refused to hear when he addressed them directly, who were vitriolic when finally replying, who let him stand unattended before their desks while they carried on thirty-minute conversations over the telephone concerning everything under God's sun and would then arise and walk away, who made it as tough as they possibly could, would some day say to him, "Why in heaven's name can't you colored people be patient?" and he would snarl at her right off the very top of his muscle, "Why you-you, why go to hell, you beatup biddy!" And he would be out of a job. All of the Negroes who ever hoped to work in the library project of the W.P.A. in Cleveland, Ohio, would be out of jobs; the whole race would feel it and he would be a traitor not only to himself but to twelve million other people who didn't have a thing to do with it. He'd have to go home and tell Clara that he blew up and lost

his job; and God knows they couldn't go hungry anymore. He hated to think of what might happen, because they couldn't take another period of that hungry hopelessness.[39]

Also in 1944, with "Cotton Gonna Kill Me Yet," Himes tried something very similar to Langston Hughes's popular Simple stories, a comic urban folktale, recounting in an approach to black jitterbug dialect the trials and tribulations of an amiable loser. His narrator, and loser, is an easily bewildered, conk-haired young poolroom hustler from Los Angeles who lets himself be conned into taking a job picking cotton in Bakersfield and is not long in discovering, that he, a shiftless loafer by conviction, has been betrayed into what is very probably the world's hardest job:

> Let me tell you, them stiffs was grabbin' that cotton so fast you couldn't see the motion of their arms. . . .
> I hauled off and started workin' my arms and grabbed at the first cotton I saw. Somp'n jumped out and bit me on the finger and I jumped six feet. Thought sure I was snake-bit. When I found out it was just the sharp joint of the cotton boll I felt like a plugged slug. . . . Then I got mad. I 'gan grabbin' that cotton with both hands.
> In 'bout an hour looked like I'd been in the rain. Hands ain't never been so bruised, look like every boll musta bit 'em. When I tried to straighten up my straightener wouldn't work.[40]

Himes's humor scrapes uncomfortably close to unpleasant reality throughout the story, both in the details of the incredibly harsh, backbreaking labor and in the fundamentally unadmirable character of his hustler–narrator. Unlike Hughes's lovable Simple, Himes's loser is not above trying to change his luck by stealing cotton from the other black pickers, a ploy that, characteristically, gains him nothing at all, beyond a very thorough, though generally friendly, gang beating.

In "Mama's Missionary Money," of 1949, Himes was still

39. Chester Himes, "All God's Chillun Got Pride," in *Black on Black*, p. 240. (Originally appeared in *The Crisis*, 51:6 [June 1944], 188.)
40. Chester Himes, "Cotton Gonna Kill Me Yet," in *Black on Black*, p. 200.

close to the manner of Langston Hughes, but he was closer to that of Mark Twain. It is the brightest and happiest story he ever wrote. It projects an idealized image of a rural boyhood that is as real as anyone's fondest memory, or the smell of a wet barnyard. The world of the story is one in which a mischievous boy's misdeeds never trouble the wall of love that surrounds him, a world in which parental punishment itself can be an act of love, carrying with it no suggestion at all of condemnation or rejection. It is a world in which life triumphs, and injustice is not even a passing thought:

> Lemuel heard his ma call him. Always wanting him to go to the store. He squirmed back to the corner of the chicken house, out of sight of the yard. He felt damp where he had sat in some fresh chicken manure and he cursed. . . .
> He got up and peeked out the door, looked around. He felt like old Daniel Boone. Wasn't nobody in sight. He went out in the yard. The dust was deep where the hens had burrowed hollows. It oozed up twixt the toes of his bare feet and felt hot and soft as flour. His long dark feet were dust covered to a tan color. The dust was thick on his ankles, thinning up his legs.[41]

The peak of Himes's achievement as a short-story writer, however, is marked by a grim tale with an unprepossessing title, "Da-Da-Dee" (two *dah*'s and a *dee*), written in 1948. It is an autobiographical fragment, but it is a perfectly structured unit so charged with its own internal energy that it could not possibly function within any larger structure. It is a short story by a writer who has chosen the form, this time at least, for its intrinsic values and not simply as a convenient substitute for the novels he really wants to write. It deals with the worst period of crisis Himes ever passed through, when his marriage to Jean was breaking up and the hostile critical reaction to the first two novels he published, in 1945 and 1947, had driven him temporarily into a state of alcoholic despair. In *The Quality of Hurt* (1972) he

41. Chester Himes, "Mama's Missionary Money," in *Black on Black*, p. 275. (The story was printed twice in *The Crisis*: 56:11 [November 1949], 303, 307; 77:11 [November 1970], 361–63.)

suggested the appalling scope of the crisis in one short sentence: "For the next five years I couldn't write" (p. 103).[42] In 1953, when it was finally over, his marriage gone but his will once more intact, he left the United States on a steamer bound for France, determined to reside permanently in Europe. His novel *The Primitive* (1955) deals with the same period of crisis, and there are some very striking points of resemblance between the novel and the 1948 story. In both the protagonist is a black novelist with a work-in-progress entitled *I Was Looking for a Street*. But the Jethro Adams of "Da-Da-Dee" is a very different character from the Jesse Robinson of *The Primitive*. His despair is purer, less complex, more fundamental.

In the spring of 1948 Himes was a guest at Yaddo, in Saratoga Springs, an estate and foundation dedicated to providing artists of all types, creative people in general, with support and working facilities, primarily in the form of living quarters in a gracious residence where they could work undisturbed and commune with their peers at fixed hours. For Himes, it proved a stormy and largely unproductive episode, and he left a very bad memory behind him, as a man who drank. The story "Da-Da-Dee" is set there. Jethro Adams is "a famous writer of two racial novels . . . the guest of the celebrated artists' colony, Skidoo. . . . something a little inhuman—a celebrity."[43] The story focuses on a single incident, a span of time of about one hour. It picks him up, very drunk, in his favorite bar and follows him through his noisy, staggering return to Skidoo, trying all the time to sing a song he can't quite remember, going something like da-da-dee. He wants desperately to be in love, and he thinks he just may be in love with the barmaid, but he is far from a romantic figure:

> He tried to hold her with his smile. Actually it was more a grimace than a smile. His face was twisted to one side and down-pulled with weariness. His skin was greasy; his eyes deep-sunk and haggard. There were harsh, deep lines pulling down the edges of his mouth. His age was showing in his face. At such times he looked a great deal like his father, a

42. It was, however, during these years that he wrote *The Third Generation*.
43. Chester Himes, "Da-Da-Dee," in *Black on Black*, p. 269.

small, black man who had faded to a parchment-colored mummy in his old age. It was hard for him to realize that he looked so old. Even blotto, at five o'clock in the morning, he still felt youthful and good-looking. He tried to hold her attention long enough for her to notice that his glass was empty. But she smiled perfunctorily and moved down the bar. By now the night was telling on her also. Although she was twenty years younger than his forty-one, her eyes were pouching slightly and slowly glazing with sleepiness. (*Black on Black*, 267–68)

The song that carries him through the dark streets, all the way to his luxurious room in the plush estate—"a melodic wailing of pain as if he were being beaten to some vague rhythmic beat. . . . as if the loud wailing notes, themselves, relieved the pain" (p. 272)—is the story's center, moving it in a single straight line with great speed, underlining and defining Jethro's perfect despair. Himes's finest story, like all his strongest work, was rooted deep in his own suffering. His unique gift was the power to transform those emotions into art. He was always the most completely an artist when he felt the least like one:

He was humming and he could feel the sharp vibrations of the sounds in his nostrils. It filled his head with a great melancholy. He felt as if nothing would ever matter again one way or another. . . . He was never meant to be anything but a cheap, smiling gambler with a flashy front, he told himself. He was a simple man. All he ever wanted was a street that he could understand. (*Black on Black*, 274)

3

The Protest Novels
If He Hollers Let Him Go
Lonely Crusade

I If He Hollers Let Him Go

In the summer of 1944 Chester Himes arrived in New York City, on the crest of a rare mood of high confidence. A major publishing house, Doubleday, Doran & Co., had accepted one of his novels, and he was to assist in the process of publication. His cousin Henry Moon, one of his father's nephews, and Henry's wife Molly had helped him to obtain a fellowship from the Julius Rosenwald Foundation, and, for the moment, finances were not a grinding concern. Henry Moon was already a highly visible figure in the Civil Rights movement, a recognized member of Franklin Roosevelt's unofficial "Black Cabinet," the small circle of black leaders who were on occasion given the opportunity to offer their advice to the President on issues affecting the black community. Under his cousins' influence, Himes became deeply involved in Roosevelt's campaign for a fourth term, losing himself completely in "the flood of humanity that worshipped at his [F.D.R.'s] shrine," "a movement that was vaguely political but also strangely religious."[1]

But both his crusading fervor and his soaring optimism for his own future were short-lived. Years of prison and close familiarity with degradation and vice had had little effect on his fundamentally idealistic bent, and the seamier side of practical politics —"Everything was used to garner votes: sex . . . money, eloquence, and intrigue" (*The Quality of Hurt*, 76)—quickly repulsed him. "I must have been a puritan all my life" (p. 13), he

1. Himes, *The Quality of Hurt*, p. 76.

confesses, a bit ruefully. The ending of his one political campaign was characteristically paradoxical, "I lost myself in sex and drunkenness and I didn't even vote for Roosevelt after all" (p. 76).

The publication of his novel, *If He Hollers Let Him Go* (1945), was only briefly a triumph, then a source of new and deeper bitterness. The book had a very strong start, with mixed reviews but rapid early sales that seemed to indicate solid profits ahead. Himes later learned that Doubleday was considering the book for the George Washington Carver Memorial Award, $2,500 offered by the company to books that best seemed to "illuminate the Negro's place in American life." The award went instead to a novel by a white writer, *Mrs. Palmer's Honey* by Fannie Cook, an earnestly plodding work about a charismatic black maid. Next, sales for Himes's book very abruptly dropped off. He told John A. Williams almost thirty years later:

> But what had actually happened to *If He Hollers* was that this woman editor—Doubleday was printing their own books in Garden City—had telephoned to their printing department in Garden City and ordered them to stop the printing. So they just arbitrarily stopped the printing of *If He Hollers* for a couple of weeks or so during the time when it would have been a solid best-seller.[2]

At the time a number of people had written to Himes to inform him that they had tried to purchase copies of his book but that the bookstores had been strangely unable to fill their orders. Some seven years later he was told by Bucklin Moon, who had been his official editor at Doubleday at the time, that a white woman editor, "whose name was never told to [Himes],"[3] had violently attacked his book: "[she] said that *If He Hollers* made her disgusted and it made her sick and nauseated, and if *If He Hollers* was selected

2. John A. Williams, "My Man Himes: An Interview with Chester Himes," pp. 35–36. In his interview with Hoyt Fuller, Himes described the telephone call ordering the printing stopped as a threat made rather than an action taken (Fuller, "Traveler on the Long, Rough, Lonely Old Road: An Interview with Chester Himes," p. 6).

3. Williams, "My Man Himes," pp. 35–36.

for this memorial award that she would resign."[4] Further, Himes told Williams, Doubleday's advertising copy for the award book, *Mrs. Palmer's Honey*, had referred to another book published by the company on the black problem as a "series of epithets punctuated by spit."[5] Himes complained bitterly about the ad and the falling sales to everyone he could talk to at Doubleday, but with no result, and he began to search for another publisher for his next book. Carl Van Vechten, introduced to Himes by Richard Wright, already a close friend, agreed to intervene, and he persuaded the Knopf company to purchase Himes's contract from Doubleday, a matter of no great difficulty, since Himes had received an advance of only $1,000 from Doubleday for his next book. By one of the ironies that seem to typify Himes's career, however, Doubleday would be once again his major American publisher in the later stages of his career. *The Quality of Hurt* (1972), which contains an account of his quarrel with Doubleday that is only slightly less detailed and emphatic than that which appears in Williams's interview article, was published by Doubleday itself (*The Quality of Hurt*, 77).

Himes's conviction that *If He Hollers Let Him Go* (1945) could easily have been "a solid best-seller" was, moreover, reasonably well founded. *If He Hollers Let Him Go* is preeminently the kind of book that compels the reader to finish it at one sitting. It is the kind of book that the purplish adjectives of publishers' blurbs—"gripping," "unforgettable"—were invented to describe. I first read the book at about the time it was published, and I never forgot its hero or his plight. Although the title and the author's name soon faded from my memory, almost all of the substance of the book, incidents, characters, even specific lines and passages, remained quite vivid in my mind for more than twenty-five years, until I began to reread Himes's work.

Although the treatment of sexual themes was much more frank and literal than was customary in America in 1945, it was at the

4. Ibid. Himes told Hoyt Fuller that he had heard about the hostile woman editor "from my own art department woman" (Fuller, "Interview with Chester Himes," p. 6).
5. Williams, "My Man Himes," pp. 35–36.

most only two or three years ahead of its time, and very few readers could have been seriously disturbed by its capacity to shock. The mysterious woman editor at Doubleday who found the book disgusting, sickening, and nauseating would have had to have been guided (if her judgments were entirely innocent of racism) by very nearly the same criteria that Victorian critics applied to Thomas Hardy's *Jude the Obscure*, or even those of earlier French critics of Flaubert's *Madame Bovary*. A few professional reviewers did express reservations concerning the book's language, but there was no general outcry, nothing that approached the vehemence of the outraged Doubleday editor.

Himes, however, his nerves taut from the war of rumors at Doubleday, was excessively sensitive at this time to any criticism, on this score or any other, and when *Saturday Review* invited him to contribute a statement to its feature "The Author Talks Back" he responded with a short piece that was—if not exactly a "series of epithets punctuated by spit"—certainly more notable for vehemence than tact. "I flayed the carping white critics," he notes in his autobiography, recalling with evident relish how he had compared them to finicky whores protesting about flies in their rice. His answer to the criticism that his book had failed to suggest any solution at all to America's racial problem was, as he later paraphrased it, triumphantly ungracious: "Let the white people solve it their own goddamn selves" (p. 77).[6]

Had all of the factors involved in the making of a best-seller meshed with better effect in the case of *If He Hollers Let Him Go*, producing something more than an exasperating near miss, the book's critics would very probably have received softer answers from its prickly author, and the subsequent career of Chester Himes would possibly have followed a classic pattern for commercially successful novelists. But such a purely promotional accident, a chance fluctuation in the book market in 1945, is in many ways curiously unrelated to a book's intrinsic qualities. Poor

6. Cf. Chester B. Himes, "If He Hollers Let Him Go," *Saturday Review* 29 (February 16, 1946), p. 13. In point of fact, the comparison to finicky prostitutes was directed at "Americans as a whole," not literary critics in particular.

first-year sales notwithstanding, *If He Hollers Let Him Go* has most of the qualities that assure wide popular appeal: an exciting backdrop, a fast pace, a tight plot, a smoothly fluid and readable style, and a hero who is easy to identify with. On the other hand, however, it is also an angry and bitterly indignant book, qualities not guaranteed to help sales in every season.

The novel is set in booming, wartime Los Angeles, toward the beginning of the hot summer of 1944.[7] Bob Jones, the narrator and central figure—and the only fully developed character in the novel—works in a San Pedro shipyard as a "leaderman," a kind of black assistant foreman in charge of a few other black workers. The sudden burgeoning of defense industries on the Pacific coast was the last great boom of the American frontier, a final outpouring of energy on a heroic scale by the world's most creative and unstable people. Bob Jones is a volatile, highly imaginative man, and he is swept up in the sheer excitement of the times, the heady sense of his own youth and new importance as a well paid, draft-exempt "key worker," and, most fundamentally, by the frenetic rhythms of the production race itself:

> I hung up [the telephone], went back out on the yard, stood for a long time in the hot sunshine. Beyond was the road leading down to the outfitting dock, flanked by the various shops, dropping off in the blue-gray stretch of the harbor. Off to the left was a row of hulls in various stages of erection, spaced apart by the craneways. Cranes were silhouetted against the sky like long-legged, one-armed spiders, swinging shapes and plates aboard. Over there the workers walked with care. Everywhere was the hustle and bustle of moving busy workers, trucks, plate lifts, yard cranes, electric mules, the blue flashes of arc welders, brighter than the noonday sun. And the noise, always loud, unabating, earsplitting. I loved it like my first love. (*If He Hollers Let Him Go*, 149)

7. The date of the action is left deliberately vague, but the reader is told, at different points, that Bob Jones came to Los Angeles in the fall of 1941, that he has been there three years, and that it is June. Himes, *If He Hollers Let Him Go*, pp. 6, 17, 143.

Life in this immensely exciting world, factories expanding with explosive speed, hordes of workers with newly acquired, half-learned skills, a nexus of pure energy in which no one was entirely certain of his precise role, could also be very dangerous, particularly for Bob Jones, a black man who stubbornly refused, for reasons he himself could not quite understand, to acknowledge the existence of the plainly marked lines of discrimination. The world of *If He Hollers Let Him Go* is more than slightly mad. In its sheer crowding, it is not unlike a prison in which the solid infrastructure of deadening routine and discipline has completely dissolved. Passions normally held in tight rein—lust, racism, anger—surge dangerously just beneath the surface. There is a whiff of conspiracy here and there—Communists playing a waiting game, native American fascists whose pockets are stuffed with hate pamphlets, union organizers temporarily more interested in obfuscating than in clarifying issues, and black men, painfully conscious in this violently racist city of their reduced and impaired citizenship. Beyond the excitement, the promises, the enthusiasm, it is a world filled with menace, threats, danger.

And Bob Jones, in spite of his moments of almost ecstatic commitment, his swaggering masculinity, his considerable strength as a man, is very much afraid, gripped by a massive, permanent fear seated somewhere near the very base of his being. Fear is the novel's major theme. It is a concentrated study of the genesis of panic, the progressive deterioration of a personality under the deadly pressure of a huge and inescapable fear. Bob Jones is an aggressive, intelligent, and adventurous man, to whom fear should be alien, to whom high confidence is a natural and normal state. But he is also acutely aware of every aspect of his environment, and much that he sees disturbs him, and shadowy dimensions that he is only beginning to grasp already have the power to terrify him. The war itself, seen in the Pacific area primarily as a war against Japan, had disturbing racist undertones. For those whose nostrils were sensitive enough, there was a faint odor of genocide in the air, and at the point at which the novel begins Bob Jones is excruciatingly sensitive in every pore of his body, more like a man with no skin than simply a man with a

black skin. His fear had begun to assume tangible form when
he witnessed the arbitrary internment of a large part of California's Oriental population:

> Maybe it wasn't until I'd seen them send the Japanese away
> that I'd noticed it. Little Riki Oyana singing "God Bless
> America" and going to Santa Anita with his parents next
> day. It was taking a man up by the roots and locking him up
> without a chance. Without a trial. Without a charge. Without
> even giving him a chance to say one word. It was thinking
> about if they ever did that to me, Robert Jones, Mrs. Jones'
> dark son, that started me to getting scared. (*If He Hollers
> Let Him Go*, 7)

His panic is that of a man who has always believed absolutely
in the sanctity of the law and who suddenly discovers that the
law can be abrogated when it becomes an inconvenience to a
sufficiently large and powerful group. In the light of this knowledge he has taken a new look at his traditional enemies, the white
racists, with equally disturbing results. He had never really believed that they were in earnest. Their malice had always seemed
somehow accidental, essentially unmotivated, almost uninten-
tional. He had believed that they recognized a basic sort of
brotherhood with him and that somehow, at some time, they
could be "reached." Now, however, he seems to see that there
is in fact murder in their hearts, inexorable determination to
destroy him and all his kind, and that there is nothing that can
prevent them from having their way. He is a black man from
Cleveland, in close contact for the first time with Southern whites
accustomed since birth to witnessing or participating in the
casual brutalizing of black people. And this contact was set in
a city where law had become an ephemeral thing.

Himes himself, as a defense worker in wartime Los Angeles,
had experienced both the excitement and the brooding sense of
incipient violence that form the supremely unsettling ambiance
of the story of Bob Jones. He marks this encounter with naked,
violent racism in Los Angeles as the most severe trauma of his
life:

Up to the age of thirty-one I had been hurt emotionally, spiritually, and physically as much as thirty-one years can bear: I had lived in the South, I had fallen down an elevator shaft, I had been kicked out of college, I had served seven and one half years in prison, I had survived the humiliating last five years of the Depression in Cleveland; and still I was entire, complete, functional; my mind was sharp, my reflexes were good, and I was not bitter. But under the mental corrosion of race prejudice in Los Angeles I had become bitter and saturated with hate. . . . I was thirty-one and whole when I went to Los Angeles and thirty-five and shattered when I left to go to New York. (*The Quality of Hurt*, 75–76)

The plot structure of *If He Hollers Let Him Go* was designed to capture the anguish of that experience, compressed into five days in the life of one man. It is one of the tightest and most neatly balanced plots that Himes ever devised, an almost flawless mechanism, reminiscent of the marvelous torture machine in Franz Kafka's "Penal Colony" that was designed to inflict maximum pain upon its victims with minimum waste motion. Himes had undertaken to demonstrate how a particular set of social circumstances can break a man, and he assembled the assorted disasters that demolish Bob Jones with the skill of a Grand Inquisitor. The device of the first-person narrator, Bob Jones himself, is applied quite literally, without tricks or gimmicks, and the book's other characters, flattened to recognizable social types in Bob Jones's distorted view, function in much the same way as the row of needles set in a conveyor belt do in Kafka's ghastly machine. Two women, one black and beautiful and the other white and vicious, are the principal barbed spurs that drive Bob Jones from point to point through his short and violent trajectory, as he is jabbed at or slashed first by one set of characters and then another.

On each one of the five days the story spans, Monday to Friday in a single week, Bob Jones awakens out of a jumbled and terrifying nightmare, into a world that frightens him even more. The dreams are minutely and vividly described and, like so many surrealistic prose poems, these accounts set the tone for the events of the day that is to follow, described in contrasting, flatly naturalistic style. Paradoxically, the significance of Bob Jones's experience is painfully clear in his muddled and murky dreams, and consistently ambiguous—until just before the end— in his waking hours. In his dangerous world the elaborate puzzles of Freudian symbolism are much easier to penetrate and interpret than the smiling facades and casual hypocrisies of a society that simultaneously practices and denounces racism.

Monday morning's dreams involve a lovable but unwanted black dog, with a wire twisted around its neck, a policeman who is certain that guilty men are black and crippled, and two white employers who burst into braying laughter when Bob Jones asks them for a job: "I didn't mind their not giving me the job, but their laughing at me hurt. I felt small and humiliated and desperate, looking at the two big white men laughing at me" (p. 8). The mood is menace, and the events of this incredibly crowded Monday more than fulfill that promise. Before the day is over Bob Jones has lost absolutely everything he values—except his new car. He and the handful of black workers who ride with him to work every day in his car arrive late at the shipyard, after a nerve-wracking race through tangled traffic. The routine drive is itself invariably an ordeal for Bob, because he never fails to notice any gesture or facial expression that seems to indicate hostility or hate, however fleeting or ambiguous, on the part of every white driver or pedestrian he passes. In his mind the freeway is a kind of psychological obstacle course, compounded of racist threats and insults, that he has to negotiate twice a day, but on this particular Monday white hostility is very evident, and even some of his riders notice it: " 'What's the matter with these pecks this morning?' Homer said. 'Is everybody evil?' " (p. 16). Bob's first official act on the job is to give a direct order to a white woman worker, a lumpish peroxide blonde from Texas named Madge, the novel's most prominent white monster. She calls him "nigger," he retorts with "cracker bitch," and he is promptly demoted from leaderman to simple mechanic, a demotion that also involves the loss of his draft deferment. Dazed, he wanders out into the yard, joins a group of workers playing

dice, wins a little money, and is then promptly knocked unconscious when a young blond bigot named Johnny Stoddart
throws a sneak punch at his chin. When he comes to, he decides
that he will kill Johnny. He heads for the shop where Johnny
works, with a knife in his hand, then abruptly decides that a gun-
shot in a dark street, with no consequences for himself, would
be a much more satisfactory revenge. When the shifts change he
follows Johnny home in his car, fondling the .38 Special pistol in
his glove compartment. Johnny sees him and is badly frightened,
but Bob Jones, Hamlet fashion, again decides to postpone his
revenge, to savor it just a little longer. He returns to his room,
changes to elegant evening clothes, makes a few perfunctory
passes at Ella Mae, his affectionate young black landlady, and
phones Alice, his fiancée, to confirm their date. Alice, daughter
of a wealthy black doctor, is a social worker with a supervisory
position, a much better job than Bob's—even before he lost his
prestigious leaderman rank. He picks her up at her home in the
poshest black suburb of Los Angeles and takes her to dinner to a
restaurant in the center of the city that is so exclusive and formal
that the racist insults come in a neatly typed note attached to the
bill by the manager. *"We served you this time but we do not
want your patronage in the future"* (p. 59). Alice is badly shaken
by their treatment at the restaurant, and she takes the wheel of
the car when they leave, driving wildly along the highway for
miles. They are stopped by two policemen who call them "coons"
and fine Bob. By this time Alice's formidable poise has been
completely shattered, and she takes Bob to a strange house in a
run-down section of the city, where he learns that his aristocratic
and breathtakingly beautiful fiancée finds an outlet for her own
unbearable frustrations in a very banal vice, homosexuality. He
gets completely drunk, punches the only other man in the place,
and almost wrecks his car on the way home.

The next day, understandably, Bob is in no condition to make
it to work, and he drifts aimlessly for a few hours, first to a bar,
then to a movie. The morning's dream had, without the slightest
trace of ambiguity, spelled out his position of helpless isolation
in a violent and hostile world; "I dreamed I was lying in the middle of Main Street downtown in front of the Federal Building and

two poor peckerwoods in overalls were standing over me beating
me with lengths of rubber hose" (p. 66). A respectable black
couple passes by during the beating, but the president of Atlas
Shipyards, who is personally supervising the beating, easily per-
suades them that they have no cause for concern. Bob awakens,
and even after a few drinks finds it very hard to restore his illusions to a semblance of working order. The movies, a standardized and usually reliable illusion restorer, prove little help:

> I never found out the name of the picture or what it was
> about. After about five minutes a big fat black Hollywood
> mammy came on the screen saying, "Yassum" and "Noam,"
> and grinning at her young white missy; and I got up and
> walked out.
> I was down to a low ebb. I needed some help. I had to
> know that Negroes weren't the lowest people on the face of
> God's green earth. I had to talk it over with somebody, had
> to build myself back up. (*If He Hollers Let Him Go*, 75)

He drives to Alice's house, where he finds in progress an uplift meeting of socially prominent young black women plus one
male do-gooder, the young, white, and very handsome Tom
Leighton. Bob smiles politely for a while, then painfully, and
finally launches a few acid home truths into the gathering, scat-
tering it in all directions. When they are alone Alice first upbraids
him fiercely, then quickly shifts to her role as social worker
when she senses the extent of his hurt, bombarding him with impeccably conventional good advice. But she is extraordinarily
eloquent—Himes did not believe in handicapping his devil's
advocates—and she carries Bob along for a time. In effect, she
explains the book's heavily ironic title: black people exist in
a white world on white sufferance, totally dependent on the support and protection of friendly whites, and if they disturb their
white overlords, if they holler, they will be let go, allowed to
fall back into black oblivion. There is no place in the world, as
it is presently constituted, for a defiant black man. On the other
hand, only minimal concessions are demanded of the black man
who aspires to worldly success. He must affirm, in his heart, with
total conviction, that racism is not evil, that the people who
maintain and support it are not evil, and that it does not under-

mine the black victim in any very profound way, amounting at most to no more than a few barely noticeable limitations imposed on the range of his physical movements. Alice then presents Bob with a clear-cut ultimatum: he must bend completely, accept his inferior status with becoming grace, or she will break their engagement.

On Wednesday morning, the novel's third day, Bob wakens from a dream in which the prevailing ambiguity triumphs, and all forms are confused and distorted. In it, Alice, menaced by a herd of wild pigs in the city park, shrinks to the size of a tattered doll as Bob rushes to her aid, his pistol protruding from the fly of his trousers. Awake, shaken, he returns to his job, with no clear direction, feeling his way along. The black workers in his crew are quick with verbal support, but they lack the courage to follow through. And the best the union representative can do for him is to suggest that he file a written protest describing the circumstances of his demotion. The plant's bigots, who have hated him all along, as a prime symbol of the black man who fails to keep his place, are jubilant at his humiliation and for the first time are openly and sadistically vindictive in their dealings with him. Kelly, the foreman, who had opposed Bob's appointment as leaderman from the beginning, deliberately tells a nauseatingly offensive racist joke in his presence:

> They couldn't have done it any better if they'd rehearsed it. I couldn't take offense because Kelly didn't tell the joke to me and he could always say if I hadn't wanted to hear it I didn't have to listen. And even if I still wanted to take offense, the girl had stepped into the picture and whatever I might say to Kelly was sure to offend her. I never wanted to get out of a place so bad in all my life. . . .
> I did something with my face, trying to make it smile. . . .
> But Kelly knew he had me. He waved me away, "Go on, go on. Get out of here." (*If He Hollers Let Him Go*, 115)

The only means Bob can think of to restore his sense of manhood is either to kill Johnny Stoddart or to rape Madge, the vicious peroxide blonde who caused his demotion. He manages to severely frighten Johnny again—"I'd never seen a white man scared before, not craven, not until you couldn't see the white for the scare" (p. 119)—and this keeps him going until lunch. He then accosts Madge in the canteen and discovers, to his immense surprise, that she is attracted to him and actual rape will not be necessary, just a mild show of force that will permit her to rationalize the act afterwards. That night, after finding that Alice has been going out with Tom Leighton, Bob goes to Madge's hotel and attempts to make love to her, but her token show of resistance—which is unexpectedly robust—and her incessant chatter about lynchings in Texas frighten him so badly that he flees in panic.

A few hours later, in Thursday morning's dream, a black boy is slowly and methodically slashed to death with a razor blade—a thousand tiny cuts—by a laughing white boy who had seemed at first to be losing the fight. "I woke up and I couldn't move, could hardly breathe. . . . somewhere in the back of my mind a tiny insistent voice kept whispering, *Bob, there never was a nigger who could beat it* . . . it kept on saying it" (p. 140). The import of his prophetic dreams, the screams of his subconscious, is again painfully plain, but Bob forces his mind away from it. At lunch, leaving the shipyard, he sets a marriage date with Alice, determined to live up to her terms. He will resume his long-interrupted university studies, try once more to become an important black lawyer. He drives back to the plant figuratively floating on air, all his troubles behind him. He is as happy as a lark, daydreaming of law cases he will try in the future. But then the long-awaited master blow falls. Back at the plant, somehow, he finds himself all alone in a room with Madge. She first attempts to make love to him, despite his resistance, then lustily screams "rape" when they are interrupted struggling. Bob is given a horrendous beating by enraged white workers, and when he finally regains consciousness, after minor surgery in the shipyard's infirmary, he learns that rape charges actually are pending against him and that the police are coming to arrest him. He breaks free of the shipyard guards, flees in his car, but can find no way out—Alice offers only more good advice on the phone—and finally, on the verge of collapse, his face almost shapeless from the beating, most of his teeth gone, he is stopped by a police car and arrested.

On Friday morning, the novel's final day, tossing fitfully on a bunk in a jail cell, Bob dreams that he finally succeeds in killing Johnny Stoddart, only to find himself immediately afterwards at the mercy of an enormous white Marine sergeant, who just happens along. The sergeant is, perhaps, racism personified. He drags Bob, effortlessly, into an alley, and tells him, chortling all the time with glee, that he has always wanted, all his life, more than anything else, to kill a black man. When Bob awakens, just in time, he is marched into a judge's private chambers and treated to a sanctimonious sermon by the shipyard president, actually present this time. Bob is told, at some length, both that he is a disgrace to his race and the company and that Madge, in the interests of racial harmony, has decided to drop the rape charges. After the shipyard president, wearing his "I-trusted-you look," has stalked out, Bob is quickly dealt a very special brand of justice, for blacks only:

> "And let that be a lesson," the judge said briskly, and began shuffling some papers on his desk he had brought in with him. "I see they want you in Los Angeles for carrying a concealed weapon," he remarked, then looked up at me. "Suppose I give you a break, boy. If I let you join the armed forces—any branch you want—will you give me your word you'll stay away from white women and keep out of trouble?"
> I wanted to just break out and laugh like the Marine in my dream, laugh and keep on laughing. 'Cause all I ever wanted was just a little thing—just to be a man. But I kept a straight face, got the words through my oversized lips. "Yes sir, I promise." (*If He Hollers Let Him Go*, 190)

His forced enrollment into a Jim Crow army, to fight racism abroad in the name of the Four Freedoms, forms a fittingly ironic finale to what Bob Jones has just begun to realize was his own private war for simple justice at home. Both the rather conspicuously neat ending and the excessively formal general plot structure are more characteristic of a play than a novel, and later in his career Himes attempted to rewrite *If He Hollers Let Him Go* as a play (*The Quality of Hurt*, 103–7).

The characterization of Bob Jones, the protagonist, or, more properly, the ball in play in the rough games of *If He Hollers Let*

Him Go, is the novel's structural center, source of both its major strengths and its weaknesses. In line with his desire "just to be a man," Bob's character has a fair number of features appropriate to a portrait of "the average man." He is the most generalized of Himes's major characters. There is evidently much of Himes himself in the characterization, segments of his own experience, his own past, that are rendered with very few fictional touches—and a few of these, indicative of a violent background, do not fit the urbane Bob too well—but there is also apparent throughout the novel a very determined effort to subordinate the autobiographical elements, to blend them into an overall impression or rugged normalcy, to achieve a characterization that would be at times recognizably close to that of the familiar hero type of popular fiction. When Bob meets Alice for lunch at "a typical Southern California drive-in," determined at last to capitulate, to conform completely, she remarks, noting his jaunty and expensive work clothes, his gleaming hard hat, "You look like a worker in a CIO win-the-war poster," and he graciously acknowledges, "I'm the twelve million black faces" (p. 154). Most readers prefer, of course, that their fictional heroes be, like themselves, just a bit better than the average man, and Bob Jones—"two years of college and a shipyard job" (p. 10)—fits the formula with tailored precision: "Taller than the average man, six feet two, broad-shouldered, and conceited, I hadn't a worry" (p. 7).

He also has a tremendous vitality, a capacity for boundless enthusiasm and a child's overwhelming appetite for life, traits that make him a basically sympathetic character. His appetite for the material comforts has an almost nonsensual dedication. He is more knowledgeable connoisseur than voluptuary, alert to the soul-enhancing properties of simple luxuries. And Himes's devotion to the detailed background descriptions traditional to naturalism—simple lists of things that stretch to the length of exhaustive inventories—effectively underscores this characteristic: "I was wearing my beige gabardine pumps, gray flannel slacks, camel's-hair jacket. . . . an aqua gabardine shirt" (p. 128). Bob's affection for his flashy new car has more than a hint of the passionate intensity of a clandestine love affair: "I had a '42 Buick Roadmaster I'd bought four months ago, right after I'd gotten to be a leaderman, and every time I got behind the wheel and looked down the broad, flat, mile-long hood I thought about how the rich folks out in Beverly couldn't even buy a new car now and got a certain satisfaction" (p. 13). The car is loyal friend, reliable tonic, infallible comforter: "When I opened the door of my car heat rolled out as from a furnace. I had to open all the doors and stand there for a moment until it aired. Then I got in, squirmed down in the soft springy seat, and felt good all over" (p. 152).

Bob brings this vitality, the verve of an expert player, even to the nasty little skirmishes of verbal combat that explode at his every contact with the white world:

> He [Hank, another leaderman, blond, from Georgia] kept his smile, but he began getting dirty. "You said it, bo." Then to the women, "This boy's really a killer, got all the little brown gals in a dither about him." To me again, "How *does* you do it, bo?"
>
> I got all set to curse him out. . . . The three of them started to laugh with me. I said, "Don't sell me *too* hard, buddy, you might find a buyer."
>
> Hank caught it first; the creases stayed in his face but his smile went. The two women dug it from the change in his expression; neither blushed; they just got that sudden brutal look. (*If He Hollers Let Him Go*, 27)

Poised and articulate, basically self-confident, with a quick mind and a ready wit, Bob Jones is a hard man to put down with an offhand sneer or racial slur, and he thrives on the easy victories he usually scores in these encounters, the "dozens" in earnest.

Like the protagonists of a thousand blues lyrics, Bob Jones infuses with a strange vigor even his moments of deep sadness, lending them a heroic dimension. His vocation is victim, but he stands ten feet all. His sadness is no polite regret, but a tremendous wail, engaging, for the moment, his entire being:

> . . . and I began feeling melancholy. I thought of my second year at State when I subbed at end on the football team— the one game I played and the one touchdown I made and the

people cheering. I had never felt so powerful, so strong, almost as if I'd become the hero I used to dream about being when I grew up. . . .

Just a simple nigger bastard, that was me. Never would be a hero. Had a thousand chances every day. . . .

My throat went tight. . . . I began to cry. Not openly. But all down inside. (*If He Hollers Let Him Go*, 71)

Bob's sheer size and power, his tendency toward excess, and his monumental instability, however, link him as closely to the great neurotics of literature as to the heroes. He is a man under maximum pressure who is running scared, always close to breaking, but whenever the dangers that surround him fade a little into the background, he appears to be partly, or even primarily, a self-tormentor, a virtuoso of suffering enamored of his own pain.

He is an idealist of the most impossibly intransigent variety. He takes people at their diplomatic value and is furious when they fail to measure up. He insists that all the glittering formulas of the pledge of allegiance to the flag be there in practical, tangible, concrete reality. He sees treason in every compromise, villainy in every attempt at adjustment. And, like Don Quixote, whose world was as savagely and brutally antipathetic to the ideal as Bob Jones inevitably finds that the wheels of windmills are very hard and turn very fast. His hold on the reader's sympathies would be firmer if his characteristic stances offered at least the possibility of survival in any world where injustice exists, any world, real or imagined, that is relevant to actual, lived human experience.

He is totally encapsulated in his private realm of pain, a man who does not reach out to other men and who cannot be reached by them. His absorption in his own dilemma is complete, perfect, and impregnated with inescapably neurotic overtones. His ever-active intelligence, his powers of observation, are invariably directed inward. Like many literary characters charged with telling their own story, he is tireless in his efforts at self-analysis, though he never approaches the true intellectual's ultimate violation of self—a full understanding of his own motives. The secondary characters in his narrative are seldom more than shadowy sketches, generally inconsistent and self-contradictory, but the character of Bob Jones, object of his own exhaustive scrutiny, remains to the end a conglomerate that involves as many unre-solved puzzles as it does clear affirmations. He can describe lucidly exactly *how* he feels at any given moment, but the *why*'s lose themselves in the gratuitous complexities of amateur psy-chology, mark of the self-conscious intellectual in the modern world:

> Outside, I stood for a time, feeling cheated, trapped. I couldn't decide whether I'd been a coward or a fool. I de-bated whether to go back and split him. I'd get a fine and some days, perhaps. Probably a sapping at police headquar-ters. I'd lose my car. I think that was what made me decide my pride wasn't worth it. My car was proof of something to me, a symbol. But at the time I didn't analyze the feeling; I just knew I couldn't lose my car even if I lost my job. (*If He Hollers Let Him Go*, 32)

An author's choice of first-person narration usually represents a sacrifice of aesthetic distance for the sake of emotional imme-diacy—and the reader of *If He Hollers Let Him Go* is uncom-fortably enmeshed in Bob Jones's world, stuck with him in the same spider web. But first-person narration can also be a kind of distancing device. It allows the author to maintain ambiguities he prefers to leave unresolved. There are aspects of his character that Bob Jones himself cannot accept. These remain cloaked in decent darkness throughout the novel, though Himes does pro-vide tantalizing clues. Bob Jones's attitude toward race is the principal clouded area. His feelings toward both black people and white people are fundamentally ambivalent. The complicated anguish he feels at every sign of prejudice directed toward him-self personally can spring from nothing so simple as resentment or hatred alone, and his sense of the brotherhood of soul that links all black men would not satisfy even a moderately radical advocate of black pride.

"I wouldn't be s'prised none," retorts Ella Mae, his landlady, when he explains his constant use of the shower with, "I'm tryna turn white," and when he flares back, with heavy sarcasm, "You know how much I love the white folks," she answers, with equally heavy sarcasm, "You ain't just saying it either" (pp. 46–47). And Alice, his fiancée, breaks into one of his tirades with the question,

"Do you want to be white, Bob?" (p. 93). Beyond question, the approval and acceptance of whites loom large in his private thoughts:

> I didn't want to be the biggest Negro who ever lived, neither Toussaint L'Ouverture nor Walter White. Because deep inside of me, where the white folks couldn't see, it didn't mean a thing. If you couldn't swing down Hollywood Boulevard and know that you belonged; if you couldn't make a polite pass at Lana Turner at Ciro's without having the gendarmes beat the black off you for getting out of your place; if you couldn't eat a thirty-dollar dinner at a hotel without choking on the insults, being a great big "Mister" nigger didn't mean a thing. (*If He Hollers Let Him Go*, 143–44)

In an argument with Alice's white liberal friend Tom Leighton, Bob rasps angrily, "The only solution to the Negro problem is a revolution . . . the only thing white people have ever respected is force" (p. 84), but he has no answers to Leighton's probing questions on the practical problems, the tactics and logistics of a racial revolution. Bob is the raw material out of which revolutionary heroes can be made, once the battle lines have been set up and the issued reduced to shoutable slogans, but he has no interest at all in social action in a context of perpetual compromises and gains measured in inches. The "Negro Problem" is for him very largely a personal problem, viewed exclusively in the light of his private anguish.

His attitude toward the black men he supervises is a mixture of affection and contempt, with the contempt often predominant— "[Smitty] was just a simple-minded, Uncle Tom-ish nigger, I told myself; he couldn't help it" (p. 25)—an attitude he shares with Ben, the only college graduate in the little group:

> I gave them the okay sign, hitched up my pants and started out. Ben stopped me. "Some folks, ain't they?" he said, shaking his head.
> "Remember what the monkey said when young Mose ran over him and cut off his tail?" I asked.
> "My people, my people," we chorused, grinning at each other. (*If He Hollers Let Him Go*, 104–5)

A full acceptance of his people is possible for Bob only in those rare moments when he has convinced himself that he has found a way out, that he is not trapped with them, as when he clutches at the illusory "discovery" that in killing Johnny Stoddart he can cleanse his own mind of the fears that torment him:

> It was a slick, niggerish block—hustlers and pimps, gamblers and stooges. But it didn't ruffle me. Even the solid cats in their pancho conks didn't ruffle me. It wasn't as if I was locked up down there as I'd been just yesterday. I was free to go now; but I liked it with my folks. (*If He Hollers Let Him Go*, 43)

Even Alice, dubbed by Ella Mae "the whitest colored girl you could find" (p. 47), is more symbol than person in the life of this supremely desperate loner. His descriptions of her are as effusive, and as fundamentally impersonal, as the patter of a gossip columnist describing the season's outstanding socialite:

> Alice . . . fell into the living room like Bette Davis, big-eyed and calisthenical and strictly sharp. She was togged in a flowing royal-purple chiffon evening gown with silver trimmings and a low square-cut neck that showed the tops of her creamy-white breasts with the darker disturbing seam down between; and her hair was swept up on top of her head in a turbulent billow and held by two silver combs that matched the silver trimmings of her gown—a tall willowy body falling to the floor with nothing but curves. Black elbow-length gloves showed a strip of creamy round arm. I gave her one look and caught an edge like a rash from head to foot, blinding and stinging. She was fine, fine, fine, so help me. (*If He Hollers Let Him Go*, 52)

Even during the ultimately romantic lunch meeting when they finalize their marriage plans, Alice sounds more like a prosy NAACP uplift pamphlet than a person. Always the sympathetic counselor, committed to the long view, she soothes Bob's spasmodic outbursts of self-pity with professional aplomb: "I understand, darling. . . . But you shouldn't feel too badly about it. That is typical of most Negroes working in a supervisory capacity where white and colored are employed" (p. 157). Alice's secret vices hold the promise of great depth and complexity of character, but Bob resolutely turns his mind away from them, refuses to probe. Preoccupied with his own problems, he has little time for the unhappy person called Alice, preferring the blinding glamor of the image she projects.

Nevertheless, the role Alice plays so well, which Bob seems to value so highly, is not completely exempted from the novel's sweeping indictment of the black bourgeoisie. Whenever Alice's parents, Dr. and Mrs. Harrison, are on stage the tone of the novel shifts from precise, pinpointing naturalism to light satire, and even Alice, with her slightly stuffy ultimatums, is not always spared. Dr. Harrison is "the kind of pompous little guy you'd expect to have a hyphenated name, one of the richest Negroes in the city if not on the whole West Coast" (p. 10), and Alice's mother is "a very light-complexioned woman with sharp caucasian features and glinting gray eyes . . . aristocratic enough looking, if that was what she wanted, but she had that look of withered soul and body that you see on the faces of many old white ladies in the South" (p. 48). They are targets too elusive for the art of the realist, because they are people who consciously identify with standardized roles, but by the same token they are also a bit too fragile to stand up to sharp satire. Pity insistently intrudes:

> "It gives me a feeling of personal triumph, too, to see our young men progress so," [Mrs. Harrison] said. "I like to think that the doctor and I have contributed by setting an example, by showing our young men just what they can accomplish if they try."
>
> That was my cue to say, "Yes indeedy." But she looked so goddamned smug and complacent, sitting there in her two-hundred-dollar chair, her feet planted in her three-thousand-dollar rug, waving two or three thousand dollars' worth of diamonds on her hands, bought with dough her husband had made overcharging poor hardworking colored people for his incompetent services, that I had a crazy impulse to needle her. . . .
>
> But she didn't even hear me. "You must read Mrs. Roosevelt's article in the *Negro Digest*," she was saying.

The old sister was so sincere I felt ashamed; I had no idea
I'd touch her that much. I got up and took her hand. "You're
right, Mrs. Harrison," I said. "Perfectly right, you and Mrs.
Roosevelt both." I had to bite my tongue to keep from say-
ing, "How could you and Mrs. Roosevelt possibly be wrong?"
(*If He Hollers Let Him Go*, 50–52)

The basis of the occasional satire in *If He Hollers Let Him Go* is
always the flight from reality involved in easy sentimentality and
enthusiastic role playing, and these are qualities that permeate the
entire fabric of modern American society, targets of every satirist
from H. L. Mencken and Sinclair Lewis. The traits that Himes
satirizes are never exclusively those of blacks, like ghetto swagger
or the barbaric yawp of the blues. The people satirized, however,
are almost invariably black—black men who have assumed pompous white mannerisms—but it is the mannerisms themselves,
the hollow, pretentious core of bourgeois American civilization
in general, that form the satirist's central target. Unfortunately,
these mannerisms are completely laughable only when they represent an infallible wall of protection against every sting that reality offers, and the Harrisons bleed almost as freely as he does
and are wounded by the same weapons. "Just the other day,"
Mrs. Harrison mournfully tells him, "the doctor went into a
restaurant downtown where he's been eating for years and they
didn't want to serve him" (p. 51).

If, however, there is a certain obvious chilly intolerance involved in much of Bob Jones's feelings toward black people, he is
also capable of sudden surges of warmth, as when he remembers
seeing an audience in a black theatre clap wildly for a white per-
former who happened to be blind:

We're a wonderful, goddamned race, I thought. Simple-
minded, generous, sympathetic sons of bitches. We're sorry
for everybody but ourselves; the worse the white folks treat
us the more we love 'em. Ella Mae laying me because I wasn't
married and she figured she had enough for me and Henry
too; and a black audience clapping its hands off for a blind
white acrobat. (*If He Hollers Let Him Go*, 9)

Bob Jones's attitudes toward the dominant white people are,
if possible, even more ambivalent than his conspicuously mixed

feelings toward his own segment of society. At times he feels such intense hostility for whites in general that he can barely keep from running them down when they walk in front of his car. At other times, much like the black theatre audience, he feels a strange, compulsive warmth and sympathy toward them. At the restaurant where he and Alice are so insistently treated as unwelcome intruders, he stares malevolently at the people at the nearby tables, particularly the "young naval officers looking very white" (p. 55), but within minutes he is observing, "I had a sudden wistful desire to be the young ensign's friend" (p. 58). Even the enormous psychological lift he gets from his fantasies of violence against Johnny Stoddart springs from a kind of awe he feels for whiteness itself:

> I was going to kill him if they hung me for it, I thought pleasantly. A white man, a supreme being. Just the thought of it did something for me; just contemplating it. All the tightness that had been in my body, making my motions jerky, keeping my muscles taut, left me and I felt relaxed, confident, strong. I felt just like I thought a white boy oughta feel; I had never felt so strong in all my life. (*If He Hollers Let Him Go*, 38)

Although his understanding never affects his hatred of white people *per se*, he is fully aware that "whiteness" is an entity in itself, a kind of weapon, a source of power in a racist society, a temptation to be abused or ignored: "I began wondering. . . . And how it was you could take two white guys from the same place—one would carry his whiteness like a loaded stick, ready to bop everybody else in the head with it; and the other would just simply be white as if he didn't have anything to do with it and let it go at that" (pp. 41–42). The loaded-stick whites are a kind of monster. They bear a special relation to the evil in the world, almost monopolizing it. They intrude obsessively into Bob's thoughts during his waking hours, and they infest and dominate his entire world, like obscene goblins, when he dreams. But even these people have a share in the prevailing patterns of ambivalence in Bob's mind.

Madge Perkins, the big blonde from Texas, Bob's personal

nemesis, who leads him, gorgonlike, to the semilynching that is his fate, is throughout an object of both aversion and desire, a confusion that he himself finds inexplicable, since she is physically unprepossessing:

> She was a peroxide blonde with a large-featured, overly made-up face, and she had a large, bright-painted, fleshy mouth, kidney-shaped, thinner in the middle than at the ends. Her big blue babyish eyes were mascaraed like a burlesque queen's and there were tiny wrinkles in their corners and about the flare of her nostrils, calipering down about the edges of her mouth. She looked thirty and well sexed, ripe but not quite rotten. She looked as if she might have worked half those years in a cat house, and if she hadn't she must have given a lot of it away. (*If He Hollers Let Him Go*, 21)

When he invades her hotel room at night, determined to establish his mastery, to humiliate and degrade her physically, he finds, attempting to wrestle her to the bed, that she is also fantastically strong:

> She was big, strong, and quick, and it was all I could do to hold my own. "Gawddamn you!" she grated once, but that was the only time she spoke. I didn't say anything. We stopped for a moment by common accord, resting. Her face was a hard, glowing red and her blue eyes were dark and furious. Her mouth was a hard brutal line. (*If He Hollers Let Him Go*, 136–37)

Madge is at the same time banal, vulgar, and disturbingly strange. And to Bob there is menace in her strangeness. She is to be the instrument of his destruction, and he senses it from the beginning, yet he literally cannot leave her alone. He seeks her out again and again, driven compulsively, only half convinced that he is trying to prove something. Madge also seems to be caught in the pattern of their odd relationship, fascinated by the dangerous game they are playing. With the regularity of ritual, whenever they meet at the plant, she acts out an elaborate pantomime of fear—"she deliberately put on a frightened, wide-eyed look and backed away from me as if she was scared stiff, as if she was a naked virgin and I was King Kong" (p. 21)—and the effect on Bob of her bizarre behavior is violently aprhodisiac:

> Lust shook me like an electric shock; it came up in my mouth, filling it with tongue, and drained my whole stomach down into my groin. And it poured out of my eyes in a sticky rush and spurted over her from head to foot.
>
> The frightened look went out of her eyes and she blushed right down her face and out of sight beneath the collar of her leather jacket, and I could imagine it going down over her overripe breasts and spreading out over her milk-white stomach. When she turned out of my stare I went sick to the stomach and felt like vomiting. (*If He Hollers Let Him Go*, 21–22)

But very little in Bob's world is exactly what it seems to be at first glance, and there are vague hints that this archetypal white monster might in fact be nothing more than a very ordinary, very unhappy person, seen through the distorting lenses of Bob's own hate, fear, and lust. It is her very ordinariness that shakes him most, the disconcerting absence of the menace he had intended to affront, when he talks to her for the first time at length, at the shipyard canteen:

> Then she let recognition leak into her look. "Oh, you're the boy I had the fight with the other day." Now she gave me a ravishing smile—at least that's what it was supposed to be —and her manner became easy, friendly, without tension of any sort. "Yo' name is Bob, isn't it? Rest the weight, Bob, you must get tired of toting it around all day." (*If He Hollers Let Him Go*, 121–22)

It is often said that the devil is an idiot, and, if so, it is appropriate that Madge, who seems to represent him very directly in the role she plays in Bob's life, should be an obvious simpleton. All that lurks behind the mysterious facade of this monolith of depravity and white hate is the limp, petulant mind of a perpetual child. As he listens to her inane and aimless chatter through lunch, he cannot possibly escape this conclusion—and with it the suspicion that all the enemies that stalk him may be for the most part creations of his own tormented imagination—and yet he does escape it, or at least rejects its full implications. His fear remains. His need to humiliate and defeat Madge, symbol of the sexual component of racism, is as great as ever.

Throughout the novel it is basically Bob's masculinity that is at issue. Both Madge's threatening aggressiveness and physical strength and the suggestions of Alice's lesbianism are challenges to this masculinity. Bob's supreme aspiration, his thwarted ideal, is to live out the American myth of maleness, with all its folklorish components: heroic fighter, dauntless leader of men, and tender lover. But this is the one role that racism denies to the black man. It is in his very masculinity that he is most seen as a threat, and directly attacked. Bob's tragedy is that, both physically and by temperament, it is the one role he was born to fill. The threats to Bob first become tangible and concrete when he accepts the role of leaderman at the shipyard, symbolically affirming the full extent of his manhood.

> I got a clean pair of coveralls out of the dresser . . . pulled on my high-heeled, iron-toed boots, slanted my "tin" hat on the back of my head, and slipped into my leather jacket. Something about my working clothes made me feel rugged, bigger than the average citizen, stronger than a white-collar worker—stronger even than an executive. Important too. It put me on my muscle. I felt a swagger in my stance. (*If He Hollers Let Him Go*, 12)

The essence of the role of the dominant male, the cock of the walk, is to throw down challenges to every other male, to affirm his own superlative excellence by the sheer dynamism of his presence, but, ironically, in its substance the role is primarily ritualistic, and it is viable only when it is accepted and applauded by society as a whole, and Bob finds that not even other black men, or the black American community as a whole, will support a black man who assumes such a role. Alice's incessant good advice, her ultimatums, are in fact only so many demands that he abandon his soaring pretensions, and the dangers they entail:

> I started to interrupt, but she stopped me. "No, Bob, this is important. Your present attitude has no place for me in your life, it has no place for anyone except yourself. When you

lost your temper with the girl you were not thinking about me."

"I suppose I should have just said, 'Yes ma'am, I'm a nigger,' and let it go at that."

She went over and sat down again. "It's not just you any more, Bob," she said. "I have to think about myself. . . ."

"Will you go to the girl tomorrow morning and apologize?" she asked. . . .

"Look, baby—" I cut in again; I was trying to stop her; I didn't want her to say it. "Look, Alice, will you listen to me? Will you let me tell you what'll happen to me if I do that?"

"No, Bob, I won't listen," she said. "It's such a little thing." (*If He Hollers Let Him Go*, 93–94)

Himes calls *If He Hollers Let Him Go* "my bitter novel of protest" (*The Quality of Hurt*, 75), and the book is in effect, first and foremost a detailed account of the brutalizing of a normal decent man by a racist society. It is a passionate indictment of a society that makes blackness a handicap. But the book's range is also much wider. Racism is only one facet of man's inhumanity to man, and it is against cruelty itself that Himes protests all the life-denying forces that are rampant in the modern world. Bob's very isolation, the absence of any close human ties whatsoever in his life—the supreme price he has paid for his independence— makes him as much a symbol of alienation in general, as a simple exemplar of the black protest novel's standard hero-victim. It is Bob alone, the man who says "no," that is most obviously under attack in the novel, rather than the black community as a whole. And the very manliness of his choice, his intransigent insistence on a full set of options, universalize him, making him a kind of modern Everyman, the archetypal protagonist of tragedy, steadfastly refusing every infringement on his full humanity, however "little" the Alices of the world may consider them.

II Lonely Crusade

Himes's second novel, *Lonely Crusade*, was published by Alfred A. Knopf in 1947. The setting was again wartime Los Ange-

les, specifically the spring of 1943.[8] Himes even took the trouble
to toss in a stray detail to point up the identity of setting in his
two novels: *Lonely Crusade*'s protagonist, Lee Gordon, a black
union organizer at an aircraft plant, casually glances through a
newspaper while riding on a city bus and briefly notes an account
of rape charges brought by "a white woman in a shipyard"
against "a Negro worker" (p. 207).[9] But the setting is one of
very few points of strong resemblance between the two books.
Lonely Crusade is almost twice the length of *If He Hollers Let
Him Go*, and its plot structure, operating on a number of different
levels, is far more involved and complicated. The prose style of
Lonely Crusade is, in many passages, much more brilliant, containing some of Himes's most successful efforts at "fine writing,"
and in its ultimate effects this long novel is a much more deeply
disturbing book, but in immediate impact it is distinctly less
powerful than *If He Hollers Let Him Go*. It is, of all of Himes's
books, the one that comes closest to failure, due to the sheer
abundance of things packed into it. It is a book that demonstrates
that richness and multiplicity run riot can be very costly virtues
indeed. But it is also Himes's supreme effort as novelist, thinker,
propagandist, and crusader, and the rich tapestry of *Lonely
Crusade* demands close study.

Lonely Crusade is, like *If He Hollers Let Him Go*, technically
a "protest" novel, anatomizing with passionately intense indignation the brutalizing and inevitable destruction of a black man
in a hostile white world, but *Lonely Crusade*'s Lee Gordon is not
simply a victim like Bob Jones, but more nearly a martyr, a man
with a carefully thought out philosophy and faith who consciously
and deliberately chooses both the manner and moment of his own
destruction, a fact that adds much to the dignity of the protagonist
but diminishes the tragic effect of his fate. And Lee Gordon is
not alone in his world, as was Bob Jones. The narrative point of
view is that of the disembodied, omniscient third-person narrator,
employed throughout with a strongly subjective bias, the narrator tending to identify with whatever character happens to be in
center stage at the moment, both recording and analyzing their

8. Himes, *Lonely Crusade*, p. 3.
9. Cf. note 7, p. 74, this volume.

secret thoughts. This technique enables Himes to develop rather fully a large cast of characters in addition to Lee Gordon, probing from within from many different angles. The result is a very big, sprawling novel bulging with memorable characters, which at times lacks central thrust and a clear direction.

Lee Gordon never achieves the solid reality that is Bob Jones's from the beginning of his story. His symbolic overtones, the "meaning" invested in his actions, tend to show. Set in a gigantic and crowded canvas, surrounded by secondary characters who are at least as vigorous and as sharply defined as he is, manipulated by an author who is clearly determined to control the directions the story takes, Lee Gordon is all too often hard put to maintain his hold on the reader's interest and sympathy. He is a college graduate, married, thirty-one years old (a few years older than Bob Jones), but he is much smaller, more slender, and somehow much more youthful in appearance than the protagonist of *If He Hollers Let Him Go*; he generally impresses other people as "a kid," boyish, winsome, and basically inept. He does not, like the hulking Bob Jones, shake people up by his sheer size and vitality when he enters a room. He is perhaps even more moody, more volatile, than Bob Jones. Himes was always convinced that black Americans are the world's most complicated people, and Lee Gordon was the first literary character in which he fully embodied that conviction.

The plot structure of *Lonely Crusade* reveals a distinctly Victorian concern for elegant overall shape, à la Wilkie Collins, that is not always perfectly suited to its severe and generally dead serious naturalistic texture. All of the numerous secondary plot lines impinge directly on the central strand—the ordeal or rites of passage of Lee Gordon—but there are also various independent interlinkings between these rather sketchy subplots, chronicling the private disasters of six major characters in addition to Lee. The stormy passage of the central protagonist alone involves enough factors to invite simultaneous comparison to at least two of the paradigmatic passage myths of classical antiquity: Jason's passage in the *Argo* between the clashing rocks, the Symplegades, and Odysseus' navigation of the straits between Scylla and Charybdis, the dragon and the whirlpool. The clashing rocks that threaten to squash Lee Gordon like an ant between bricks are the twin monoliths of class struggle, communism and capitalism; while the multiheaded sea beast is represented by dangerous tendencies toward psychopathic violence in three other black men, and the giant whirlpool is the agonizing turmoil of Lee's collapsing marriage, agitated by the surging currents of an equally troubled interracial love affair. Most of Lee Gordon's actual efforts are devoted to threshing in the whirlpool, for the novel is first of all a great love story, but the resolution comes with his decision, or "discovery," as he gains new insights into the pathology of racism and his own role as a black man, that his destiny is immersion in the class struggle, the struggle of all humanity for social justice. In the novel's rather melodramatic denouement, Lee Gordon signals his abandonment of all concerns that are purely personal with a symbolic gesture of defiance against the forces of social repression, heroically committing himself to the brotherhood of the modern Argonauts, all those who shed their blood willingly in the fight for a better world.

But this novel that ends on a high note of pure affirmation—without parallel in the rest of Himes's fiction—begins darkly enough, in accounts of pain and frustration. Lee's "lonely crusade" is launched—though he doesn't know it at the time—at the very moment that he accepts a job as union organizer at Comstock Aircraft, a "Negro First" for the Los Angeles area. At first this "opportunity" evokes only fear in his heart:

> He had once again crossed into the competitive white world where he would be subjected to every abuse. . . . Now suddenly he hated this urge in him that always sent him sowing in the fields where the harvest was nothing but hurt. . . . To keep going back where he was not wanted. Where the penalties for just going were so great. (*Lonely Crusade*, 4)

In the fifty days the novel spans, these fears are first massively reinforced then abruptly abandoned. His first day at the union hall starts with a snub from the union president, a white Southerner, followed by sympathetic pep talks from Smitty and Joe Ptak, the union's top white organizers and its real leaders. The two are a formidable team. Smitty supplies the sentiment and Joe

Ptak the guts, the will, and the anger. Though Himes was dealing with a strictly contemporary situation, his approach is suggestive of the historical novel. He seizes upon random opportunities to unload background data, presumably all new to the reader. Joe Ptak's preliminary instructions to Lee provide one such opportunity. The workers of this brand-new Los Angeles warplant, Joe ponderously explains, are for the most part new to the area, and also completely new to industry itself and to unions. Many are from the rural South, and they are "against the union on general principles" (p. 23). The plant manager, Louis Foster, an old enemy of Joe Ptak's from the East and a deadly enemy of unionism in general, is thwarting the budding union's every move to win new recruits with Machiavellian cunning. This "rotten fascist bastard"—epithets Louis Foster manages fully to live up to in the course of the novel—"keeps 'em hopped up on patriotism" (p. 24), and placates the black workers, whom he despises but needs, with the "even ten per cent," holding the proportion at precisely three thousand black workers out of a total mass of thirty thousand workers on three shifts.

Lee's task is to organize the black workers, to win their votes, which will be vital in the pending election that will determine the future of the union's power at the plant, though, Joe notes, "The union can't show any special interest in your people or we antagonize the Southern whites" (p. 25). Further, while Lee pursues the black workers, the Communists, who are determined to seize control of the union, will be stalking Lee in his turn. "Play the discrimination, and play the Communists, too" (p. 25), advises the rocklike Joe, a walking compendium of stolid working-class virtues in a very un-Californian blue-serge suit. The tactics of the Communists, however, are as clichéd as Joe himself, and he is able to describe them in detail to Lee with what proves to be complete accuracy: two people will attempt to become his personal friends, one an apparently simple black man, the other a young and attractive white woman. And, sure enough, by the end of the first afternoon Lee has been approached by the black Communist, a huge and dangerous looking man with a jagged scar on his cheek, named Luther McGregor, and on Saturday at a party at Luther's house, he meets the Communists' young white woman, Jackie Forks. Lee distrusts and resents all Communists, having been thoroughly disillusioned by the failure of a Communist antidiscrimination group to protect his previous job at the post office. He sees their wartime insistence on national unity and the resulting de-emphasis of their former strong stand against racial injustice as a betrayal. Their vaunted "sympathy" for black Americans seems to Lee to be only a more cynically hypocritical brand of exploitation. But he is strongly attracted to Jackie Forks, agonizingly responsive to her smothering maternalism, and totally indifferent to hints of condescension in her manner, as well as to the fact that to her he is an "assignment." His life has been an unbroken succession of failures, all stemming from his open resentment of any hint of racial discrimination, and his wife Ruth has finally lost all confidence in him. His marriage has been reduced to brutal sexual aggression on his part and emasculating withdrawal and indifference on Ruth's. The sudden availability of Jackie Forks, this "attractive, single, white girl" (p. 198), proves an irresistible trap, and he plunges at once into an affair, willfully ignoring Jackie's pathetic weaknesses and his own dubious motivation, the fact, supremely humiliating to both, that it is only her "whiteness" that he desires.

What little success Lee has in organizing the sullen and distrustful black workers at the aircraft plant is due primarily to Luther McGregor's skill in manipulating simpler people, part tough ghetto savvy and part Marxist training. But the work bogs down when a rumor spreads through the plant that Louis Foster, the plant manager, has "bought out" a key union official. To Lee the focus of the rumor seems to be Lester McKinley, the aging and scholarly black worker who had first mentioned it to him. Unaware that the strangely gentle McKinley is actually a dangerous psychopath plotting Foster's murder, Lee slowly convinces himself that Lester McKinley is Foster's "traitor." Foster, acting always very much in character as the standard capitalist villain of a proletarian novel, invites Lee and Ruth to Sunday dinner at his house in Pasadena, a mansion only slightly less opulent than the Huntington museum, where he offers Lee a job in the plant's personnel department, and then, barely concealing his rancor at Lee's refusal, confidentially "confirms" the rumor of a highly placed union traitor. Next, the Communists, led by Bart, the black chairman of the party, approach Lee at Jackie's apartment, anxious to use him to denounce Lester McKinley and end the rumor that is defeating the organizing campaign.

Lee believes that the revelation that the traitor is a highly respected, educated black man would "kill a race" (p. 216), and he is painfully resisting the Communist pressure when, suddenly and dramatically, he learns that the "traitor" is the brutish and sinister Luther McGregor. Lee and Luther are stopped on the highway in Luther's car by four white sheriff's deputies in Foster's pay. They offer Lee money to cooperate with them and savagely beat him when he refuses. They force Luther to admit to Lee that he is on Foster's payroll. Luther then drives Lee, battered and unconscious, to a union hospital. Bart, called by Luther, meets them at the hospital and accepts with wry humor Luther's statement that he has taken Foster's money but given nothing of value in return. To Bart, Luther's value lies precisely in his ingrained criminality, his capacity for violence, his fundamental dishonesty, and his maniacal but well-hidden hatred of all authority.

To Lee, however, the knowledge is an open wound, and the determination of both the Communists and the union to protect Luther is shattering beyond endurance. Bart arranges to have Jackie Forks denounced as the traitor at a union meeting, backing the play with elaborate fabricated evidence, and Joe Ptak and Smitty, the union organizers, the "good guys," offer no protest, happy to see the rumor squelched, and not caring very much how it is done. However, Smitty, the sentimentalist, has become deeply concerned for Lee, moved by pity for his excessive sensitivity to every setback, and he keeps Lee's name on the payroll even after he has indignantly resigned.

After a six-day interlude of passionate eroticism with Jackie has ended with a complete collapse of the relationship, demolished by her surfacing racism, Lee slinks to a skid-row hotel, exhausted in spirit and body, tasting the bitterness of ultimate and absolute defeat. There Luther finds him, sent by Foster, who had sadistically baited Lee when he had gone back to ask for the personnel job, rejecting his final surrender with vast satisfaction, but now ready to offer tiny sums for small services, petty acts of betrayal.

Lee, hysterically embracing his degradation, allows Luther to drive him to the house of one of Foster's corrupt deputy sheriffs for his first assignment. But the deputy is maladroit, pushes Luther too hard, too brutally, too arrogantly and even allows that supremely dangerous man to see how much of Foster's money he has in the house, and with explosive suddenness, Luther draws a switchblade knife and stabs the deputy repeatedly, in a spasm of uncontrolled violence. The room is spattered with blood before his victim finally dies. Lee lapses into shock, apathetically helps Luther clean up after the murder, and then wanders off to seek refuge with Jackie, blankly oblivious to the finality of their rupture.

Jackie, fearfully, hysterically, agrees to offer an alibi for him, then denounces him to the police as soon as he falls asleep. After Luther has been shot to death resisting arrest, Lee is beaten at the police station and charged with the deputy's murder. Ruth, abandoned by Lee, half-heartedly toying with the notion of suicide, sitting alone in her dark house with a bottle of poison before her, is also arrested, lodged in a cell, questioned. At this point, however, all the currents of the novel change direction. Smitty, Lee's union boss and secret friend, who has all this time stubbornly retained Lee's name on the roster in the vain hope that he would adjust in time to the hard realities of union politics, now comes to the rescue. He mobilizes the union's lawyer and even obtains perjured testimony alibiing Lee to support the lawyer's demands for writs releasing Ruth and Lee. He offers Lee the full support of the union in the coming murder trial if only Lee can somehow complete the job of organizing the black workers in the six days that remain before the plant election.

Lee is at first resentful of the strings attached to Smitty's help, and deeply suspicious of Smitty's "whiteness," but he quickly yields to the overwhelming evidence forcing the conclusion that this oddly soft white man is truly his friend. Lee attacks the job with new fervor, refusing to give way this time before the unyielding realities that have made the job from the first a practical impossibility. Still separated from Ruth, who will need much time to forget his affair with Jackie, still living in the skid-row hotel, Lee draws philosophical and moral support for his dynamic new stance in life from long conversations with Abe Rosenberg, a gentle little Communist who had been expelled from the party for supporting Lee's charges against Luther and who now quickly becomes the most important of Lee's newly found, highly committed white friends.

On the day of the final rally staged by the union outside the plant, Lee is on hand, eager and full of enthusiasm, though hiding in the sound truck, since Foster has forced the authorities to issue new warrants for his arrest. He watches Foster's army of deputies brutalize the marchers, watches rocklike Joe Ptak fighting heroically, holding the union banner aloft, only to be beaten to the ground, the flag staff sadistically rammed into his crotch, the banner still fluttering in the air. Then Lee Gordon, his great moment finally come, springs from the sound truck, crashes through the line of deputies, and, as the novel ends, he snatches up the staff of the union banner, brandishing it aloft, seeing at the same time out of the corner of his eye the drawn gun of one of the deputies who had beaten him on the highway "come leveling down on him" (p. 398).

The ending is equivocal, failing to resolve questions of life and death, success and failure, dismissing them as irrelevant beside the overriding importance of Lee's inner rebirth, his spiritual awakening. Yet, until the last section of the book, Lee is almost entirely a passive character, tightly responding with stock responses to the impacts of other personalities, like a billiard ball in play. The ending, in fact the entire structure of the novel, depends for credibility upon the believability of Lee's sudden shift from reaction to action, from billiard ball to cue stick. Even the reader's confidence in the author's sincerity in centering this novel around one black character's emphatic "yes" to life in a strongly racist society depends to a very large extent upon the success of this one characterization.

"No one man could be as contradictory as Lee Gordon seemed" (p. 354), broods Smitty, but Himes's omniscient narrator decisively undercuts the competence of Smitty's judgment: "He simply did not have the imagination to put himself, a white man, in a Negro's place" (p. 345). Yet Himes was clearly aware of the problems posed by the extraordinary complexity of his central character. And, just as clearly, the complexity was not accidental, but a reflection of Himes's most basic convictions about the paradoxical nature of black Americans.

The contradictions in Lee Gordon involve even his physical appearance. To his wife Ruth he seems prematurely old, with an aging man's "bitterness in the droop of his mouth that marred his whole appearance" (p. 12). But to the book's other characters he is "this thin, too tense, tightly hurting boy" (p. 75), "this tall, thin Negro youth" (p. 154), or "this kid. . . . the simple son of a bitch" (p. 324). He is thirty-one, and it is only at the very end of the book that he discovers his first gray hair, "And he was glad to realize that he had safely passed his youth" (p. 385). As with Bob Jones, Himes put much of himself into this character, but also much that he had observed in others. Lee's ability to accumulate hurts and show them, while maintaining intact the essential qualities of extreme youth could come from either source.

Lee is a native Californian, son of house servants in suburban Pasadena, and a graduate of U.C.L.A. with a degree in sociology —all qualities that should distance him from Chester Himes. But his elegantly complete education is visible primarily in an occasional pomposity of manner. He does not possess—as did his largely self-educated creator—the true intellectual's toughness of mind. He invariably responds to reasons with emotions. A young Tuskegee graduate working at the aircraft plant "bucking rivets" counters Lee's efforts at persuasion with the hard Himesian line, "I'm seeking the truth about myself and my heritage, and I don't give a damn what it proves," and Lee can only reply, with earnest sentimentality, "But why accept a conclusion that in the society of your times makes you appear inferior?" (p. 61). Yet Lee does have a scholar's broadness of perspective, a firm awareness that most social problems extend throughout the fabric of American society, far beyond the confines of the black community. The subjects of his reflection range from America's national obsessions, "a nation rooted in heroism, built on heroism" (p. 106), to its weaknesses and incipient sicknesses, "In a nation where so many millions of people kept getting drunk for drunkenness, there must be something deeply wrong" (p. 96). Lee has also the scholar's confidence that phenomena can be explained rationally, a willingness to turn and return in his mind every event of his experience in search of answers.

Many of the apparent contradictions in Lee's behavior arise from the uncomfortable combination of his deep-seated fear of all whites and the extreme and slightly absurd belligerence he sometimes assumes to mask it. He is gentle, reserved, and shy, but he can blurt out in a conversation with Abe Rosenberg, in answer to Abe's arguments against black anti-Semitism, "There is a certain repulsiveness in the Jew's basic approach toward life" (p. 158). Lee's long history of joblessness is partly due to his pride, his justifiable refusal to submit to the humiliations of discrimination, but also to his "high-shouldered air of bravado, disdain, even arrogance": "Those to whom he applied for work. . . . resented his tight-faced scowl, his hot, challenging stare, his manner of pushing into an impersonal office and upsetting everyone's disposition with the problem that he rolled in front of him, as big and vicious and alive as if it were a monster on a chain" (pp. 36–37).

Lee suffers from an acute identity problem. He has not been able to discriminate between his rejection of the penalties imposed on blackness and a rejection of blackness itself: "He had learned nothing to make him proud of being a Negro and everything to make him ashamed of it. . . . He came to believe that something was lacking in Negroes that made them less than other people" (p. 33). As he goes through the procedures of recruiting Comstock's three thousand black workers, side by side with crude, violent, black Luther McGregor, his indispensable volunteer helper, Lee becomes agonizingly aware both of his own ignorance of black Americans and the prejudices he carries. At first this new awareness is no more than the source of a vague discomfort: "Lee's vision sought out the Negro workers. All seemed either too loud or too sullen. Their demeanors set them apart. Lee felt an odd, unwanted embarrassment for them that they should always be so different" (p. 27). In the beginning his personal confidence is such that he can terminate an intreview at a black worker's home with a single curt remark to Luther:

"I'm going. It's bad enough to be a nigger but this man is a fool" (p. 55), and he can interrupt Jackie's sympathetic white Communist patter with a flat rejection of any broad involvement on his part: "I'm not trying to solve the Negro problem, Jackie. I'm trying to solve my own problem" (p. 149). What Lee fears from the white workers is not so much the possibility of violence toward himself as the inevitable "rebuffs, humiliations, sneers, scorn, rejection, exclusion" (p. 5). "He could feel their antagonisms hard as a physical blow; hear their vile asides and abusive epithets" (p. 5). In the normal operative level of his consciousness he has no feeling of difference from the whites, no feeling of special kinship with the blacks, and every event that jars these feelings from the depths of his consciousness is traumatic. His mind rejects his exclusion from the mainstream with something stronger, more instinctive and spontaneous than logic or reason. His whole being rejects inclusion in the special classification society insists he accept. Through the years his personal defense mechanisms have grown continually stronger, more and more automatic, effectively shutting him off from the rest of humanity: "He did not like people that much, anyway—neither Negro people nor any people. He did not feel that much involved in humanity or the struggle for humanity" (p. 28). But his job as black organizer forces him to be involved, hammers open the wall of his defenses. For the first time in his life he is acquiring some insight into the enormous complexity of the black experience. He finds that even his prejudices, of which he is increasingly ashamed, are not his alone:

> Yes—he was learning the Negro, Lee Gordon thought. And most of what he learned was hurting knowledge. It brought fear and hurt and shame to learn of the beaten, ignorant Negro laborer, so indoctrinated with the culture of his time that he accepted implicitly the defamation of his own character and was more firmly convinced of his own inferiority than were those who had charged him thus. (*Lonely Crusade*, 61)

He finds an immense range of characteristics within this small group of three thousand black people:

They did not look alike, act alike, or think alike. Their emotions were as different as their intelligence; and their educations as different as their environments. That what was a joke to one might be an insult to another; that what one saw as beneficial, another saw as detrimental. (*Lonely Crusade*, 60)

Lee's voyage of discovery into blackness provides Himes with a platform for extensive editorializing, none of it entirely gratuitous, though much is seemingly contradictory, and, in the end, Lee's expanded horizons provide Himes with machinery to reshape his protagonist's outlook, to wrench him from his bitter isolation:

For the knowledge of them was like looking into a mirror and seeing his own fear, suspicion, resentments, frustrations, inadequacies, and the insidious anguish of his days reflected on the faces of other Negroes. It frightened him all the more because he could not divide himself from the sum total of them all. What they were, he was; and what they had been, he also had been. . . . What life held for them, it also held for him—there was no escaping. (*Lonely Crusade*, 60)

In Lee's final crisis of disillusionment, when he has withdrawn to the skid-row hotel—"when the taste of salt came into his mouth, he knew that he was crying"—all of these strands begin to intertwine, "For this was the end of the line for all those who did not embrace the color of their skins and live by it, he told himself with cynical self-depreciation" (p. 307).

Yet, there is no one factor that explains Lee, no one string that is pulled to produce any and all of his reactions. Even at the expense of the neat functioning of his plot, Himes cherishes the complexity of this character, which closely approaches the complexity of a real person. There is in Lee a rejection of his blackness, but also a willingness to fight for it. His fears seem primarily to be fears of humiliation, but there is also a basis in his experience for a purely physical terror of the violence of whites, and this too functions in the story. He has never seen a lynching, but reading and imagination have filled this gap, "Had he never known the long history of brutalities toward Negroes, he might not now be so afraid, he told himself" (p. 10). The same terror that came to Bob Jones through witnessing the injustice meted out to Japanese Americans had come to Lee Gordon in the reflective quiet of his sociology classes at the university. Even in the banal routine of passing out union leaflets at the plant gate, the knowledge chills him: "Suppose the plant guards came out and attacked him? . . . Declaring that he was within his rights as a citizen had never been of any protection to a Negro—that he could recall" (p. 27). At first this fear appears more a product of imagination than of knowledge. His first reaction to the incredible insults directed at him by the deputies who stop him on the highway is a civilized man's disbelief, "Lee's tight, hot gaze searched the speaker's face for signs of levity but found only a blunt bestiality that frightened him" (p. 217). And it is as a civilized man that he fights back, with his bare fists, against the pistol butts of four dangerous men. Luther's knowing "shuckin' n' jivin' " reaction to the same insults and threats is to Lee just one more proof of "the cowardice of Negroes" (p. 238). When Ruth looks into Lee's battered face after the beating, she recognizes in it a semblance of "that naked look of protest seen in the face of a young girl just ravished trying to absorb the effects of the brutality" (p. 235). The exquisitely painful passage from imagined to lived experience is a major part of Lee's odyssey. The union lawyer's advice not to press charges against the deputies, since he can "prove" nothing and they will only rebound against himself as countercharges for false arrest (p. 242), is one more step, perhaps more important than the beating itself, toward full realization of the helplessness of the black man in a society whose elected officials refuse even to listen to his protests. "Every time something happens to a nigger, he says a deputy sheriff did it" (p. 242), snorts the novel's sheriff, an absurd figure who is in no way comic.

It is Lee's complex of fears, real, imagined, and dimly or clearly foreseen, that has poisoned his relationship with his wife, the omniscient narrator assures us. Himes dipped deep into his knowledge of human love and marriage under the unique and killing pressures of life in black society to depict this marvelous and irreparably damaged love. It is by far the most real, the most powerful, and the most moving of the book's many components, the most vital of the many facets of Lee Gordon's life. Wherever he is, whatever he is doing, Lee's thoughts continually turn toward Ruth, "His love for her was so intense he could feel it like a separate life throughout his body" (p. 185). They had loved each other from the moment of their first meeting in 1935. She had entered his life as a promise of "the end of loneliness and the faintest stir of meaning in a meaningless world" (p. 38). For the first two years of their eight years of marriage they had known great happiness, in a world of their own, a world rich with promise: "They could lie together in the warm, dark nights and imagine things.... She had taught him to enjoy literature" (p. 8). But the pressures had slowly mounted. They were both college graduates, but he had to accept demeaning work as a laborer, and she became a personnel counselor in a large industrial plant: "He thought that with Ruth he would never be afraid again. But it merely changed the pattern of his fear. Now it was the fear of being unable to support and protect his wife" (p. 39). Their total openness to one another, their complete vulnerability demanded from each a special effort of kindness, an infinite tenderness, and, little by little, both had begun to forget how to be kind: "When you were a Negro, so many things could happen to keep you from fulfilling the promises of yourself.... Yet now he was of a mind to blame her for all of it" (p. 8). There was at last no joy at all in their lovemaking, only a dull anguish, a deadly compulsion—"He hated her because he could feel no desire. Yet he had her anyway, because she was his wife" (p. 9). They had drifted into separate worlds, forever walled off from one another.

> Now prone with one of her large, ripe breasts overflowing in brown warmth the blue night gown, her lips flowering prettily against the darker brown of her heart-shaped face, she looked more desirable and voluptuous than in many a long, lonely night. But he did not see her. He put his flat, cold lips to the pressure of her kiss, and when arms came up to encircle him, he broke quickly away. (*Lonely Crusade*, 13)

And all of this suffering, this waste, had come from the economic and social pressures on Lee, his sense of inadequacy, his gnawing fears:

> Ruth? . . . She could not even understand his necessity for dominance, or anything at all about his ego—his warped ego, his sickly, dwarfed, cowardly, cringing ego that his fear had given him. . . . So what if he did need such a wife to know that he was not the lowest person in the world? And what if he did make her the lowest instead of himself? It would just be her unfortunate predicament of being married to a Negro man. . . . But, Lord God, a man had to stand on somebody, because this was the way it was. (*Lonely Crusade,* 143)

Driven by pain to inflict pain, finding in his marriage bed the only outlet for his terrifying angers, Lee had methodically debased not only his marriage but his wife as well:

> She had been absorbing Lee's brutality for six long years. . . . She had not minded absorbing his brutality, allowing him to assert his manhood in this queer perverted way, because all the rest of the world denied it. But at so great a price, for it had given to her that beaten whorish look of so many other Negro women who no doubt did the same. (*Lonely Crusade,* 7)

In the end, the bright promise held only unbearable despair: "No one but his wife had ever truly liked him, and she didn't like him anymore" (p. 198).

In his brief affair with Jackie Forks, Lee seeks a safe outlet for his sexuality and his considerable capacity for tenderness in a relationship that is reassuringly simple: "Jackie? . . . But he could better bear the thought of her not understanding since there was no reason why she should" (p. 144). Pity, pure and simple, is the foundation of his feeling for her, and he finds it an enormously bracing sensation: "To be able to pity this white girl gave him equality in this white world. With the equality of his pity for her he could now love her; and he did. He loved her desperately, violently, and completely" (p. 279). Jackie's sexuality is as blatant and uncomplicated as "the strong musk scent of sex—a woman scent" (p. 104) she brings to their embraces, but she is also an empty vessel, undeveloped in both mind and emotions, and Lee's attraction for her is tempered by his sharp awareness that "Ruth . . . had all that Jackie feigned" (p. 196). He can achieve no real intimacy with this essentially dull woman, her sensations keyed to a far lower level of intensity than his can ever be: "Shock showed clearly in her face when she looked into his eyes and saw the grinding hurt. It confused the attitude of three-fourths sex and one-fourth understanding which she had so carefully rehearsed, and brought dismay" (p. 247). Yet, as always, Lee's expectations are inordinate, unreservedly sanguine, and he manages to experience considerable pain in the wreckage of this flimsy affair. In fact, he succeeds in communicating some of his own intensity to the relationship, and for a brief moment of time it burns with a hard, clear flame:

> . . . he was hers, and she was of no race and of no color but only of the people of the world. For this was the way God made it, and now she knew it was the way He wanted it to be. . . .
> And thus they started up the ladder to the way it might have been. (*Lonely Crusade*, 279)

Lee radiates his complexity and pain into every corner of the novel. However, the book was not intended, or constructed, as a neurotic's case history, but as the detailed account of a crusade, a struggle that gains in coherence and meaning as it advances. An author who respects words as much as Himes would not use the word *crusade* in a title unless he intended to invoke ultimate questions, to venture into the religious and philosophical dimensions of experience. But Lee Gordon, eminently convincing as failed lover and tormented victim, is not an entirely satisfactory crusader. In the first place, the precise nature of the faith that sustains him is left vague, and, in the second, little foundation is laid for the appearance of traits that run counter to the prevailing negativism of his character.

To Luther McGregor, Lee is clearly set apart from other black men by "his university education and his white folks' ethics" (p. 325), and the omniscient narrator assures us that much of Lee's behavior is determined by "the Anglo-Saxon trait of emotional repression he had inherited. . . . he was bound by it as he was by all white traits he had inherited" (p. 313). It is not too surprising, then, that when idealism comes to Lee it comes in familiar, standard-brand, mainstream forms. The confusion arises from the fact that it flows from three distinct mainstream sources: the cult of patriotism, the philosophy of Marxism, and sentimentalized Christianity.

A line from a speech made by a Southern white army colonel to a group of black American aviators, given to him to read by Jackie Forks, "etched itself in Lee Gordon's mind and crucified him to his seat." The magic line was: ". . . that you, as Negroes, have not been particularly encouraged to be heroic in the past" (p. 106). At first, Lee responds angrily, rejecting what he feels to be hypocritical condescension, but phrases from the speech keep returning to his thoughts, until at last he has completely bought what the colonel was selling: the notion that there is a peculiar grandeur in the willingness to die for a cause and that the black man's greatest deprivation in "this nation rooted in heroism" (p. 106) has been his exclusion from the ranks of those who die for causes (p. 367). Lee firmly believes that all black men, and he himself in particular, lack certain essential qualities, and in his thoughts he always identifies these qualities with references to the men of the mainstream:

> Once again he was held by the knowledge that he could run, but he could not escape; for what he wished to escape was not in the City of Los Angeles, or in the offices of Louis Foster, but within himself—not an actual thing, but a lack of something. . . . in the indefinable essence of manhood there was something missing. Something in the hope that kept man struggling throughout all history for a better world; in the faith of man on which were built all civilizations; in the charity by which man sought an understanding; in the love from which man has drawn man's humanity to man; in the self-reliance, honesty, integrity, and honor that

have always kept man above the beast; in the convictions
that are the measure of a man; and—most of all—in the
courage by which men die for these convictions. (*Lonely
Crusade*, 365)

The task of defining these convictions is not left entirely, however, to rampant internal-monologue editorializing. The novel's
penultimate thirty-first chapter is devoted to an exhaustive bull
session in Lee's skid-row hotel room, in which Abe ("Rosie")
Rosenberg, a Mensh with overtones of Messiah—"he began
seeing Rosie not as a Jew, but as a savior" (p. 376)—expounds his
personalized and highly humanitarian version of Marxism. "All
people die—that is a little thing," Rosie insists, "Once you resolve your indecision toward life and embrace your own reality,
you will not be afraid to die" (p. 383). The inexorable forward
march of historical change will in the end reduce everything to
relevance: "This is change, Lee, and out of the rivers of blood
will come a different world" (p. 383). Lee responds, but only
to the immense hopes Rosie embodies, and not to the specifics of
Marxist dogma: "Standing there watching Rosie's fat, frog-
shaped body go carefully down the stairs, Lee felt the joy come
back into living. The man must set his watch by God, he thought
wonderingly" (p. 375).

The next morning, the day of the ultimate confrontation, Lee
awakens humming "Oh, when the saints . . ." (p. 385). He bub-
bles over with ecstatic religiosity: "Yet everything he saw was
with compassion and all he heard was with a prayer. And the
odor of garbage from the uncleaned gutters gave place to a fra-
grance of friendliness in this living world" (p. 385). He is trans-
ported to the dizzying peak of absolute certainty: "and the faces
of the people of the race—the human race—each with its story
of the crusade. . . . he did not feel lost or black or unimportant,
but a part of it, contained by it, as a ripple in the river of humanity.
. . . Values had taken new meanings and people new forms"
(p. 386). The ultimate form into which his ecstasy flows is traditional Christianity: "But what kept ringing in Lee Gordon's
mind like some forgotten liberty bell was not the words of Rosie
nor the words of Marx, but the words of Jesus Christ: 'Blessed
are the meek, for they shall inherit the earth' " (p. 394).

Until this point in the novel, only Ruth in her most wistful moments has sensed the seeds for such a metamorphosis in Lee:

And the hope that he would find himself had never died. For paradoxically she saw within him a quality of belief in human nature that kept this hope alive; a slender thread of integrity between him and his God that she had seen conditions bend but had never thought would break. (*Lonely Crusade*, 236)

This is, however, a very slender thread indeed, almost completely buried in the morass of Lee's nihilism. Shock at the murder he witnesses stirs it only briefly: "But the horror of death made life no less dreadful, only more meaningless.... deep within him was still something that did not want inclusion in a murder" (p. 324). Depressingly enough, the essential lever in the mechanism of Lee's awakening is a rejection of the "blanketing excuse of race" (p. 362), not quite, but almost, a rejection of the fact of blackness itself:

A fact, first of all! But if this fact could justify vicious, immoral, criminal behavior, if it could offer absolution, provide a valid excuse, or even pose a condition for sympathetic judgment, then the Negro was subnormal and could never fit into a normal society. (*Lonely Crusade*, 362)

Lee's soul-searching leads him to positions similar to those that Alice had urged on Bob Jones, positions that had proved fragile illusions in the nightmare realities of Bob's catastrophe. Lee escapes from his own nightmare by a process as simple as pushing a button. He finds somewhere deep within himself the energy for a simple but heartfelt "yes" to the universe, a "yes" that is also a "no" to all the debilitating habits of thought that a lifetime of living the black experience had forced on him and into him. Himes's interest is always primarily in the psychological effects of the black experience on its victims rather than in the petty details of repression or in the social mechanisms that produce it, and he traces with overwhelming authority the stages of the slow breakdown that immediately precedes Lee's abrupt recovery, "It was as if he were drugged, or entering into some mental state resembling amnesia where he had not so much actually forgotten who he was, as that it did not matter" (p. 311). Despite all of the documentation and all of the rationalizing that prepare the reader for Lee's emergence as a crusader, a true believer, a freedom fighter on the barricades of a predominantly white humanity, this event nevertheless comes as a very big surprise. It is, of course, not difficult for a man to believe in the importance and purposefulness of other men and of the universe as a whole once he has come to believe in the importance and purposefulness of his own life, but Lee seems at all times far from the possibility of any such apprehensions. If his transformation is not totally gratuitous and unmotivated—and Himes provides too large a field of action with too many elements in play, too much going on, to make this a safe conclusion—its suddenness is at the very least a massive flaw in the management of this central characterization. Too much had been said, and said with clarity and conviction, about Lee's isolation and bitterness, suspicions and fears, too much weight had been piled on the other side of the scale, for his metamorphosis to be easily acceptable to the reader, and, in the novel form, what is not easy for the reader does not work. "Well—Yes" is Lee's habitual response to situations he cannot quite accept but has to anyway, and it is bound to be many a reader's final reaction to Lee himself.

The impressive portrait gallery of secondary characters the book also offers, each one at least as well developed as the central figure of a short story or novella, presents no similar problems. The other characters in Lee's world are "flat," in E. M. Forster's classic sense of the word, since they neither evolve nor hold surprises for the reader, but these characterizations are nevertheless fully detailed and complex, as real as Himes's own experience. Many are easily recognizable as literary types, particularly the white characters, but all embody patterns of internal conflict that give them a lifelike solidity. The keys to their characters are always the mainsprings of a precisely defined psychological dynamism.

In the case of Ruth, for instance, this basic conflict is between stubborn remnants of girlish idealism and the harsh cynicism life has forced upon her. Her essentially strong character is rent by the clash between the confidence in humanity that is instinctively hers and her ever-growing sense of disillusionment, specifically centered on Lee. Though her parents had disapproved of her marriage—"could see no future for a Negro of Lee's temperament" (p. 38)—to Ruth herself, whose early years had been "one long odessey of books," spawning dreams as compellingly real as those of Emma Bovary, Lee had appeared at first as "a tall, proud Negro youth with hurt eyes and a tormented smile and a touch of Byron in his make-up" (p. 187). After eight years of marriage, though, "her faith in him was gone. . . . she did not believe that anything would ever help Lee Gordon" (p. 7), a man who "failed, as if failure was his destiny" (p. 187). She is, to a greater degree even than Lee, a victim of the prejudices of the world they live in: "A man could not be less than a man to the world and more to her. Whatever of a man the world rejected, she rejected too. For her values were common values and her thoughts common thoughts" (p. 293). Her love for Lee remains intense, however, almost unbearably intense. After he is beaten by the sheriff's deputies, shock and fear begin slowly to destroy her: ". . . she had suffered this stiflingly intense trepidation every moment he was out of her sight. She could not concentrate on her work; she was nervous and irritable, uncertain and absent-minded" (p. 263). All that restrains her from suicide after Lee has left her for Jackie Forks is her fear that it would hurt Lee (p. 336). Yet, in spite of the constant tenderness of her deepest feelings, she more than holds her own in the savagery of the verbal infighting that fills the last bitter months of their marriage, ending only when Lee leaves to take up his monastic sojourn in a skid-row hotel. She taunts Lee for his pride in a job his blackness alone has brought him (p. 6), calls him "pimp" because her earnings have long supported them both (p. 266), venomously ridicules his claims that he may have found another love: "You envy white men. . . . you are a Negro. You are cheap and vicious and craven. . . . she wouldn't have you. I am the only fool who ever wanted you. And I don't want you any more" (p. 300). Ruth has some idea of how much her job, a job far better and more prestigious than any he has ever held, "her little cute office and white secretary" (p. 5), contributes to his sense of failure, but she cannot bring herself to abandon it, "for what would become of both of them if she did quit her job?" (p. 191). She sees his pain and longs to comfort him, "but in her state of discontentment she could find no voice for words as these" (p. 186). In the end, after Lee has left her, these conflicts rob her of all direction, all coherence; she can neither reject Lee completely nor forgive his betrayals: "At first she simply hated him, but finally the awful terror came again. For now that it had finally happened, she could not see how she could live without him. But God knows she could live with no man unfaithful to her for some white bitch" (p. 267). For Ruth, firmly rooted in the class of "successful" black people, who had long before quietly assented to the rules of the game as prescribed by the dominant whites, the black experience had begun to be traumatic only after her marriage to Lee. Her resistance to Communist propaganda, described in a letter to Lee, is stolidly middle class, resolutely mainsteam: " 'What they apparently can't see is that I like being a Negro regardless of what color I am; that I like being an American even more so and that I wouldn't exchange this democracy I live in for all the Utopias they can possibly picture' " (p. 85). From her job and her background both, she has learned the mannerisms of success, including even a "tiny professional smile she had developed for the working class" (p. 166). Lee had brought the first fear she had known into her life. "I've always been afraid with you and I wasn't afraid before" (p. 122), she tells him in one of their calmer exchanges. Lee had dragged her out of her safe, orderly, contented world into his own perpetual nightmare of self-rejection. For a time their love, a very great love, had sustained her, proved itself a strange and truly fantastic source of solace:

> There had been so many, many things in the slow tortured movement of the years, while watching his slow disintegration under the impact of prejudice and feeling the tearing, hurting, awful inadequacy at not being able to help. There had been the sublime joy when she had first learned she could absorb his hurts—the great feminine feeling of self-immolation when he struck her, the sharp hurt running out of his arm into her body. (*Lonely Crusade*, 293)

When this love falters, however, Ruth's whole world topples with it. Staring at her face in the mirror after Lee has left her for Jackie, Ruth hysterically powders it "a sickly white," "the first time in all her life she had ever felt a sense of inferiority because her skin was brown" (p. 294). Her reaction away from this moment of despair severs her forever from Lee: "And though Ruth's love for him was deeply compassionate, inspiring the desire to comfort him, she could not touch his body—it was a very personal feeling" (p. 359).

Within Jackie Forks there is a similar conflict between lovingly cherished dreams and unwilling perceptions of very ugly realities, but in her case both dreams and "realities" have something cheap and fundamentally fraudulent about them. Hers is a portrait etched, for the most part, in acid. She recites John Donne's love poetry from memory in intimate moments with Lee (p. 104), and lectures him constantly on the glories of the Marxist vision of material progress (p. 107). But she is not at all shocked at the Party's plans to "frame" some innocent bystander in order to free Luther of Lee's suspicions that he is a hireling of Louis Foster's. Yet she is filled with righteous and unbelieving horror when she herself is picked to be the victim offered: "Her white gentile soul was utterly outraged that they would sacrifice her to save a nigger's reputation" (p. 268). In response to Lee's confused speculations over the special bonds that draw a black man to a white woman, she smugly proclaims, "In your mind we are the ultimate" (p. 196), but she is incapable of a normal response to his desire for a life together: "She would not fight for him with a Negro woman—she would not sink so low, she thought" (p. 301). Clinging desperately to the illusion of her own nobility, her own unique worth as a person, she destroys their relationship with unconscious but deadly cruelty:

> "I'm white, Lee—white! Can't you understand? I'm a white woman. And I could not hurt a Negro woman so."
> For a long, emasculated moment, during which he suffered every degradation of his race, Lee Gordon stood looking at the whiteness of her face.
> "Well—yes," he finally said, and accepted his bag from her hand and went out of the door. (*Lonely Crusade*, 303)

To Himes race is more a psychological than a physical reality, an entity that has its being, its undeniable reality, only within the mind. He labels it here "an emotion," and he invites no condemnation of Jackie, a product of psychological realities she cannot change, "In the end she would always find race her strongest emotion" (p. 334). Even Lee can sense the power of the constraints at war within Jackie, the forces that will never allow her to be the splendid and free person she wants to be, and dreams of being: "He felt sorry for her. For she too was caught in this dirty hell of race, he suddenly realized. And it made her into what she was when she allowed it to, as it made him into what he was when he allowed it to" (p. 369). In the beginning of their relationship Lee had judged her to be "strangely good" (p. 149), and there are moments when she manages to fulfill the promise of her dreams and ideals, to escape briefly from the prison of racist emotion. And Himes endows her with a strangely flawed, jarring beauty:

> Her hips were too broad even in the dark blue skirt. And the saddle-leather loafers made her legs seem too large and her ankles too thick. From the neck down she was any girl Lee might see anywhere. But there was something in her face, the zestful mobility of finely cut, sensitive features framed by brown wind-blown hair . . . the vitality of her large brown eyes, the irresistible challenge of a candid mouth. There was an unconscious maternalism that seemed to come from within, as if she not only mothered the meek, but had given birth to them. (*Lonely Crusade*, 92)

Inexorably, the events of the novel destroy the best that is in Jackie and draw out all of the worst. They reduce her from easy, amiable, warm arrogance to cringing hurt, to knowing the same fears and hates that Lee knows, though she exits with a kind of apology, at the very moment of her final act of betrayal: "Please don't hurt me, Lee. I never meant to hurt you" (p. 332).

Bart, the aging black Communist leader who makes the decision that flings Jackie out of the sheltering arms of the Party, an act that impresses Lee as tantamount to a lynching (p. 259), appears only in a few brief scenes of the novel, and always as a wily and unscrupulous revolutionary, but he too is seen to be riddled with conflicts, and his internal contradictions run curiously parallel to Lee's. His ability to adapt instantaneously to every minor fluctuation in the wildly veering Communist "Party line," has brought him power, backed by his reputation for cold logic, which the omniscient narrator calmly undercuts: "For within Bart, as within many Negroes, there had developed a defense mechanism similar to a sixth sense whereby he could reach agreement with his masters with greater accuracy and rapidity than by logic" (p. 256). Yet, though he conquers with a black man's special weapons, Bart shares Lee's mainstream cultural hang-ups:

> There were times . . . when his American instincts were diametrically opposed to the ruthless nonconformity of revolutionary maneuvering . . . when the voice of his Baptist mother could be heard in the night of his soul; when virtues such as honesty, loyalty, courage, and kindness, charity and fair play had meaning and value; when his mind rebelled and could not follow the merciless contradictions of reality. . . . He felt no pride in the things he had done. For he had done so many things against his innate convictions. His Protestant, puritanical, Negro inheritance rose to torture him. . . . It was not that the Communist Party lacked integrity; it simply did not recognize it. For integrity was the virtue imposed by the *bourgeoisie* upon the proletariat to stabilize oppression. And materialism not only embodied flexibility, but in itself was change, breaking the bonds of all oppression. . . . "Motion is the mode of existence of matter," he quoted in his thoughts. (*Lonely Crusade*, 254–55)

Himes is less interested in the cogency of his characters' thoughts than in the psychological harmony or disharmony their thoughts generate, and Bart jangles noisily as he bulldozes his way through life, an oddly pathetic man of power.

Lester McKinley, scholarly black factory worker and former professor of Latin, also appears very briefly, all too briefly in fact. He leaves the novel by the simple expedient of getting on a train for Denver before any of the murky and murderous schemes hatching in his troubled mind have had time to mature, an abrupt, unexplained departure is, of course, precisely what one would expect of an unpredictable type like Lester McKinley, in real life, but it nevertheless runs counter to the canons of the big well-made novel, the subgenre to which *Lonely Crusade* seems to have been intended to belong. But, during the short time that McKinley is on stage, Himes weaves around him arguments for the intriguing theory that the psychological reality that is "race" may not only be a distinct emotion, as in Jackie's case, but even a fully developed, identifiable psychosis—a theory similar to those later developed in great detail by Frantz Fanon, who was, incidentally, perhaps the first major international "thinker" to take Himes's work seriously.[10]

In a chapter of the novel devoted almost entirely to this minor and transient character Himes quickly sketches a case history of this strange new variety of psychosis. Lester McKinley had once actually consulted a psychoanalyst to help him "to overcome the psychosis of race," only to be convinced that "in this society there was no cure." He had come to believe that his personal confusion of mind had a very broad general basis: "an oppression composed of abuses that had completely destroyed the moral fiber of an entire people. ... the Negroes of America had actually become an inferior people" (p. 70). On the advice of his analyst he had married a white woman, buxom, blonde Sylvia, and they are reasonably happy, despite the fact that "she believed him capable of killing her and their three children and himself in one of his fits of fury" (p. 67). On the surface Lester radiates culture, sophistication, and calm. "May I fix you a highball?" is a typical conversational gambit in his interviews at his home with Lee Gordon, "He appeared stiffly formal in collar and tie and a blue-bordered, gray flannel smoking jacket" (p. 73). "Well ... scholar or mountebank?" wonders Lee at their first meeting, when Lester solemnly intones, "*Labor omnia vincet*" (p. 21). But this distinguished and gentle little man's private thoughts are a writhing, paranoid maelstrom of violent plans, to murder, subvert, destroy. He is aware that he is insane, but the thought does not greatly perturb him, for to him insanity is one of the norms of existence for black men; even the relatively unrepressed Lee Gordon "was also insane, but did not know it yet, as were all Negroes, he told himself" (p. 75). This characterization, though something of a gratuitous irregularity in the

10. Williams, "My Man Himes," p. 87.

generally smooth texture of the novel, is nonetheless one of the major triumphs of the book. With it Himes probes as deep as any writer ever has into the tight coil of unbearably intense pain that is at the center of the black experience in America.

Along with the irritating similarity of their names, intimate knowledge and total awareness of this pain are the major points of resemblance between the suavely urbane and dangerous Lester McKinley and hulking, dangerous Luther McGregor. Both are black men bedeviled by their own conviction that black men belong to a lower order of humanity. Both have acquired white wives as props for their diseased egos. But while Lester McKinley has slipped across the border of rationality into the limbo of a permanent and stable paranoia, Luther's portion in his bargain with the devil is a diamond-hard mental clarity that is closely akin to the absolute freedom from illusion of the standard existentialist anti-hero, which is at the same time, in his case, the brutal cynicism of the conscious criminal, the criminal who devoutly believes in crime. Luther is possibly the most complex in this gallery of complex characters, but Himes, ever the connoisseur of paradox, cloaks him in an extreme, almost exaggerated, exterior simplicity:

> . . . a man who normally looked dangerous. Fully as tall as Lee, his six-foot height was lost in the thickness of his torso and the width of muscular shoulders that sloped like an ape's, from which hung arms a good foot longer than the average man's. His weird, long-fingered hands of enormous size and grotesque shape, decked with several rings. . . . On his left cheek a puffed bluish scar, with ridges pronging off from it in spokes, was a memento of a pickax duel in a Southern chain gang. . . . eyes as yellow as muddy water. (*Lonely Crusade*, 28)[11]

"One is black and the other is off-black," remarks one of the deputies that taunt and brutalize Lee and Luther on the highway, and throughout the novel Luther's purely African heritage is contrasted with Lee's mixture of "Anglo-Saxon" and black American. As Lee is being beaten by the deputies, looking up toward the car, "He saw Luther standing there looking down at

11. See pp. 47–97, this volume.

them, the flat black features of his face set in Negroid negativism"
(p. 221). Mollie, Luther's blowsy, sluttish white wife, calls him
"Caliban" and exults over his sexual prowess, his sheer animality:

> She was ready again to lose herself in sensuality, because
> what the coarse animal brutality of this nigger did to her
> was more than any drug. It intensified the perceptions of her
> five senses to a sexual grotesqueness, where the merest touch
> of his hand upon her body produced a sensation either acute-
> ly exciting or nauseating—an aphrodisiac stimulant either
> way. And at such times the warm velvety surfaces of his arms
> could feel as delicious as silk against her fingers, and the
> rough texture of his kinky hair could leave the sensation of
> a bruise. The whiteness of his teeth, the yellowness of his
> eyes, the redness of his tongue, and the blackness of his
> skin became writhing hues in her frenetic ecstasy . . . build-
> ing up . . . sexual bliss until at times she thought her guts
> would retch completely out. (*Lonely Crusade*, 323)

Often in this novel Himes treats interracial sex as a kind of
pathological symptom, at times almost as a perversion bred of
self-hate, something destructive that the black man's hurt, his
need for retributive violence and his hunger for physical mastery
and violation, compel him to seek out. And, from one point of
view, Luther appears as the personification of all such hungers,
all the bestial urges racist mythology attributes to black men,
or "uncivilized" men in general. He is, indeed, Caliban. In the
scene in which Luther murders the deputy, named Paul, in that
unfortunate man's own kitchen, before Lee's horrified eyes, there
is, as it were, a kind of apotheosis of Luther, a transformation
into, or revelation of, the dark demonic gods of mankind's primitive past, embodiments of chaos, all the uncontained violence of
an emerging universe:

> The instant Paul's back was turned, the curtain of submis-
> siveness dropped from Luther's face and malevolence stood
> out with the shock of sudden nakedness. His neck roped like
> a growth of blackened roots and his thick white-shirted torso
> knotted with muscles. Abruptly he was caught up, meta-
> morphosed, embodied with a violence that shed evil like rays
> of light.

Clutched in a presentiment of horror, Lee opened his mouth to cry a warning but it stuck in his throat like a rock. For before his startled vision, paralyzing his vocal cords, Luther rose like a great black monster, shook open a switch-blade knife, and stabbed Paul in the left side of the back, reaching for his heart. He saw Paul's body snap taut. A vacuum-tight concentration sealed his mind. He saw Luther stab Paul twice rapidly, low down on the right side. He heard Paul grunt. He watched him put his hand flat against the icebox and strike back with the other as he tried to straighten up.

Each stark detail poured into his consciousness to be for-ever etched in memory. But his mind would not take it, would not rationalize, would not perform.

"Mother—!" he heard Luther curse with an animal sound as he stabbed Paul in the side of the neck. He saw the muscles of Paul's neck tighten with the stab, saw the blood spurt in a geyser, saw his body strain to straighten and turn. He heard Paul's last gasped words, half cursing, half begging: "You don't have to kill me, you black son of a bitch!"

The next time Luther stabbed, the blade snapped off against Paul's spine, and Paul's body, like some gory gar-goyle, began slowly crumpling to the floor. As Lee watched him fall dying, he saw his tremendous effort to live, and from behind his wall of nausea, came an icy trickle of horror down into his soul. (*Lonely Crusade*, 318)

In a literary chat with Alice's friends in *If He Hollers Let Him Go* Bob Jones impatiently rejects an affected black woman's stock protest against Richard Wright's brutish black hero, Big-ger Thomas—"It just proved what the white Southerner has al-ways said about us: that our men are rapists and murderers"—with the flatly provocative line: "Most white people I know are quite proud of having made Negroes into Bigger Thomases" (pp. 83–84). Himes's Luther, like Wright's Bigger, may be seen as the deliberate projection of a racial myth, a hated stereotype, utilizing it as an instrument of protest. But Luther is no simple brute, no frightened child-man striking out blindly at an op-pressive world. Even Lee, not the most perceptive of men, comes in time to see the mental power embodied in Luther: "Against his will he had to admire the Communists for the job they had done on Luther. They had taught him poise, restraint, the skill of adjustment, how to time a parry. . . . within the short period of time he had known Luther he had come to lean on him for emotional support" (p. 58). Lee is immensely impressed when Luther reduces one group of fiercely squabbling black workers to chuckling harmony by smoothly reciting from memory the now classic ghetto ballad "The Signifying Monkey," though at the moment he doesn't really understand what Luther means when he concludes with "Thass me," identifying himself with the fantastically adroit trouble-making monkey, master manipulator of the jungle (pp. 202–4). Lee is mildly surprised when the phonograph record Luther plays in his own house turns out to be Sibelius's First Symphony; he is slightly surprised again when he learns that for a time, under the tutelage of an earlier white wife, Luther had written short stories about his boyhood in Mississippi (pp. 79–81). When Lee later attempts to force the Communists and the union to denounce Luther he discovers that this crude and seemingly simple man has a formidable record and reputation. "He's been out there in the field working for the union for a long time. . . . always considered him very reliable. . . . a few years back he was up at Bakersfield trying to organize the agricultural workers almost singlehanded," protests one white organizer (p. 230), and Bart piously pronounces him, "one of our most militant members, Luther McGregor, a tried and true Communist" (p. 245). It is, however, only in their last conversation, in Luther's house after the murder of Paul, as Luther for the first time openly expounds his brutally cynical philosophy in a long and rambling tirade, that Lee begins fully to understand the man:

> "In this goddamn world they's all kind of wars always going on and people is getting kilt in all of them. . . . And they's the nigger at the bottom of it all, being fit by everybody and kilt by everybody. And they's me down there at the bottom of the bottom. I gotta fight everybody. . . . Just like you always knew, I been taking Foster's money right straight along. And taking money from the party. And from my ol' lady too. And selling 'em all out. 'Cause why? 'Cause they is white. 'Cause to Foster I ain't nothing but a nigger. Ain't

never gonna be nothing but a nigger. . . . But if'n I can help it, don't nobody sell Luther out. 'Cause I sells 'em out first. . . . And I can do this 'cause I is a nigger. And I know I is a nigger. And what I do don't make no difference noway. . . . Do you think I love the Party? Or even believe in it? What the hell does I know about Marx? Or give a damn 'bout him? But I knows how to be a nigger and make it pay. . . . Look, man, as long as I is black and ugly white folks gonna hate my guts. They gonna look at me and see a nigger. All of 'em. Foster and the white folks in the party and the white women in the bed. But I is gonna always make it pay off, man, just as you could if you had any sense. (*Lonely Crusade*, 327–29)

Lee is staggered, faced with a man who not only lives the unthinkable but articulates it complacently.

At least he knew what Luther expected of him—to be a man without a soul. The white people had always said a nigger didn't have a soul, and Luther proved them right. Yes, maybe Luther was the only right one after all. For he, Lee Gordon, felt more like the murderer for having seen it done than did Luther who had done it. Being a murderer to Luther was just being a nigger after all, since being a nigger was being anything. (*Lonely Crusade*, 330)

Luther's views on Lee are similarly absolute: " 'You is a fool,' he said. 'Not only is you a fool but you is a *square* and a *lain* and a *do*' ' " (p. 324). Yet Luther has a great deal of sympathy for Lee, almost a father's love, and it is his failure to silence him as the one witness to his crime that leads to his own death at the hands of the police a few hours after the murder. As a literary character Luther suffers from gigantism; everything about him is outsized like a figure out of folklore, from his affections to his hatreds. That he is nevertheless entirely believable, even terrifyingly believable, is a measure of Himes's skill and the extent of his knowledge of men like Luther.

In the opening pages of Ernest Hemingway's *To Have and Have Not*, the narrator-hero Harry Morgan describes a black man killing another man in the streets of Havana, first shooting him in the stomach with a Tommy gun and then blowing his head apart with a shotgun at close range. "Some nigger," is Harry

Morgan's classic comment. In that novel, far from his best, Hemingway never again reaches quite that emotional peak. Though it is a minor and apparently irrelevant incident, the horrific passage of this one violent black man, brilliantly evoked, makes much of what follows after appear somewhat anticlimactic. A similar effect, enormously magnified, applies to the parts of Himes's *Lonely Crusade* in which white characters play important parts. In juxtaposition with the book's supercharged black characters, all triumphantly alive, Himes's few important white characters—with the notable exception of Jackie Forks—seem excessively flat, almost lifeless. They are either very good people or very bad people, but in either case their motivations seldom reach a truly human level of complexity.

Louis Foster, the Comstock plant manager, is little more than a villain out of Victorian melodrama with a few modern American touches. He affects simplicity of manner—a "tall, gangling man in a plaid woolen shirt and old corduroy trousers" (p. 168) [12] on the Sunday he welcomes Lee and Ruth to his palatial home—but domination is the name of the only game he cares to play. Mrs. Foster, "a fifty-year-old Ophelia," has "deliberately let her body go to seed as a defense against her husband's brutal passion" (p. 173). "They are my pets," he remarks of his three daughters, a sufficiently sinister statement in itself, which the omniscient narrator nevertheless hastens to contradict in a stage aside: ". . . an untrue statement. . . . Martha, his oldest, who was nineteen and feeble-minded, he wished had never been born; and he resented Abigail" (p. 172). Foster loathes Roosevelt and the New Deal and is aggressively patriotic in the standard America-first manner: " 'Are you proud to be an American, Lee?' he asked with sudden sharpness" (p. 180). He is fond of black people—the decor of his mansion includes "two cast iron statuettes of pickaninnies" (p. 168)—provided they have "the right attitude," that is, accept servile positions with open and frank enthusiasm. Roy, the Fosters' chauffeur, who drives Lee and Ruth to the informal dinner at the great man's home, is a prime example: " 'My name's Roy,' he announced, letting them know they were Negroes too" (p. 166). To Lee, Foster's offer of a

12. See p. 30, this volume.

better job is all too visibly weighed down with spiritual and psychological strings, "a handout with condescension, like old clothes given to a servant" (p. 181), despite the high salary Foster is willing to pay to buy him: "Foster could not bear to have a Negro, any Negro, dislike him. And before he would allow a Negro to really hate him, he would make the Negro rich" (p. 181). There are no limitations upon the ploys Foster will resort to in his endless and compulsive maneuvering for mastery over other people—even to secretly punishing refractory black house servants by "arranging the meals so as to keep them late on their half-days off" (p. 180). Lee's quiet, and reluctant, refusal of his offer immediately converts Foster into a tirelessly malevolent enemy:

> But it was shock that showed in Foster's face, stronger than his control. In the sudden fury that raced through his mind he thought with deadly venom: "You goddamn black bastard, you'll pay for this—" And then he composed his features to a stillness and kept his voice on an even keel: "I won't try to persuade you, boy, for I can understand your loyalty even though I know it to be misplaced." (*Lonely Crusade*, 182)

The characterization of the virtuous whites—Smitty, Joe Ptak, and Abe Rosenberg—is even less subtle. Joe's single-minded dedication to unionism amounts to monomania. But, though more rock than man, pure essence of unionism in a stone jug, Joe's final, fraternal "Okay, boy" (p. 389), to Lee, after Lee had actually toyed with the notion of treason to the union, clearly places him in the ranks of those white people who, Lee thinks, "must have been his friends right down the line from slavery" (p. 361). These "good" characters are frankly allegorized, symbolic less of actual segments of society than of hypothetical human potentialities, and in his relations with them, Lee briefly becomes similarly symbolic. Smitty, the fount of infinite compassion, oversteps, in his devotion to protecting Lee, all boundaries of literary verisimilitude. In suborning perjured affidavits from other white union leaders to alibi Lee and get him out of jail, he risks delivering the entire union leadership into the hands of Foster's deputies. A father could do no more for an idolized son, yet Smitty scarcely knows Lee; nothing really explains why he should so desperately "want to protect Lee from . . . almost certain hurt" (p. 232). Abe Rosenberg, self-avowed "unsuccessful Jewish philosopher" (p. 376), who plays sympathetic chaplain to Lee's melancholy martyr—"and he knew suddenly that Rosie had been working to save something in him in much the same manner as a minister works to save a condemned man's immortal soul" (p. 383)—is no less eager to throw himself under the locomotive's wheels for sullen, surly Lee. He listens to Lee's anti-Semitic diatribes with smiling patience, responds with eager, warm understanding, indeed almost with cloying sweetness (pp. 152 ff). Communism is his whole life, but he cheerfully accepts expulsion from the Party as the price for supporting Lee's futile charges against Luther. Such characters might be, if not convincing, at least less surprising if they were not so very rare in Himes's work, but his somber fictional world has ordinarily little room in it for the bright faces of the entirely virtuous. The notably good characters in the entire range of his work can be counted on one's fingers, with fingers to spare. And Smitty, Joe, and Rosie would be perfectly at home with Charles Dickens's Messrs. Pickwick and Micawber. They seem definitely out of place with Luther McGregor, Jackie Forks, and Lee Gordon. They are one more indication of the strain between Himes's naturalistic bent and his apparent determination to give *Lonely Crusade* a traditional plot structure and an upbeat theme, to mould it into a hopeful statement on "the Negro problem."

The first critical reaction Himes had to *Lonely Crusade*, which was to be the most extensively criticized and discussed of all his novels, came from his wife Jean while the book was still in its first draft, and it was disastrous. During the summer of 1946 he and Jean had gone to live in a secluded shack on a rundown ranch in the mountains near the California-Nevada state line, owned by Jean's brother, Hugo Johnson, a chief petty officer in the navy stationed in the San Francisco area. There, between bouts with sand lizards, invading field rats, and six-foot rattlesnakes, Himes had completed the first draft of *Lonely Crusade*. One night, after an expedition with the visiting Hugo to the nearest large town, seventeen miles away, to try to obtain parts for a damaged car, Himes returned to find the shack completely dark and Jean mysteriously gone. It was a moment of high drama, and Himes, a conpulsive storyteller, did it full justice in his autobiography:

> I fetched my rifle and we searched the nearby hills, calling her name, then all the area about the house, both of us with torches. Then we crossed the street and searched the barns and dilapidated farm buildings. It was approaching midnight and we had found no sign of her. Now thoroughly alarmed, we set out for Janesville to try to enlist the postmistress's family to help us organize a posse.
> About three miles down the highway we found her stumbling aimlessly along, sobbing to herself. We thought at first she had been attacked. . . .
> But she threw herself into her brother's arms and denied that anyone had approached her, but begged him to take her away. We were both flabbergasted. She said she didn't want to live with me. (*The Quality of Hurt*, 92)

The sole cause of Jean Himes's shocked and dazed condition, her open hostility toward her husband, Chester Himes soon learned, was his manuscript of *Lonely Crusade*:

> She had been reading some of my manuscript, which I had advised her not to do. . . . Jean thought that I had patterned the character Ruth after herself, and she was chagrined and hurt to learn I had this opinion of her after all the years of our marriage. I think it was chiefly the complex about color which I ascribed to Ruth. Jean was a very beautiful woman and she knew it and she was hurt to think I thought she had any kind of inferiority complex because of her color. As a point of fact I didn't . . .
> Hugo dismissed it with a laugh, which I don't think she considered very brotherly. But I spent many hours then and for years afterward trying to convince her I had never thought of her as Ruth. But I'm afraid she never really believed me; and I often wondered if I had drawn a true picture of which I was not consciously aware. (*The Quality of Hurt*, 92–93)

Himes completed the book in New York during the winter of 1946, and Alfred A. Knopf was prepared to launch it with heavy publicity. The official publication date was October 8, 1947, and to Himes it dawned like the first real Christmas in a life filled with dark winters:

> My father had come from Cleveland and was staying with us to celebrate the great event, and I was scheduled to appear on the Mary Margaret McBride radio program, and on a CBS program for books, and on the day of publication I was to speak to Macy's booksellers; from there I was to go to speak to Bloomingdale's book department.
>
> I got up early that morning to catch a Seventy-ninth Street Ferry, which would take me to Manhattan on time to get to Macy's at eight-thirty, the time for my appearance. (*The Quality of Hurt*, 98–99)

But nothing happened. The promotion had been canceled. It was as though a great many powerful people had launched a determined underground campaign against the book. In his interview with John A. Williams, Himes attributed the earliest assaults to the Communist Party,[13] but acknowledged that eventually almost everyone had gotten into the act: "It had some of the most terrible reviews, one of the most vicious reviews I ever read."[14] Himes was at first determined to fight back, and he had devised an ingenious scheme, which he described with some satisfaction to John A. Williams many years after:

> Knopf had given me an advance for another book, but then they . . . [*sic*] I had trouble with Knopf too. I tried to have some kind of dialogue with Blanche [Knopf] to discuss some of these reactions. I said, "Now, you have all of these reviews from *Atlantic Monthly, Commentary, New Masses*, the *New York Times*, the *Herald Tribune*, and *Ebony*, the black

13. Williams, "My Man Himes," p. 37. In his interview with Hoyt Fuller, Himes stated in more detail his conviction that the Communists were actually systematically harassing the booksellers to force the withdrawal of the book (Fuller, "Interview with Chester Himes," p. 9). Lloyd L. Brown's review of *Lonely Crusade* in *New Masses* (Sept. 9, 1947, pp. 18–20) openly called for "action" against the novel: "The issuance of this book ought to be met with more than passive anger, more than contempt. It should call for action. It should be buried deep beneath a rising mountain of protest, boycott and condemnation."

14. Williams, "My Man Himes," p. 37.

press. All of these reviews have different complaints about this book, different ways of condemning it. Well, this doesn't make any sense, and these reviews should all be published in an advertisement showing that all of these people from the left, the right, the blacks, the whites, that if all these people dislike the book there must be some reason. It would stimulate interest; people would want to know why."[15]

But, as he records in *The Quality of Hurt*, the company was not at all interested in openly fighting generally hostile reviews: "[Blanche Knopf] thought it best to let it alone. She said every writer must expect a certain amount of adverse criticism. Perhaps she was thinking only of my own good. But just then I needed support badly" (p. 102). The new protest novel he had planned for Knopf was never written. Himes was badly shaken, and it would take him years to recover: "Of all the hurts which I had suffered before . . . and which I have suffered since, the rejection of *Lonely Crusade* hurt me most" (p. 102). He had, by pushing his own deep angers and bitterness to one side, succeeded in writing a book that said "yes" to the whole of life, and the world had rejected his "yes." "Everyone hated the book," he notes in *The Quality of Hurt*, and proceeds to quote, with obviously painful scrupulosity, a few choice excerpts from the most biting reviews: ". . . *Ebony* magazine ran an editorial . . . in which it said: 'The character Lee Gordon is psychotic, as is the author, Chester Himes' " (p. 100).[16] He had written one protest novel with an angry, negative hero and the white critics had hated it; he had written another with a wistful, positive hero and the white critics had hated it even more, and this time the black critics had joined them. He would never again attempt so ambitious a work as *Lonely Crusade*, never again attempt to construct a novel that would spell out his personal solutions to all the

15. Ibid., p. 38.
16. Himes's "quotation" is, more exactly, a paraphrase. The context, and statement, in the *Ebony* editorial was: "The novel's [*Lonely Crusade's*] hero is a good example of many Negroes who suffer from what psychiatrists would call a color complex. Gordon—and his creator Himes—are infected with a phychosis that distorts their thinking and influences their every action in life." "*Ebony* Photo-Editorial: Time to Count Our Blessings," *Ebony* (November 1947), p. 44.

world's major problems. When he was psychologically ready to write productively again, a few years later, he would confine himself to a very narrow autobiographical vein. For years he concentrated all his efforts on telling his own story, trying to see it clearly, understand it fully, a task he was to find unexpectedly difficult, but ultimately rewarding.

4

The Autobiographical Novels
The Third Generation,
Cast the First Stone, The Primitive

I Question without Answer

Apparently as corollary to the arguments he remembered using in his efforts to convince his wife that *Lonely Crusade*'s pathetic heroine, Ruth Gordon, was not in fact a close portrait of her, Chester Himes argues briefly in *The Quality of Hurt* for his own remoteness from his character Lee Gordon:

> But then Lee Gordon had nothing in common with me, either. After all, I had been to prison; I didn't believe in the sublimity of people, black or white, any more than I believed in their depravity; I believed that people were capable of anything. But for the purpose of my story I had to give this couple a belief in the integrity of whites, and at the same time certain fears and complexes resulting from their race. Jean hated it.[1]

The argument is both reasonably convincing and obviously disingenuous in that it insists on regarding a multidimensioned reality in one dimension. A literary character molded to fit particular plot situations must differ markedly from its author in many ways. But it is equally evident that an author must invest a part of himself in every character he creates. For example, the great French novelist Gustave Flaubert—a physically impressive man, a brilliant intellect, and a great artist supremely conscious of his special gifts—could state, with the force of truism, that he was Madame Bovary, a very small, insignificant, and rather silly young woman. The genesis of literary characters is not an easily explained process, to be resolved with simple affirmations pointing

1. Himes, *The Quality of Hurt*, p. 93.

in any one particular direction. It is one of the deeper mysteries of the mind, as ultimately inexplicable as creativity itself.

And, so long as literary characters appear in situations that are for the most part invented for the purpose of displaying some facet of the characters' personalities, a particular character's precise degree of resemblance to its creator need not be a pressing concern for the reader. The question is in fact not only irrelevant but counterproductive as well. A writer creates his own reality, which the reader must fully accept if the reader-writer relationship is to function effectively. But when the literary characters consistently appear in situations that differ only in minor points of detail from the actual events of the author's own life, the reader's curiosity about author-character and fiction-reality relationships is naturally very strongly aroused. When a reader knows that what he is reading is very close to autobiography he inevitably wants to know exactly how close it is.

Unfortunately, Himes did not choose, in his autobiography *The Quality of Hurt* (1972), to clarify in any detail the exact relation of fiction to fact in his three autobiographical novels of the early 1950s—*Cast the First Stone* (1952), *The Third Generation* (1954), and *The Primitive* (1955). The sections of his life that he explored so exhaustively in the novels are hastily sketched in *The Quality of Hurt* in a few pages. His seven and one-half years in prison, for example, subject of *Cast the First Stone* and numerous short stories, are given less than six pages in *The Quality of Hurt*, and all the events of his youth and his parents' bitter marriage, subjects of *The Third Generation*, are compressed into a single chapter of the autobiography. The love affair that furnished the central theme for *The Primitive* is given only three pages. It is firmly established that almost all of the basic events that make up the plot structures of the three novels are factual, but no light at all is shed on the validity of the characterizations and patterns of motivation developed in the novels. And the brief descriptions of the novels themselves in *The Quality of Hurt* tend to be both vague and contradictory. *The Third Generation* is described both as "my semi-autobiographical novel" (*The Quality of Hurt*, 121) and "my autobiographical novel" (p. 201).[2] In a

2. Cf. Hoyt W. Fuller, "Traveler on the Long, Rough, Lonely Old Road:

conversation with John A. Williams, Himes described the same novel as his "most dishonest book," because he had not used much material from a manuscript memoir that his mother had written telling the story of her family, a mixture of almost-white slaves and affectionate slave owners:

> Well, she had produced this novel in detail and I thought that that should have been part of the book. The reason I didn't use it was that—I needed for it to be published and I thought that would be offensive to the publishers and would make it difficult for publication at that time.[3]

Himes's comment in *The Quality of Hurt* on *Cast the First Stone* mixes, characteristically, phrases like "I don't know" and "but obviously": "I had made the protagonist of my prison story a Mississippi white boy; that ought to tell me something but I don't know what—but obviously it was the story of my own prison experiences" (p. 117). His formula for *The Primitive*, in which a love affair that lasted almost two years was transformed into a one-week encounter, in order to make a more elegant plot structure, is the unsatisfying phrase, "rather exact": "My book *The Primitive* was about our affair, and although it doesn't tell the whole tedious story of my eighteen months with her, it gives the essence of the affair; in fact it is rather exact except that I didn't kill her" (p. 136).[4]

It is doubtful, however, that any artist could be more definite in describing an "autobiographical" work. He is guided as he writes by twin poles—his sense of the formal exigencies of art and his sense of the unalterable reality of his own experience—without ever being certain which he is following at any particular moment. Experience has many levels and can be seen in many lights. Just as a gifted actor can play Hamlet many times, giving the role each time a radically different interpretation, all equally

An Interview with Chester Himes," p. 12, a conversation in which Himes described *The Third Generation* and *The Primitive* as "autobiographical" in the same sense as *The Quality of Hurt.*

3. John A. Williams, "My Man Himes: An Interview with Chester Himes," p. 74.

4. In a comment contributed to a *New York Times Book Review* piece on authors' own favorite works, June 4, 1967, p. 7, Himes called *The Primitive* "largely autobiographical."

valid to the text, a good novelist can write a dozen different accounts of an incident giving the event each time a radically different interpretation, each one firmly grounded in his personal "truth," his sense, at the moment of writing, of the way it had to be. Himes's dilemma, as he tried to explain to his wife that she was not at all like his character Ruth Gordon, finding himself at the same time wondering "if [he] had drawn a true picture of which [he] was not consciously aware" (*The Quality of Hurt*, 93), is one the artist never escapes. He cannot "explain" his art, only create it. The measure of its truth rests entirely in its effect on the reader, who must recognize everything that is clearly specious without help from authoritative explanatory footnotes.

II   The Third Generation

Following the bad reviews of *Lonely Crusade* Himes had for a very long time great difficulty in writing and then, when he was able to begin again, he had difficulty finding a publisher for his work. His agent at the time, Margot Johnson, diligently circulated for some time manuscripts of both his prison novel, *Black Sheep*, eventually to be retitled *Cast the First Stone*, and his new novel *The Third Generation*. It was a trying and confusing time, and in his autobiography and his interview with John A Williams, Himes gives slightly blurred accounts of the publishing history of the two books (pp. 139, 142).[5] Apparently all that he remembered clearly were the frustration and his decision to use the relatively large sums of money he had finally obtained in publishers' advances to leave for France in April 1953. In point of fact the prison novel was the first of his two manuscripts to be published in 1952, and *The Third Generation* followed in 1954. Paradoxically, the much-revised prison novel, though written and published first, is essentially a sequel to *The Third Generation*, dependent on it for the vital background that molded the character of its protagonist and explained his presence in prison. *The Third Generation* is, in every important regard, the first piece in the set.

5. Williams, "My Man Himes," p. 31; cf. Fuller, "An Interview with Chester Himes," p. 9.

In construction *The Third Generation* is perhaps Himes's least contrived work. It flows easily, irresistibly, organically, retracing the course of Himes's troubled childhood and youth, seemingly driven solely by its own internal forces, without apparent management or manipulation. The characters develop freely, moving toward fates that they must both invent and discover, and the novel is shaped by them.

The structural center of the novel is the relationship between the two main characters, mother and son, her struggle for domination and his struggle for freedom and personal identity, extending over fifteen years. The character of the mother, Lillian Taylor, develops in a straight line, inexorably, tragically, a few traits that exist from the beginning becoming more and more dominant, until all flexibility is lost, and madness begins. The character of the son, Charles Taylor, is a continual seeking, resisting, groping, striving, an activity more than a structure. He is about four years old, "gleeful and spontaneous with a mischievous twinkle in his eyes,"[6] when the novel opens and a very old eighteen when it closes. The book is Himes's *Bildungsroman*, and it is one of the great classics of the genre.

By coincidence of experience rather than literary influence, Himes's novel bears close resemblance to D. H. Lawrence's *Sons and Lovers*. Lawrence had used the closely autobiographical format of the *Bildungsroman* to define symbolically a fundamental conflict in British society that would preoccupy him throughout his writing career. He reduced the complexities of class struggle to the confrontation between one plebeian male and one aristocratic female, father and mother, and their struggle for control of their own sons, a struggle finally centered on one son, the most sensitive and the most loved. Himes found in his own experience a similar social paradigm, ready made, and personally lived. His novel reduces the traumas generated within the black American community itself by the pressures of racism to the story of a single black family, rent by the conflict between a black-hating mother and a black-accepting father, and the sons caught in between—Himes's own story. Just as in Lawrence's *Sons and Lovers*,

6. Himes, *The Third Generation*, p. 11. (First published by World Publishing Co. of Cleveland in 1954.)

the battleground on which the mother and father wage their deeply symbolic fight is the soul of the most loved and most sensitive son, and, with the father's decline and the escape of the other sons, the struggle eventually becomes primarily a struggle between the mother and this one son. It is a war that assumes some of the forms, and the essence, of love. It is at the same time a search for identity in a world split into hostile camps, each holding equally legitimate claims to love and loyalty.

For young Charles Taylor, who gradually assumes the role of the novel's protagonist as he emerges from childhood, the painful choice every black man must make, to accept or reject his outcast people, in his own heart, becomes inextricably confused with the even more painful choice between affection and loyalty to his very black and defeated father and his overwhelming love for his almost-white mother, who is infected, deep in her being, with the deadly sickness of racism. The path Lillian Taylor follows, the denial of self, is an impossible one, leading only to madness, but it has the fatal attraction of the impossible, the realm of dreams, wish fulfillment, escape from bitter reality, and Charles is always powerfully, and at times irresistibly, drawn by Lillian's supremely demanding and somehow very beautiful love for him. To reclaim him, to force him back to the realm of reality, the world will have to come very close to rending him into pieces. In the progressive characterization of Charles Taylor, a detailed account of the genesis of an artist's special sensitivity, Himes's novel also has important points of affinity with another celebrated *Bildungsroman*, James Joyce's *Portrait of the Artist as a Young Man*, but Charles Taylor's story ends rather abruptly, before the artist has begun to emerge from the tormented teenager. Himes's novel is more nearly a portrait of the artist as traumatized child and suicidal delinquent.

The characters of *The Third Generation* have a largeness of size that is without parallel in the rest of Chester Himes's fiction. They are creatures of epic, of romance, of allegory—and of life itself, remembered with love and anguish. Charles is invested with all the beauty and potentialities of a slightly narcissistic author's fondest memories of his own distant past. Lillian is every passionate and sentimental man's memory of the mother whose perfect love he somehow lost. In the dynamics of the novel she functions as the negative principle, the primary destructive impulse, but she is nevertheless a heroic figure, as awesome as Medea, and as chilling, both superhuman and inhuman. And even the father, Professor William Taylor, called "Fess" Taylor, and Charles's two brothers, Will, Jr., and Tom, are clearer in outline and purer in substance than ordinary mortals. Himes's parents had both died before *The Third Generation* was published—his mother just before his first novel was published in 1945, and his father just before his departure for France in 1953 (*The Quality of Hurt*, 121, 139)—and it is very unlikely that fear of their personal reactions could have been a factor in his choice of approach. Throughout his career Himes inevitably assumed that the people he knew would have the good sense to separate themselves from the characters in his books; in fact, he lost innumerable friends that way, including his helpful cousins Henry and Molly Moon. The need for idealization, the seeds of generalization and exaggeration, were doubtless latent in the story itself, the story of his own past, as it presented itself to his mind at the time he wrote. The narrative point of view of *The Third Generation* is omniscient, invisible third person, but it is employed so flexibly that it effectively embraces a wide range of possible viewpoints, from precise and pompous sociological objectivity to outrageous bias and special pleading for Lillian.

References to Lillian's strength and incidents that demonstrate it are scattered throughout the novel: "She was a tiny woman, but she carried herself with such implacable determination that her size was seldom noticed" (p. 12); "Only the mother's indomitable will saved them. Now that she had overcome the attack of paranoia, she was stronger than before. She wouldn't admit defeat" (p. 155). Not even the menace of a pointed rifle in the hands of a savagely enraged white Mississippi farmer, whose mules have been frightened by the Taylors' primitive automobile, can intimidate "the grim, white-faced woman" (pp. 73, 84):

> The coal-black driver turned gray with fear. William began to whimper. Charles was rigid with rage and terror. But Mrs. Taylor's eyes glinted and her mouth set in a cold, deadly fury. When the driver got down and went to calm

the mules, she took a small revolver from her purse and aimed it at the white man's back. Charles hated the uncouth, bestial man and hoped his mother would shoot him.

But William begged hysterically, "Don't, Mama. . . ."

His mother lowered the pistol and held it in her lap. (*The Third Generation*, 91)

On another occasion, however, when a black professor at the Mississippi college where Fess Taylor was teaching attempted to thrash her little boys for peeping into the girls' latrine, Lillian actually fired the gun she brandished, an antique double-barreled shotgun:

> Deliberately, Mrs. Taylor encircled the house. In his haste, Professor Saunders had stumbled, but he was up, running again, when she came into view. Although he was out of range, Mrs. Taylor, unfamiliar with firearms, raised the gun and fired. The gun kicked her sharply and she uttered a cry of pain. The children dashed from beneath the house to aid her.
>
> Professor Saunders had been running in the direction of the Pattersons' field. But the sound of the shot panicked him and, wheeling suddenly, he jumped the picket fence, snagging his coat. As he tore off down the road in a cloud of dust, she raised the gun and fired again, the bird shot kicking up spurts of dust far behind him. He was well out of danger, but at the sound of the second shot he leaped high in the air, as if he'd been hit, and howled in fear.
>
> "Shoot him again, Mama!" Charles screamed. (*The Third Generation*, 83)

She also has the capacity for great warmth, at least in scattered moments, and her icy reserve can let slip past an impulsive gesture of affection for a clumsy black servant girl: "Tears brimmed in Mrs. Taylor's eyes. She put her arm about the girl and hugged her spontaneously" (p. 44). Nothing in the physical descriptions given of her—a white face, thin lips, reddish hair, an erect carriage—is indicative of great beauty, but in the eyes of her sons and her husband she is incomparable and, with her studied charm and sense of ceremony, she does bring into their lives unforgettable moments of great beauty, as she plays the piano and sings for them, or reads a poem she has composed for Christmas Eve:

> The children listened to her light, lovely voice with eyes as big as saucers; and afterwards carried their potties upstairs and went to bed, breathless with excitement.
> Professor Taylor felt such pride in his lovely, talented wife, he could scarcely contain it. These were the moments he lived for. (*The Third Generation*, 64)

Her culture, her passion for music and literature, are to a large extent functions of her snobbism. Personal superiority, in her view, is an attainment to be earned, and education and culture are the consecrated instruments through which this goal is to be reached. But the harmonies and reassuring rhythms of music and poetry are nonetheless very real passions in her life. In her moments of deepest melancholy she turns to her piano and plays for hours, losing herself completely in an ideal world in which ugliness is not even a disturbing echo. In the little family's endless and chaotic wanderings, as Fess Taylor loses position after position, defeated by his wife's refusal to accept the life he offers in the segregated black world of the rural South, the only world in which a Fess Taylor can function effectively, Lillian's tinkling piano and fragile singing voice along with the rudiments of classical literature she drills into her boys are essential symbols of continuity. She is the family's soul, providing its only direction and coherence, lifting it above the ordinary by her determination and the ardor of her aspirations, however naive and conventional they might in fact be.

But Lillian is also the source of the hysterical fears that haunt the family. The slightest accident, every minor mishap, drives her immediately into mindless hysteria, before she rallies her strength and grimly takes her stand. She is fervently religious, but her god is a deity of savage ill humor and petty revenge, on the order of William Blake's rancorous Old Nobodaddy, the only possible god for a person who can sense only threats and menace in the surrounding world. She nags and scolds constantly, both husband and sons, in her fear that they will do something to enrage the sullen, lurking deity. "God doesn't like ugly" (pp. 86, 127), she reminds them, again and again. And when Will, Jr., and Charles seem about to die of smallpox, she pleads desperately: "God take my life . . . give me the disease . . . please, dear God, spare them . . . I'll do anything. . . . God in Heaven, what have they done? . . . What have my children done that You should punish them like this?" (p. 122). It is not the oppression of white people she fears, for they are remote figures in the closed and segregated world she lives in; it is the universe itself, the very fact of being alive in it, unjustified and pathetically puny, that terrifies her. And she transmits her terror to her sons. Will, Jr., is blinded by an explosion during the chemistry demonstration he and Charles were to perform together on parents' night at their school. Charles, guilty earlier in the day of a supreme sin, blasphemy, had been denied permission by Lillian to assist his brother in the demonstration. The accident is the direct consequence, and both Lillian and Charles are quick to recognize their harsh God's familiar handiwork in this grim sequence of events:

> They all knew that William was blind. And Charles knew that God, who had taken his sight, would never give it back.
>
> It left him with a sense of shock that never wore off. He might have been able to adjust to his brother's loss of sight. But he never learned to rationalize the error of God's judgment—the profound and startling knowledge that virtue didn't pay.
>
> Before, life had held a reasoned pattern. There was good on the one side and bad on the other. . . .
>
> Now it was complex. . . . God didn't like ugly his mother always said: God would punish him. God didn't even know the difference, he thought bitterly. (*The Third Generation*, 131–32)

On the novel's last page Charles finally "understands" that Will's accident had demolished the entire family, not just Will alone. It plunged them all into torment, and they had never succeeded in fighting their way free: "Now he knew: *God didn't make a mistake, after all*" (p. 316).

The novel's title, "The Third Generation," has, like almost all of Himes's titles, a hidden edge of irony. On the one hand, it refers to Charles and his brothers, the third generation from slavery, the grandsons of the freed slaves. But the novel's epigraph is a quotation from Exodus, "For I the Lord thy God am a jealous God, visiting the iniquity of the fathers upon the children unto the third and fourth generation of them that hate me" (p. 6). Lillian's god, the chastiser of peoples, races, generations, is a very real presence in the novel. A kind of cosmic malevolence seems to stalk the Taylor family, inflicting crippling accidents upon them, blinding them to every possibility of tenderness, turning their loves to bitterness and hate.

The curse borne by Lillian herself, received from her parents, the first generation, to be passed on to her sons of the third generation, is "the tradition that Negroes with straight hair and light complexions were superior to dark-complexioned Negroes with kinky hair" (p. 11). She had married William Taylor because he was a professor and seemed ambitious and able, but from their wedding night the blackness of his skin had stood as an impassable barrier between them: "His naked body assumed a sinister aspect, its very blackness the embodiment of evil. She felt a cold shock of terror" (p. 22). For years after, she taunted him in their quarrels with the fact of his blackness, lashed him with racist epithets: "black devil," "shanty nigger," "cabin brood." "Your father's people are black like your father and think differently from us" (p. 58), she cautions her son Tom, when he leaves to live with his father's sister. In a world in which a whole people could be doomed to undergo the monstrous ignominy of slavery and its aftermaths, a "tradition" that enforced self-hatred and self-rejection on a large segment of that same people might well seem a gift from capricious and malicious gods, a divine scourge.

Fess Taylor, a sturdy, energetic, and talented man, slowly loses both his confidence and his sense of direction under the goad of his wife's blatant racism:

> Only his wife could make him feel inferior. In the presence of most people he felt a wonderful assurance. But she was so

conscious of her white blood she kept him constantly on the defensive. He could never be natural with her. He was either indulgent or resentful. She seemed destined to bring out the worst in him.

Now, added to her contempt for himself, was her attitude toward their children. She wanted to rear them in the belief that they were, in large part, white; that their best traits came from this white inheritance. He wanted to prepare them for the reality of being black. Between them the battle of color raged continuously. But he still wanted her; he still loved her; and deep down he was proud of being married to her. (*The Third Generation*, 32–33)

Despite his great love for Lillian, however, Fess's capacity for verbal violence almost equals hers. He fires back retorts that she finds bruising, shattering, unforgivable: "yellow bitch," "bastard," "white man's leavings" (pp. 25, 37). In fact, for a secondary character, subject of only a handful of relatively short passages in the novel, he is extraordinarily complex, a mass of contradictions, proud and humble, aggressive and servile, skillful and ineffectual; and the omniscient narrator needs every bit of his omniscience in those passages—tricky exercises in prolonged antithesis—that are devoted to explaining this inconsistent, improbable, and entirely real character:

Most persons thought him lovable. He had the guile and intuition of the born comedian and could be extremely entertaining, yet he was never quite a clown. Along with an innate servility, which he had almost completely submerged beneath an aggressive demeanor, he had a strong and bitter pride. But unlike many proud men, who carry their pride in silence, he was boastful. . . . Deep in his heart he wanted to be a rebel. Had he ever become a hero in the eyes of his wife he might have been a leader. He had the physical courage. Often he thrashed grown students half again his size. But his wife and the circumstances of his life had put out much of his fire. For the most part he was disarmingly ingratiating, not only toward his superiors but toward most persons. (*The Third Generation*, 10–11)

William Taylor is a simple man whose life is passed among simple tasks, simple scenes, but he has learned that he must display

Machiavellian cunning simply to survive. And Fess's guile, deep, habitual, and expert, permits the narrator to tie together a dozen disparate traits into a plausible whole, though the character remains fundamentally enigmatic:

> In part his popularity came from his being a magnificent actor. None knew this so well as his wife, who had learned it to her regret. He could dissemble and pose with such validity that his innermost thoughts and emotions were seldom revealed. Mrs. Taylor despised this characteristic almost as much as she did his color. She thought of it as a slave inheritance. Whenever she saw him scratch his head and assume his attitude of subservience, she was reminded of the fictional character, Uncle Tom. Ofttimes she was struck with a queer notion that he, also, might have been a slave. (*The Third Generation*, 32)

The black colleges in the deep South at which he teaches throughout the first half of the novel are really vocational-technical schools for students on the secondary-school level, and his field is more blacksmithing than academics, but he brings impressive talents and skills to his profession. He is "an artist at the forge and anvil," creating in his classroom-shop an amazing variety of objects: "jewelry and lamps and dishes. . . . the wrought-iron gate. . . . ornamental silver bridles. . . . sleds with fine iron runners, rocking horses, and miniature garden tools. . ." (pp. 26–27). It is oddly appropriate, since there is so much insistence on his African ancestry, that he should be a master of the art that reached what was probably its highest point of development in West Africa.

He is a warm and companionable man, a man who reaches out to other men, easily and naturally, without demanding anything from them in return beyond an answering warmth. He has many friends, called "cronies" in the novel, and even the white Southerners, the oppressors, respond readily to his gentle good humor, repay him with a fond affection that will go as far as small favors and patronizing indulgence. Compared to Lillian or Charles, he is doubtless superficial, shallow. And he is careless, forgetful, absentminded. Almost all of the acts that Lillian considers his darkest and most diabolical crimes spring from simple forgetfulness, or inability to imagine their effect on others. He traumatizes Lillian on their wedding night and irreparably damages his marriage by casually removing his clothes—"*He's naked!* she thought, horrified as by some startling obscenity" (p. 22)—without giving a passing thought to the fact that the slightly hysterical girl he had just married had never seen a naked man. He is equally blind to the effects on his growing sons of life in segregated and backward communities, dismissing Lillian's exaggerated fears concerning them. His own perfect adjustment is suggestive of emotions that do not add to his stature: "Professor Taylor always held a deep, secret fondness for those white southerners in authority" (p. 61).

Despite the limited respect he receives from his friends and colleagues, and Lillian's complete contempt, he does succeed, as long as he can remain in the South, in supplying his little family with impressive and spacious houses, expensive clothes, lavish food, and a certain standing in the community. He provides comfortable homes, in spite of the destructive effects of Lillian's color complex on his career, and he manages to establish himself as master in hs own household. Lillian's hatred for him is not strong enough to offset her deeply ingrained respect for nineteenth-century social conventions and structures, and she does bend her fierce pride sufficiently to fit into the role of Professor Taylor's wife. But the accident that blinds Will, Jr., gives Lillian the lever she needs to force her husband to leave the South. Will, Jr., she insists, must be closer to the best doctors. They move first to St. Louis, then to Cleveland. And, once he ceases to be a professor, Fess's life becomes one long, catastrophic decline:

> Professor Taylor had no ability at all for city life. At heart he was a missionary. He'd lived his life in southern Negro colleges. There, a professor was somebody. He counted in the neighborhood. His family counted too. But in St. Louis he didn't count.
> He'd gotten a job waiting on tables in a roadhouse out near Carondulet. . . .
> . . . He was a pathetic figure coming home from work; a small black man hunched over and frowning, shambling in a tired-footed walk, crushed old cap pulled down over his

tired, glazed eyes, a cigarette dangling from loose lips. . . .
. . . once, going to the bathroom, Charles saw his father
slowly trudging up the stairs. He looked so old and stooped
and beaten. It frightened him. Suppose his father died. What
would become of them? (*The Third Generation*, 143–44)

Ironically, Fess Taylor's decline, his defeat, is accompanied by an
equally rapid disintegration in Lillian, who is no better able than
he to bear the shabby circumstances of their new life in Northern
ghettoes. Her hovering hysteria crystallizes into something very
close to insanity:

> . . . she felt that Charles actually hated her.
> Later she discovered they were doing little things to hurt
> her physically, to drive her insane. One would put too much
> salt in the stew pot, or turn the fire up on the roast. Charles
> —she was certain it was him—sprinkled water in her bed-
> room slippers so that she would catch a cold. But she was
> afraid to accuse him of it; he looked at her so strangely now.
> And she was positive her husband sprinkled red pepper in
> her bed, although she couldn't catch him at it. But she knew;
> she'd wake up in the morning with her skin all red and
> blistered. . . .
> At times she became so frightened of them she'd dress and
> slip out of the house. She'd go downtown and mingle with
> white people who didn't know her. . . . On those days she ate
> in the white restaurants. Her desire to talk was overwhelm-
> ing. She got into long, involved conversations with strang-
> ers. Most times it ended in unpleasantness.
> She'd say at some point in the conversation, "I destroyed
> my life by marrying a Negro."
> The shocked, indignant people would rise and stalk away.
> (*The Third Generation*, 153–54)

Charles dominates center stage throughout the second half
of the book. The novel then becomes largely the story of his high
school years and his gradual decline into delinquency as he is
slowly pulled into the most sordid aspects of ghetto life. In his
concern for structure, Himes ended the novel with a catastrophe
that abruptly cuts through the curve of Charles's decline and
heads him back to normalcy, before he has taken the irreparable
step to serious crime. When his parents' marriage finally ends

in a bitter divorce, Charles lapses into mindless, drunken despair and takes refuge in the squalid house of an underworld friend, Dave, gambler and pimp, a character cast in the mold of *Lonely Crusade*'s Luther McGregor. There Lillian and Fess, briefly united in their overriding concern for their lost son, seek him out, and precipitate the novel's violent, and melodramatic, finale:

> He saw his mother push Dave aside and come quickly into the room, calling, "Charles!" He saw Dave clutch her arm and jerk her about.
>
> "You son of a bitch! That's my mother!" he cried thickly, pushing to his feet. His legs buckled and he was trying to get his feet underneath him when he heard his mother say sharply, "Don't you dare touch me," and then he saw her slap Dave.
>
> Fury rent his heart as he saw the sudden pimp rise in Dave's flushed face, the moronic bestiality in the character of men who murder women, and heard Veeny shriek, "Don't hit her, hon!" He knew that Dave was going to strike her, . . .
>
> As he tried vainly to move, his will still severed from his mind, he saw his father strike Dave across the forehead with a chair. He saw Dave stagger back, the white cut over his eye not yet beginning to bleed, whip out his knife and loom above his father like an enraged monster, stabbing him in the chest. (*The Third Generation*, 311)

Fess dies, and Lillian, lost in shock and memories, can no longer respond to Charles. He must make his way alone, and he determines that his course will be back to responsibility and hope.

In life, where climaxes that suit artistic scruples can seldom be arranged, Himes's parents both lived to see him charged with armed robbery, serve seven and one-half years in prison, marry, and become a published author. But only an exceptionally violent denouement could have resolved the inexorable patterns of conflict and defense that the novel's characters had become locked into. The ending Himes chose is not entirely convincing in realistic terms—Charles seems at that point to be already too badly damaged to be rescued by a single shock, however cataclysmic—but it is artistically valid. It satisfies the structural demands of the novel form. These demands are the one major difference between the autobiographical novel and straight autobiography—characterization in both being equally dependent on the creative imagination—and Himes's sense of structure was one of the major factors in the success he had with the autobiographical novel.

The character of Charles, one of Himes's many self-portraits, is a study in excessive sensitivity and the harsh defiance that cloaks it. He is little more than an infant as the novel opens, but he is already deeply involved in his parents' quarrels, finally and fatally committed to his mother's side:

> Their parents fought a great deal during that time. Hearing their screaming voices, followed by the sounds of scuffling, Charles would crawl to the head of the stairs and crouch, trembling in rage and fear. He didn't hate his father. But when his parents quarreled he wanted to cut off his father's head with the chopping axe. He felt violently protective toward his mother. (*The Third Generation*, 74)

Will, Jr., sixteen months older than Charles, is curiously immune, a calm, reflective child, safely lodged in the exclusive world of childhood, but Charles has already the intense, uncontrolled emotions and the exaggerated defense posture of the neurotic. He is brittle and inflexible, as prone to hysteria as Lillian herself, but he never cries when his parents whip him—and both parents feel that "sparing the rod" would be an unforgivable dereliction of parental responsibility—and he permits himself no reaction to the thronging terrors that fill a child's world, like the sudden, thunderous, threatening approach of a train locomotive:

> When the train came hurtling in, William broke from his father's grasp and ran screaming. His father caught him halfway across the road and held him in his arms until his trembling stopped. Charles had been as frightened as his brother. But he'd stood rigid in defiance. Both children gave their mother pause, but Charles's reaction worried her the more. She couldn't understand what was hurting him, what was he holding himself against? (*The Third Generation*, 69)

Lillian is drawn to her hysterically intense child with a passionate love that is equally intense and hysterical, but, almost always, her impulses of tenderness are blocked by her gnawing fears of the cosmic order, by her own neurotic defenses, and a barrier builds between them. Himes further complicates this strained, hurting relationship by giving Charles extraordinary physical beauty:

> Mrs. Taylor rarely kissed her youngest son. All of his intense emotion poured out through his kiss and she was shocked by her own passionate response. She didn't want to favor one child above the others. He was a beautiful child with perfect rose-tan features and deep dimples when he smiled. His dark brown eyes were deep-set like her own, but large and very clear. They were fringed by long black shiny lashes that curled upward. Each time his mother looked at him she could see in his shockingly beautiful face the girl she had wanted when he was born. But he was the most uncontrollably violent of all her children. (*The Third Generation*, 73)

Charles's explosive temper and reckless daring, the savage fist fights with other boys, the near-fatal accidents that befall him with numbing regularity, become the focus of Lillian's instinctive fears, the terror that had somehow been bred into her:

> She lived in constant dread of his killing some other boy, or getting himself killed or maimed for life. She became obsessed with the fear that God was going to punish her for the strange passion she had for him. She brooded for weeks, worrying and fretting between moments of intense anguish. She doubted if he'd live to see his twenty-first birthday. Life would never take his reckless challenge; it would kill him. (*The Third Generation*, 121)

But Charles's sensitivity runs far deeper than a penchant for violence or hysteria. It is different in kind from Lillian's own aching vulnerability. It is his response to life itself that is overwhelmingly intense. The reveries of his childhood and adolescence betray a completeness of response, a total giving of self, an agonizing openness, that call to mind the letters John Keats wrote to his brother, literature's most eloquent testimonies to the pangs of awakening poetic consciousness:

Spring affected him physically. He could feel it rising within himself like a great turbulence and when it boiled out, strangely, he was a flower, a deep red flower, or a green whispering tree. He could change himself into a bird, or he could become a yellow-winged butterfly. It was almost all a dream; he could turn everything into a dream. (*The Third Generation*, 77)

Charles's response to literature is similarly absolute, ecstatic and uncontrollable. A silent reading of Poe's "The Raven" on a stormy winter evening can trigger a frightening spasm of involuntary cursing. Even movies, routine and banal, galvanize his exorbitant imaginative powers, hurtling him into an impossible and fascinating world:

His emotional turbulence quieted to a steady pulsation; his trembling slowly ceased. The picture came on and in the quiet darkness he devoured the youth and beauty of the heroine's face. His stare never left the soft, mobile mouth, the tender smile, the expressive eyes, and the thousand exquisite movements of the facial planes. For a time he was lost in his spell of adoration. Then the picture ended.

He returned to the street, forced to face living people in this living world. He shrank from them as if he had leprosy. At last his thoughts caught up with him. (*The Third Generation*, 230)

His sensitivity is almost entirely passive, however, a source of suffering with no avenues of sublimation open, no relieving spurt of creativity. Only in very late adolescence does he begin to give proof of poetic powers that match his poetic temperament. And then it is his father, the player of roles, who furnishes the model he follows, not Lillian, with her worship of "culture," her music and poetry, her uncritical attachment to everything she has been taught to believe elevating. Charles first affirms his own personality, his complete originality and independence in his early contacts with the confusing world of the Cleveland ghetto. He slowly begins to manifest a strong sense of personal style in his choice of clothes and the mannerisms he assumes. The ghetto drastically undermines Fess Taylor's ability to provide a home, and for a time following their arrival the family is scattered in widely separated residences around the great city, rooming with relatives and friends, until Fess finally succeeds in buying a house. During this period, Charles, separated both from Will and his mother, forges a new circle of acquaintances, first among the black bourgeois youth, who flaunt a brittle and spurious sophistication, then among the most depraved elements of the city's underworld of vice and crime. He adds a studied grace and an easy volubility, verging on eloquence, to his striking physical beauty. He struggles to overcome his innate shyness and lack of confidence with such vigor that he achieves an air of impudence and cold arrogance. Nothing that he does during this period is unpremeditated, coming naturally and effortlessly. His personality is a deliberate construct of his will, his conscious striving to emulate models of poise and elegance. But he brings to all of these basically painful efforts the mark of his exuberant imagination, a touch of the artist, evident even in the "line" he uses to mask his nervousness with girls:

> He could talk to one girl at a time. He sang a rapid monologue to keep his courage up, and the girls thought he had a sly, sweet line.
>
> "Your eyes are like rare wine," he told Marie as they sat swinging on the porch. "Your lips burn like eternal fire; I'd like to quench them with my kisses. Your throat is a pillar of gold, brushed by the lips of men who worship at your feet. Your breasts are softly distant mountain peaks at dusk; between them flows the dark disturbing river down to the mysterious sea."
>
> She was entranced. "You're sweet," she said, her arm stealing about his neck as she leaned forward in the dark and kissed him wetly. (*The Third Generation*, 170)

He falls in love with speed, the fast cars of the time—"The big car leapt forward in an open-throated roar, throwing him back against the seat, and the road came up over the hood like a tidal wave. Nothing in all his life had equalled that sensation. He leaned forward into the onrushing road, his mind sealed shut in a feeling of invincible power, the whole past dropping away behind him" (p. 250)—and he is involved in three major automobile accidents in rapid succession, with ruinous damage to the cars and a few pedestrians, though no serious injury to himself. But unendurable physical pain, and the terrors and despair it inspires, come to him with shattering suddenness when he falls down an empty elevator shaft at the hotel where he has just begun working for one of his father's many old friends, the head-waiter Dick Small.[7] He passes without warning from perfect health and dashing good looks to the state of a semi-invalid, with the grim prospect of years of pain, and slow recovery, ahead of him. When he awakens after the accident, he begins to sense the true fragility of his resources, his enormous vulnerability, his total dependence on luck, the accident of good health, and his overpowering need for the physical strength and beauty that had seemed unchallengeably his. He had, without realizing it, already accepted the peculiarly American snobbism of physical vigor and grace:

> It was late that night, while the hospital slept, that the first blind panic shattered him. He was going to be a cripple, confined to a wheel chair, with a wizened, useless arm. He lit a cigarette, fighting a losing battle. He couldn't bear it. Everything he'd ever dreamed of doing depended on his body. How could one be brave, noble, gallant, without phys-ical perfection? He might never be in love, because it was of the flesh also; might never know what it was like to be with a woman. That was the bitterest thought of all. He pulled the covers over his head to muffle his sobbing. (*The Third Generation*, 217)

He becomes obsessed with the fear of aging, of physical decay or debility in any form. He becomes agonizingly aware of the wounds his parents have inflicted on one another and of the pre-mature old age that has enveloped them both:

> He saw sharply the gray in his father's hair, his old, seamed face, now fading to a saddle color; he saw the deep lines about his mother's eyes, how the flesh had sagged down from her high cheekbones, making her jaws more pro-nounced, squarer. Her lips had thinned and her eyes had become sunken, the lids age-lowered, so that their steady

7. See pp. 54–55, this volume.

glint was almost baleful. With advancing age her face had taken such a great sternness as to appear mean. He was stricken with pity for them. Once as he tenderly brushed her hair he felt an impulse to cry, "Don't grow old, Mama. Please don't grow old." He yearned to make some great sacrifice to bring back youth to her face. (*The Third Generation*, 197–98)

Shortly after the hotel accident, while he is still in the early stages of recovery, Charles begins college. There he discovers that his parents' endless battling, and Lillian's borderline madness, have left him with psychological injuries far more serious than the fractured spine he suffered in his headlong fall down the hotel elevator shaft:

Had his mother been there she would have pushed him. Subconsciously he had come to depend on her pushing. He was not complete away from her, not a whole person. He was still joined to her by an artery of emotion. Independently he could only exercise his will against her, never against others. Against others he needed the joining of her will. (*The Third Generation*, 238)

He quickly fails his way out of college, never to go back, experiencing actual physical nausea whenever he attempts to study. Still in his teens, a failure and a pensioned invalid, he plunges deep into the ghetto's morbidly fascinating, lurid half-world of prostitution, drunkenness, and petty thievery. He and a chance associate are caught passing bad checks, and he is given a bench parole into his father's custody. Strangely, it is often Fess, the ineffectual, the ultimately defeated, who rescues Charles when his rash adventures miscarry: "The court attendants looked curiously at the strange couple, the old, short, black man who seemed shrunken in his seedy clothes with a son a half-head taller, lighter complexioned, wearing an expensive white flannel suit with an air of arrogance" (p. 259).

Charles's experience with women is confined largely to prostitutes, including Dave the pimp's lecherous and aging whore Veeny, "a paralyzing evil in her consuming desire. . . . the sweet acid shock of utter evil" (pp. 301–2), with whom he experiences every extreme of passive perversity, submitting like a terrified and mindless virgin to her voraciously aggressive lovemaking. He also experiences, once, a love that is genuine and almost complete, with a young girl who sees in him the man he is afraid to be. But Lillian and her desperate smothering love stand in the way. When the girl, Peggy, tells him, while they are riding in his car, that she is pregnant and that they must marry, the extent of Lillian's control over him is abruptly evident:

> To marry her was beyond his comprehension. It seemed impossible; impossible that she would even think he would. She didn't know. He just couldn't marry a common ordinary colored woman like herself. What would his mother think? She'd feel betrayed after all the things she'd told him about his white forbears. She'd really die, he thought.
> It was the first time he'd been faced with such a choice. He knew, at that moment, he could never leave his mother.
> "Well, let's go inside and talk it over with your sister," he said.
> She got out. He reached over and closed the door and sped off, driving as if the demons were chasing him. (*The Third Generation*, 253)

The relationship of Charles and Lillian has in it much of the pathological absoluteness of a *folie à deux*. Lillian's bizarre racism, her morbid rejection of reality, somehow become part of the fabric of his being. It is as though her spirit had invaded his, absorbed it completely. The paralyzing patterns of her neurosis gradually come to dominate his own thoughts. This sinister process is delineated with ruthless clarity in the last sections of the novel, as Charles's fatal weakness of will is demonstrated in incident after incident, then abruptly negated in the novel's bloody denouement. A tragic pattern is laboriously established then arbitrarily dissolved, a process that is all too frequent in life, but introduces an unfortunate note of confusion and indecision into a novel's structure.

By contrast, the characters of Charles's two brothers, Will and Tom, and the effects on them of their parents' bitter quarrels, are left largely unexplored. Tom, the eldest by almost a decade, is little more than an interloper in the novel, glimpsed briefly as he hurriedly passes by:

> For a time Tom was home that summer. . . .
> He was a tall, dandyish man with pretentious manners and an affected laugh.
> "Hello, Dad," he said, and when the two shook hands it was as if he was greeting a subordinate.
> The children resented him. (*The Third Generation*, 151)

The similarity in the ages of Charles and Will, Jr., is used primarily to point up contrasts; Will's paradoxical normalcy and perfect adjustment, unruffled even after the accident that blinds him, form a perfect antithesis to Charles's unmotivated frenzies:

> William clung tightly to his father's hand as they walked up the pitch-dark hill. He was a natural child, in that he was afraid of the dark and strangeness, and expanded only in the familiar. But Charles was drawn to the unfamiliar darkness, and created fantasies he found more real than what the light revealed. (*The Third Generation*, 64)

Descriptions of Will are rare and invariably consist of little more than short preambles to long disquisitions on the unfathomable strangeness of Charles:

> William screamed bloody murder when he was whipped. The neighbors, hearing him, thought Mrs. Taylor was unreasonably cruel to her children. But Charles never cried. He gritted his teeth in silence. This made his mother whip him all the harder. Her mouth closed in a grim straight line and her deep-set eyes blazed as she lit into him. And his little mouth tightened and his eyes hardened as he faced her in silence. The grim, white-faced woman and the defiant brown boy looked a great deal alike at such times. (*The Third Generation*, 72–73)

The novel's background, however, in contrast to the dearth of well-developed secondary characters, is the subject of lavish attention and effort. Structurally, this was essential. Strongly marked, even exaggerated, contrasts of time and place were needed to emphasize the insecurity and instability of the Taylor family's wandering life, constantly jolted from one place to another, its roots inevitably wrenched loose before they had even begun to take hold. Fortunately, this structural necessity furnished Himes with an occasion to exploit fully his remarkable flair for descriptive prose, and *The Third Generation* contains some of his finest set pieces. Perhaps the most brilliant example is the description of the family's arrival in Mississippi, after Fess had lost his job in Missouri:

> ... They moved like a boat down a shallow river of darkness beneath a narrow roof of fading twilight. As the road deepened, roots of huge trees sprang naked from the banks like horrible reptilian monsters. Now high overhead the narrow strip of purple sky turned slowly black, and it became black-dark in the deep sunken road.
>
> The mules moved down the tunnel of darkness with sure-footed confidence as if they had eyes for the night. They knew the road home. Professor Taylor tied the reins to the dashboard and gave them their head. It was so dark he couldn't see his hand before his eyes. The black sky was starless. As they moved along the old sunken road the dense odor of earth and stagnation and rotting underbrush and age reached out from the banks and smothered them. It was a lush, clogging odor compounded of rotten vegetation, horse manure, poisonous nightshades and unchanged years. Soldiers of the Confederacy had walked this road on such a night following the fall of Vicksburg, heading for the nearby canebrakes. (*The Third Generation*, 41–42)

III Cast the First Stone

Cast the First Stone (1952) is the most selectively focused of Himes's three autobiographical novels. It explores one sharply defined segment of Himes's experience in great depth.

The protagonist, Jimmy Monroe, is "a Mississippi white boy"[8] but in every other important respect he is Chester Himes. He is serving a twenty-year-minimum sentence in a state prison for armed robbery against private citizens in "Lake City"; he was apprehended in Chicago immediately after the robbery when he

---

8. See p. 137, this volume.

tried to pawn a stolen ring, and a confession was then quickly beaten out of him in a Chicago police station; he has an injured back and receives monthly compensation checks from the state Industrial Commission; his parents—a dominating, bitter, nagging, whining mother, whom he loves with blinding devotion, and an ineffectual father, who can't even prepare a Christmas package to mail to the prison without making ludicrous mistakes—have recently been divorced; he had been a student at the state university, but his parents' divorce had pushed him into a spiral of delinquency that had culminated in armed robbery. He has Charles Taylor's excessive sensitivity and ungovernable temper, and the scattered incidents of childhood and youth he occasionally recalls, first rural and then urban, are, with a few variations, those lived by Charles Taylor.

But Jimmy Monroe's past is all but ignored in *Cast the First Stone*; information of this type is limited to broad, general statements that would hardly fill three pages if they were brought together. The novel begins during Jimmy Monroe's first days in prison, when he leaves the prison's classification center, and it ends six years later when he is transferred to the prison farm to begin a probationary period prior to parole. The novel is a highly detailed account of one man's prison term. Prison is its one and only subject, its unique and exclusive concern.

And in making Jimmy Monroe white, Himes effected an even more drastic narrowing of scope. He eliminated the entire subject of racism, the central theme of his first two novels. It is the most radical change imaginable, a basic alteration in the nature of the reality portrayed. But racism is not an easy truth for an artist to handle. It is a lurid, obtrusive, noisy truth, usurping to itself all of the center stage. It distorts and obscures all lesser or subtler truths. The most obvious of these distortions—in evidence whenever a black writer accepts racism as his central subject—involves the depiction of white characters. In any account of a racist society seen from the victim's viewpoint, the white characters, as oppressors, are automatically reduced in stature, diminished, to the point that they appear scarcely human. Their very whiteness, which, as Bob Jones noted in *If He Hollers Let Him Go*, they are free to use "like a loaded stick,"[9] is a dehumanizing trait. Logic itself, the logic of the victim, rules out the possibility that the perpetrators of injustices as monstrously inhuman as slavery and institutionalized racism can themselves be human. The most serious weakness in William Styron's attempt, in his Pulitzer Prize novel *The Confessions of Nat Turner,* to write from the standpoint of a slave in violent revolt was his failure to understand exactly how repellently inhuman the white oppressor must appear to his black victim, an error no black writer would have made. George Jackson stated without equivocation, "They do not possess the qualities of rational thought, generosity, and magnanimity necessary to be part of the human race."[10] It is only when racism is not an issue—that is, when he has made some rather drastic alterations in the nature of reality itself—that the black writer is free to treat his white characters, not as oppressors or potential oppressors, but simply as people, and to develop them fully and sympathetically.

To remove racism from consideration, in any story of modern society that aims at completeness, is, of course, much like taking the sun out of the firmament. It is a massive distortion, leaving a gaping hole. It does, however, throw into sharper relief myriad points of detail that are normally blurred. It is a deliberate choosing of the night sky over the bright light of day, but the night sky does have its own special clarity, limited but cool and definite. And prison, like racism, is also a very demanding subject, tending to push to the side, as secondary, all other considerations, including concerns for completeness or unbiased objectivity. The writer who is recording the facts of his own incarceration, attempting to reshape them into the substance of a novel, has necessarily to accept radical limitations in scope. Prison is too grotesque a reality to share the stage with any more broad and normal concern, such as the eternal struggle for a social order that is not grounded in hate and fear. Prison permits the writer who attempts to describe it with total accuracy no second overriding concern.

9. See p. 92, this volume.
10. George Jackson, *Soledad Brother: The Prison Letters of George Jackson* (New York: Bantam Books, 1970), p. 47.

Although the narrative point of view in *Cast the First Stone* is first person, Himes, as usual, introduced a number of complex variations into the basic approach. Jimmy Monroe is both the narrator and the convict described, but the qualities that the first-person narrator unintentionally reveals in himself, the qualities implied by the narrative style itself, tend to differ slightly from the traits of character that are all too clearly implied by the recorded acts and statements of the young convict Jimmy Monroe. The single important trait that Jimmy Monroe's two avatars, narrator and protagonist, have in common is a confusing volatility. Both seem to be forever in a state of change. The character of the protagonist is subject to a steady process of evolution under the pressures of prison. The narrator, on the other hand, is constantly adopting radically new tones in efforts to adapt the narrative style to the endlessly shifting faces of Himes's mysteriously kaleidoscopic prison. The narrator can be close enough to the action to reflect the protagonist's own hysterically intense emotions:

> In the silence following the echo of the gun shots I could hear the three buttons of his uniform coat scrape across the back of the bench as he slid to the floor. I could hear, distinctly, the stiffled breathing of the convicts and the hard, fast thumping of my own heart.[11]

Or totally detached, long years away in a mysteriously undefined future:

> The first . . . was Giuseppe playing "In My Solitude" on his electric guitar every morning, just before breakfast. . . .
> I never understood why that should have affected me so then that always afterward upon hearing it I could see again that goddamn dormitory and those gray convicts and those gray winter mornings with the fog and the walls and the deserted morning look of the prison yard, and feel again that utter sense of being lost in a gray eternity. (*Cast the First Stone*, 60)

The narrator's most clearly marked trait is the ruthless lucidity with which he displays and analyzes every facet of the deplorably weak and shoddy character of young Jimmy Monroe, his pathetic

11. Himes, *Cast the First Stone*, pp. 92, 93.

vanity, arrant cowardice, cold selfishness, and, above all, his general confusion of mind. The book's title, "Cast the First Stone," is an invitation to the reader to consider his own state of sinlessness before he attempts to judge Jimmy Monroe, but the narrator seems bent on putting Baudelaire to shame in his zeal to place a tempting target for stoning before the "hypocritical reader, my fellow, my brother":

> "I looked around at Warren. You hit me, I said, biting my lips. I was going back to the hole anyway. I just may as well bust him one, I thought. I kept biting my lips, trying to get up enough nerve to sock him one. But it wouldn't come." (p. 48)

The protagonist is too busy attempting to dodge the slings and arrows of outrageous fortune, usually unsuccessfully, to betray any capacity for humor, but the narrator finds many subjects for dry, wry humor in the general prison scene, and even in various traits of the battered psyche of young Jimmy Monroe, his childlike vanity in particular:

> I found the *Preface* the most illuminating part of the entire [correspondence law] course. It explained all about the "legal mind." To succeed in the profession a lawyer needed most of all a legal mind, that is the ability to be reasonable and logical and to think concisely and quickly and sharply in the clinches. I felt certain that I would make the ideal lawyer as I felt there was probably no one in all the world more reasonable and logical than I; no one who could think more concisely, quickly, and sharply in the extremities. I became slightly obsessed with the cold clear reasonableness of my thoughts and if anyone disagreed with their reasonableness I was ready to fight. (*Cast the First Stone*, 162)

What saves Jimmy Monroe from the reader's contempt, as the evidence of his basic sinfulness steadily accumulates under the first-person narrator's pitiless "introspective" probing, is partly the fact that Jimmy is seen in a continuous process of growth and partly the extreme brutality of his situation. The prison itself, the great gray brute, easily and inevitably emerges as the villain of the piece.

In the novel's concluding passage, Jimmy Monroe bids a triumphant farewell to the prison he is about to leave, "You big tough son of a bitch, you tried to kill me but I've got you beat now, I thought" (p. 303). The novel's story is Jimmy's struggle against the prison, his ultimately successful struggle to forge an identity in an environment that negates identity. Jimmy and the prison itself are the story's two central "characters," the antagonists squared off in the book's one major conflict. But the prison, despite all the description, all the details given, remains curiously insubstantial, more an absence than a presence, a set of fundamental deprivations that dehumanize by withholding the fullness of experience that is essential to full humanity. Seldom has a prison been painted in less melodramatic terms. The fabled horrors—homosexual gang rapes, sadistic guards—are not excluded, but they are presented as rare and somewhat incidental, threats that exist but seldom materialize, and are of only minor importance in the system of repression and depersonalization the convict confronts. The one outstanding feature of Himes's prison is its dirtiness and sleaziness. The uniforms the convicts wear emphasize their derelict status:

> Over in the commissary, where I'd been outfitted, there were stacks of coats, vests and pants of different sizes, some new and some used. The commissary clerks gave out the used clothes first. They were the uniforms left by the convicts who'd gone out. All of my things were used except my Sunday shirt. My coat was patched at both elbows. It was much too small. My vest was too big and my pants were too short. I had used shoes also; the heels were run-over and the soles were thin. But I was dressed as well as anybody, better than most. (*Cast the First Stone*, 21)

The state's obsessive concern with immediate penny-pinching economy is everywhere in evidence:

> . . . the head porter. . . . opened a box and gave each of us a pair of cloth gloves. The gloves were made out of old uniforms. The imprint of a mammoth hand had been cut out of the cloth. Two pieces of the cloth had been sewed together. That was a glove. (*Cast the First Stone*, 24)

Overcrowding is fundamental, a simple fact of life: "There were four thousand convicts in that prison which had been built for eighteen hundred" (p. 36).[12] Many of the buildings clustered together within the high stone walls are "temporary" wooden structures, ancient and ramshackle:

> It was the 2–10 company of the second tier of 10 cells in the 10&11 cell block, the last of the old, crumbling, dark, damp, dim cell blocks of a past era when prisons were patterned, it seemed, after the dungeons of the medieval ages. It now seemed ready to crumble and fall. There were rotten wooden ranges, that trembled beneath each step, enclosed by waist-high iron railings. The cells had flat latticed bars, so closely interlaced as to make it almost impossible to see inside of them. (*Cast the First Stone*, 75)

Whether housed in dormitories or cells, the convict can never escape for a single moment from the noises, and smells, of other convicts. Plumbing is either primitive or nonexistent:

> Each of us had a bucket. The 2–11 company on the opposite side of the cell block from us, came around each morning after breakfast and emptied the buckets in a sewer down at the end of the first range. . . .
> . . . They rented the newer, cleaner, better buckets and kept them disinfected for you. If you couldn't afford to pay them you always got the oldest, most battered buckets, and they were never rinsed or disinfected. It didn't help much if both of the convicts in a cell didn't do it.
> On summer days the odor hung in the cells like some vile miasma, thick and putrid, with no relief. There was always an argument and generally a fight when one of the cell mates had to take a physic. (*Cast the First Stone*, 78)

However, nothing is ever so bad that it can't be made worse, and the prison's punishment and isolation cells manage to provide a substantially heightened level of physical discomfort:

12. Newspaper accounts of the April 21, 1930, fire in the Columbus penitentiary give the figures as: designed for 1,500 convicts; actually housed, 4,300 convicts.

I tried to go to sleep. I said to myself if I sit in one position and keep my eyes closed I'll go to sleep. I'm tired, I'll go to sleep. I'm tired, I'll go to sleep. I'm tired, I'll go to sleep. . . . I sat perfectly still. A bedbug bit me. Something crawled over my bare leg. My neck and throat and legs itched intolerably. I itched all over. And then a trickle of pain crept into my body. It began at the base of my spine. It flowed down my legs, up my back. I'll be asleep in a minute, I said. And then it came in a rush. The pain and the itching and the biting and the cold.

"Goddamn, goddamn, goddamn," I sobbed.

"Take it easy, Jimmy," Glass said. (*Cast the First Stone*, 51)

The prison's guards are perfectly suited to the prevailing atmosphere of filth, decay, and corruption. Almost all of those that are given close attention in the novel are elderly, misshapen, bloated, decrepit, with grotesque nicknames like Short Britches, Froggy, and Donald Duck. It is the warden himself, however, a figure reminiscent of the portrait of Dorian Gray, in its final stages, or a minor demon by Hieronymus Bosch, who most disturbs Jimmy's sense of the rightness of things. His response is grounded in his reverence for the beauty and power he believes natural to the human body and his violent prejudice against anyone in poor physical condition, traits Jimmy shares with every major Himes protagonist:

The warden had us new men over to talk to us. He was the remnants of a large man gone to seed, dressed in an expensive suit. . . . His head was practically bald and his face, seamed and sagging, looked as if it had melted through the years and had run down into his jowls which, in turn, had dripped like flaccid tallow onto his belly. His shoulders had sagged down onto his belly too, so that now his whole skinny frame seemed built to keep his belly off the ground. He had sickly white, vein-laced hands which made one nauseated to look at them. He wore a huge diamond on his second finger.

What he said, boiled down, was simply that he was tough. That any man so completely decayed could wield the power to make himself tough to four thousand human beings so much stronger was a sickening realization. (*Cast the First Stone*, 87)

The deputy warden, who actually runs the prison, is only slightly less appalling: "His head was bald as an egg, with big dark freckles and he had a flat-nosed pug's face. He was a big man. His body shook from some sort of nervous disorder. They called him Jumpy Stone because on his bad days he was a sight to see" (p. 38). When this distinctly Dickensian character is uncontrollably jittery, and he almost always is, he repeats everything he says exactly three times, very rapidly, and the narrator draws heavily on this eccentricity for comic relief throughout the novel:

> Later that morning one of the guards hit a convict in school. There was a lot of yelling and gesticulating, and a few blows were passed. A couple of the guards got rubbed up a little. They had to send for the deputy. The deputy was in his sins by then. He was irritable and impatient and twitching like a wino with the shakes.
>
> I waited until he'd gotten the men quieted down a bit and then I grabbed him by the arm and said, "Look at these pants, deputy. These are the pants that Captain Henshaw got for me."
>
> He tried to break away but I held on to him. He was so angry his face turned purple but he didn't do anything to me for fear of stirring up the riot again. Everyone was waiting tensely for him to slap me.
>
> He looked down at my pants. "What's the matter with them, what's the matter with them, what's the matter with them?" he snapped.
>
> "Hell, you can see," I said, holding up one leg. "They're too small. . . ."
>
> "Wear those, wear those, wear those," he said, pulling away again. (*Cast the First Stone*, 107)

He is a fair man, though. Jimmy gets his new pants, and Jumpy Stone then twitches out, mumbling, "the trouser freak, the trouser freak, the trouser freak." The only guard who breaks from the pattern is named Cody, "the most feared man in prison" (p. 35); he is grotesquely violent rather than grotesquely funny, capable of quelling a riot single-handedly, and barehanded:

One man came through the door. Just one man—Cody.

He wore a dark blue uniform cap, with the gold legend of a sergeant, low over his eyes, and a black slicker buttoned about his throat and wet with rain. He did not rush or hesitate but came steadily through the doorway, his empty hands hanging at his sides, his lips tight and bloodless, his face a burnt-red—raw-edged and hard as baked clay—his eyes a half-hidden tricky gleam beneath the brim of his cap. He came straight ahead across the floor, never hesitating once, and up to the two convicts who had had the guns. He slapped one of them on the side of the head so hard it laid him his full length on the floor. The other one broke to run but he grabbed him by the collar, and holding him at a distance, slapped him until his face was raw and swelling, red and turning blue. . . .

. . . Cody picked up the guns, then stood there for a moment looking us over. A convict went crazy from the strain. He jumped up, his arms outstretched to the ceiling as if hollering hallelujah, his fingers stiffened and extended out like prongs, and his hair rising on his skull. He screamed, "Oh, you goddamned dog!"

Before his feet touched the floor Cody shot him five times with one of the guns, so that when he fell he must have already been dead. (*Cast the First Stone*, 92)

"What I saw shocked me deeply, violently, as I have never been shocked before or since," the narrator remarks of this incident. The two fictional black policemen who would be the heroes of Himes's later detective novels, men capable of pushing violence several steps farther than anyone else was willing to go, men so violent that even the most dangerous criminals tremble before them, would be cast in the dread image of Sergeant Cody.

The strangest feature of Himes's prison, which is passing strange in every way, was not, however, the product of memory, observation, invention, dramatic instinct, or humor, but a simple accident of rewriting. The prison seems to be caught in a kind of time warp. The prison Himes observed was the Ohio State Prison in Columbus between 1928 and 1936. In the last of the many rewritings of *Cast the First Stone*, just before publication in 1952, he changed the time period to that between 1946 and

1952, shortly after the Second World War instead of shortly after the First World War. The "updating," however, was limited to changing the few actual dates that are mentioned and dropping in a few references to well-known figures of the time, like General Patton (pp. 10, 64, 156). The prison itself, substance and essence, remains in the time period of the early 1930s, with convicts who wear vests and white string ties for Sunday, shave with straight razors, and listen to the prison orchestra play jazz. The sounds that inspire travel nostalgia are the whistles of freight trains, not the roar of airplanes overhead. The one word used to describe homosexuality is "degeneracy," indicative of a whole climate of attitude held in a particular period of time. Most important of all, there is absolutely no racial tension within the prison involving the black inmates, a state of affairs that places it years away in time—from the racist-oriented prison conditions described by militant black writers of the 1960s like George Jackson.

Jimmy Monroe's long war of attrition against the prison is divided into four distinct campaigns, each associated with a particular "buddy." The first stage is one of fear, panic on a day-to-day basis, bluffing to survive, and the buddy is Mal, steady, soothing, more prissy than effeminate, perfectly adjusted to the prison. Mal befriends Jimmy from the moment he enters, a particularly nervous "new fish," cast into the coal company dormitory, his first prison assignment. Mal is a murderer, who had served almost two years on death row before his sentence was commuted, a fact that at least partially explains why he seems somewhat dead inside. He helps Jimmy to ward off the blandishments and seductive advances of the dormitory's most aggressive homosexuals, taking him under his wing like an old mother hen, though he is only eight years older than nineteen-year-old Jimmy.

Homosexuality is very much on Mal's mind. He never lets pass an opportunity to denounce "degeneracy," warning Jimmy about convict after convict: "He's a damn degenerate, too. Half of these guys in here are degenerates. Filthy sons of bitches. I don't like that stuff and I don't care who knows it" (p. 12). Mal is an elegant figure in oafish company: "a tall clean-looking man . . . with brown hair parted on the side and a nice-looking face. His pants were pressed and his shoes were shined, and his shirt starched and ironed and bleached almost white, and he wore a tie and a slipover sweater" (p. 12). Under Mal's tutelage Jimmy learns that he can bring a measure of dignity back into his life, purchase small luxuries with the money from the disability pension he receives for his back injury, manage a faint suggestion of style in his dress even in prison. Jimmy's greatest fears are for his masculinity, fears that he will somehow be maneuvered into a role of passive homosexuality, fears so great that he dare not even acknowledge their full scope: "half scared of everything and trying not to show it; half scared of someone thinking I was a girl-boy, half scared of someone running over me or taking advantage of me" (p. 205). His relationship with Mal seems safe, reassuring, because he has so much stronger and more definite a personality than that oddly passive man, but the specter of homosexuality, Mal's own secret obsession, casts a permanent shadow over their friendship:

> . . . we got warm and passionate thinking about the women we'd had. We kept talking about it until every time we'd accidentally touch each other we'd feel a shock. I was startled at the femininity a man's face could assume when you're looking at it warmly and passionately, and off to yourselves in prison where there are all men and there is no comparison.
> Mal looked very pretty and his eyes seemed very bright and after a time he said, "You don't believe what Jeep said about me, do you?"
> "Hell, naw," I said.
> "A lot of guys do that in here but I'm bitterly against it," he said. (*Cast the First Stone*, 41)

Mal is soon transferred to a neighboring dormitory, and a softer job than the coal company, leaving Jimmy to fend for himself. The friendship lingers on, however, for a very long time, by exchange of messages and brief conversations at peepholes and in the yard. Mal seems quite content with their ambiguous and highly detached friendship, even with his reputation as Jimmy's "old lady," but as Jimmy becomes stronger and increasingly secure in his capacity to deal with convicts, guards, the prison itself, he begins to see Mal more as a not entirely welcome "responsibility" (p. 126) than a friend. The great fire that breaks out on Easter Monday[13]—in 1930 in fact, in 1948 in Jimmy's fictional world—devastating the entire central area of the prison, wiping out whole companies of convicts, dissolving every shred of order into a hellish chaos, marks a dramatic turning point in Jimmy's prison career and ends his relationship with Mal. Jimmy reaches such uncontrollable peaks of excitement during the fire and the disorder that follow that he finally has to be hospitalized and given medication to put him to sleep. At one point, during the height of the fire, when he is already uncontrollably hysterical, he confronts Mal and demolishes their fragile friendship with a proposal of open homosexuality:

> "You don't know what you're saying, Jimmy," he said. "Come on and sit down." He tried to pull me around the desk. "Come on and sit down and take it easy. You've gotten too excited."
> "I know what I'm saying," I said. "I want you for my woman. . . ."
> He released me and stepped away. He was looking at me queerly. . . .
> Suddenly I felt repulsed. "You can go to hell," I said. "Once and forever." (*Cast the First Stone*, 140)

The great prison fire touches off a wave of enthusiasm for prison reform in the hearts of the people of the state, conscience stricken at having locked up so many men in a moldering firetrap. New laws are rushed through the legislature, reducing sentences to more reasonable lengths to offset the earlier trend in the state courts toward terrifyingly harsh sentences. Jimmy sees thirteen years cut from his twenty-year minimum and finds he can breathe again. After the warden has restored order, with an egregious but happily brief show of rampant brutality, the dismally archaic prison itself actually tries, lumberingly and awkwardly, to assume a more humane character. With a new buddy, Blocker, "a little hump-backed, sharp-faced fellow" (p. 101), Jimmy is transferred into the cripple company, the prison's softest assignment: "We convicts in the cripple company seldom

13. See pp. 44–45, this volume.

felt the heavy, merciless, brutal weight of prison as the others in the mills and shops did. We went along smoothly, serenely, easily, spoiling away the years. . . . It seemed as if we were more on the edge of prison than actually inside" (p. 166). Blocker is a skilled professional gambler. He and Jimmy set up a permanent poker game in the dormitory, and other convicts soon follow suit. The day guard, Captain Tom, instead of repressing the open gambling, organizes it systematically, with important profits for himself, and he puts Jimmy in charge of "the organization," scheduling games and collecting percentages both for himself and Captain Tom:

> And that was the way we ran it. It made me a sort of boss of the gambling racket. . . .
> There must have been four or five thousand dollars in cash in the dormitory at that time. . . . Those convicts had too much good old government money right through there to sit on it and not gamble, and by having the gambling controlled we kept the fights and disputes down to a minimum. (*Cast the First Stone*, 187–88)

Jimmy fancies himself as a poker player, a shrewd gambler. Before coming to prison he had frequented "Bunch Boy's gambling joint" in "Lake City" (p. 9)—a name straight out of Himes's own autobiography and his memories of Cleveland (pp. 32ff).[14] But Jimmy lacks the necessary emotional control. He has fast hands and perfect muscular control, is a dazzling prestidigitator in shuffling and dealing, easily able to conceal the marked cards he and his partner use, but it is his partner Blocker who is the true gambler, with iron nerves and perfect concentration. When Blocker is paroled, Jimmy's reputation as a poker player soon collapses in an unbreakable losing streak. The reliance of Jimmy and Blocker on marked cards is generally known throughout the dormitory—Himes himself had attributed the use of marked cards to an obviously autobiographical character in one of the stories he had published in 1933 early in his own prison career[15]—but the convicts actually seem to prefer the atmosphere, the superior sophistication, of a crooked game (p. 187).

14. See pp. 26–27, this volume.
15. Himes, "Prison Mass," *Abbott's Monthly* 6 (April 1933), p. 56.

Jimmy's friendship with Blocker is the most normal and least complicated of the close relationships he forms in prison. It is presented in highly idealized terms—"He had always been on my side, right or wrong, and not once since I had first met him in September, almost four years ago, had a harsh word passed between us" (p. 187)—but it is nevertheless very similar to a whole series of other relationships Jimmy forms at the same time, relationships in which that mysterious entity called companionship is all that is asked or given. Jimmy and Blocker form the nucleus of a dormitory clique, a circle of cronies made up of secondary characters so briefly sketched that they remain little more than names, a few of which, like Black Boy and Signifier, had already appeared in Himes's early prison stories.[16] Throughout this time Jimmy enjoys great popularity—another mysterious entity. He is the most admired and best-liked convict in the cripple company dormitory, almost in the manner of Melville's Billy Budd, though his lavish generosity with the money he rakes in from the poker games and his pension is a definite factor: "No kid could say that I refused him his beg, whether it was for a fin or a bag of weed. So what? I didn't get anything but what I had always wanted most in life, and that was adulation. I got too much adulation" (p. 112). Jimmy had discovered the potency of what Eric Hoffer has called "substitute gratifications"—companionship, popularity, prosperity, the artificial excitement of gambling—and prison had temporarily lost its sting:

> And the days passed. Square and angular, with hard-beaten surfaces; confining, restricting, congesting. But down in the heart of these precise, square blocks of days there was love and hate; ambition and regret; there was hope, too, shining eternally through the long gray years; and perhaps there was even a little happiness (p. 112).

He repulses occasional homosexual advances with cool contempt, confident that they can no longer "touch" him.

The dormitory guard, Captain Tom, is a fanatic softball fan, and Jimmy, whose disability amounts to little more than an occasional spasm of pain in the back, requiring a brace no larger

16. See pp. 35ff, 46ff, this volume.

than a wide belt, cements his already solid popularity by becoming the manager and star player of the dormitory's intramural (very intramural) softball team. He is a spectacular and
dramatic player, a superb athlete, though he never quite succeeds
in upstaging Captain Tom:

> You should have seen Tom walking up and down the
> firstbase line, with his big belly sweating in the sun and his
> white shirt sticking to his body, and his face red as paint,
> his cap cocked on the back of his head with a lock of hair
> down in his eyes; talking a mile a minute in a disjointed
> babble of sighs and prayers and curses and cheers. At the
> end of each game he would be utterly weary, with sagging
> shoulders, and his eyes registering the beginning of a heart
> attack. His unlighted cigar, which he had lighted a hundred
> times, would still be unsmoked but now chewed to a frazzle
> with slimy strings of tobacco hanging from his slack mouth.
> The first thing after we got back to the dormitory, even be-
> fore we sainted players got our rubdowns, someone would
> get out a bucket of warm water for him to soak his feet, and
> someone else would have to apply hot towels to his arms
> and cold towels to his head and work on him until it was
> time for him to go off duty, so he would be able to get away
> on his own power. He played each game harder than all
> twenty players combined. (*Cast the First Stone*, 196)

But "doing easy time" runs counter to Jimmy Monroe's passionate and intense nature, and neither lotus leaves nor poker
chips nor baseball bats can beguile or bemuse him indefinitely.
There are days when the cards, sports, and casual chatter that
nourish him seem repellent, days when his substitute gratifications fail to gratify:

> I couldn't work up even a passing interest in gambling any
> more. It seemed like a senseless pastime and I couldn't see
> for the life of me how I had spent so much time and thought
> on it before. For a time I lay on my bunk and read novels
> and magazine stories, when I wasn't studying. The only in-
> teresting things that happened any more were the things
> which happened in the stories I read. (*Cast the First Stone*,
> 175)

He discovers that he has intellectual needs, and he tackles a series of correspondence courses with fierce diligence: law, typing, short-story writing. Metz, a murderer, though not a "criminal," since he had been a successful businessman in civilian life, who had shot his wife, becomes his mentor, his guide to intellectual pursuits, in this third stage of Jimmy's struggle with the prison, which for a time runs concurrently with the second, sociallion stage. Metz involves him in a course he himself is taking in short-story writing, but little is said of Jimmy's progress in this field. Himes provides Jimmy with the temperament of an artist but no solid vocation, remaining true throughout the novel to his determination to present Jimmy as a convict, pure and simple. In all of his intellectual pursuits Jimmy remains an amateur; he is intrigued and involved but never fully committed:

> It was more the companionship of Metz than the course in short-story writing that interested me. His conversation was a relief from the stale, monotonous babble of the prison. I'd get away from that when we talked. I'd get away from all the sex. I'd get away from all those fags that had leaned on me, surrounded me; and those would-be wolves who had kept shooting at me on the sly, long after they'd concluded that I wouldn't go. Metz was the first really decent fellow whom I had met in prison, although Blocker was my only true friend. (*Cast the First Stone*, 126)

The accidents of convict transfers separate him from Metz, however, and in time Jimmy learns that not even "worthwhile" intellectual pastimes, pursued in isolation without plan or encouragement can shelter him from the dead weight of prison, or the full realization of the utter emptiness of the life he is forced to lead. His frustrations accumulate until, entirely unaware, he finds that he has drifted to the borderline of insanity. He toys with the notion of suicide during a brief period of hysterical depression, which, like the great prison fire, was the subject of one of the prison stories Himes published in *Esquire* in the 1930s.[17]

The fourth, and ultimate, stage of Jimmy's struggle, the one campaign he wins, begins immediately after his abrupt recovery

17. See pp. 42ff, this volume.

from the brief fit of psychotic depression. Having weathered the worst, actually seen himself as a "stir crazy con," and recovered, he is stronger and calmer than he has ever been before. For the first time, he undertakes practical measures to secure his release. He writes a humble and sensible letter to the state governor requesting commutation of his sentence, and after long ceremonial delays and many polite form letters, his release in the near future begins to seem a genuine possibility. He is twenty-four years old, sober and steady, even a bit learned, very different from the hysterical boy he had been when he entered the prison at nineteen. It is at this point, in the last fourth of the novel, that Duke Dido enters the story, a "new fish" who has just been transferred into the idle and crowded cripple company. He is also twenty-four years old, yet he is in many ways similar to the frightened boy Jimmy had been five years before. He is extraordinarily attractive and extraordinarily helpless, and Jimmy responds to him with an openness he has never permitted himself with any other convict, immediately extending his protection, as one of the dormitory's dominant figures, over this erratic and troublesome newcomer, and Dido's response is instant "adoration."

Dido had broken both his knees jumping from a freight train years before, and he walks like a hobbled horse whenever he is not perfectly calm, but this slight deformity only heightens the effect of his striking physical beauty:

> At first he looked startled. And then he blossomed like a morning-glory and smiled, showing white, even teeth. Smiling, he was beautiful. It was as if his face contained an inner life which changed its expression with each passing emotion. It looked so delicately alive I felt a strong impulse to touch it with my fingertips. His eyes would grow bright, dim, serious, earnest, mischievous, bitter, sparkling, and then suddenly cold; so that you knew instantly, as if touching piano keys, which note you had sounded. I had never seen anyone so sensitive to moods. (*Cast the First Stone*, 225)

"Not the brother of the Princess?" Jimmy remarks, flashing his knowledge of Virgil, when he first learns that the new boy's name is Dido. From the very beginning he sees Dido as a romantic figure, fascinating and unreal. To the rest of the dormitory it seems apparent that cool, aloof Jimmy Monroe has been caught in a homosexual infatuation, but the thought of abandoning his "normalcy" never crosses Jimmy's mind, and Dido repeatedly assures him that he too has never taken the final step toward physical intimacy with another man. To Jimmy, it seems that what he has found is the perfect friendship, another human being so like himself that he can cast aside all restraints and commit himself completely, emotionally and spiritually:

> On those hot summer days we'd lie side-by-side on my bunk and look out the window at the clouds in the sky, rolling by in great dirty flocks beneath the sun, and he would call them sheep. They did look something like sheep. Once we got a pair of smoked glasses and looked at them and everything was purple-tinted and fantastically beautiful. It was swell to be young and alive and have such a wonderful friendship, even if we were in prison. (*Cast the First Stone*, 276)

He teaches Dido to play softball, and together they sweep the team to victory after victory.

But Jimmy soon becomes uncomfortably aware that there is a dark side to Dido's nature, qualities that are perverse and corrupt, events in his background that suggest more than a passing acquaintance with evil. Dido seems to be a second version of the saintly character called the Kid in Himes's 1933 novella "Prison Mass,"[18] but the second time around Himes left the character little sanctity:

> When he stopped he was crying.
> I wanted to hold him in my arms as I would have a little baby and comfort and reassure him; I felt so tender toward him. "You're all right," I said. "You're all right, kid."
> A spark of worship flickered in his eyes. "Sometimes you're wonderful," he choked.
> "It's only that you brood too much," I said. "It's only in your mind that no one understands you."
> Suddenly he was laughing. "But of course you don't understand; how could you? You don't have to be afraid of yourself. You don't have to be afraid ever—" and now he was deeply bitter, "of doing something so sickening that

18. See pp. 36ff, this volume.

you want to hang yourself a moment afterward, and still not being able to help it."

"I don't know, I've done a lot of things that I'm not proud of," I said.

"But they'd still stand telling," he said.

"Let's don't talk about it," I said. For the instant I hated him for everything he had implied; all the moments and all the men. (*Cast the First Stone*, 245)

Jimmy somehow fails to note the similarity of Dido's conversation to that of all the other homosexuals who have approached him through the years, fails to note the unmistakable significance of remarks like "Aren't I brazen?" (p. 229) and "You're so masculine" (p. 238), but when Dido types out on Jimmy's typewriter a detailed program of physical intimacy, he can no longer fail to comprehend. His infatuation changes to sudden, heartsick revulsion.

But the other convicts, many of them confirmed and practicing homosexuals, have long found something basically unacceptable in the idyllic and intense relationship Jimmy and Dido have managed for so long, and the prison authorities have been literally deluged with letters written by indignant convicts denouncing Jimmy and Dido. Sex between men, an expedient without evident alternatives, does not shock Himes's convicts, but passionate friendship does; Damon and Pythias would have been lynched. Finally, the guards decide to transfer Dido to the "girl-boy company," and Jimmy abruptly discovers how much Dido had given him in permitting him to unleash his immense capacity for tenderness and love, qualities long wasted in a desert of empty, shallow men, men incapable of any deep response. He has somehow become a complete man, and he acts the part in this crisis, standing up for Dido against the entire world, actually throwing away his commutation, which was about to come through, in his insistence that he must share Dido's punishment, that he too must be transferred to the girl-boy isolation cells:

My mother hated Dido after that. She hated him forever and unrelentingly. She said some very nasty things about him, most of which had been told to her by people in the front office. She blamed him for everything. But I couldn't blame her for that, though. She didn't have any way of knowing that in the end—in the full, final decision—I had done it myself. I had done it to be a man. . . . I had done a lot of time and I could do plenty more. But I couldn't be a man later. I couldn't wait. I had waited long enough as it was. I had to be it, then. (*Cast the First Stone*, 295)

The warden however, refuses to believe Jimmy is guilty of the official sexual perversion charges and has him transferred to the prison farm as a preliminary to parole. Dido, who is to be left behind, with a long sentence to serve in the prison he cannot adjust to, hangs himself in his isolation cell. Jimmy sees in this tragedy proof that there had been love between them, pure and strong, and it had left them both whole and strong men:

I knew, beyond all doubt, that he had done it for me. He had done it to give me a perfect ending. It was so much like him to do this one irrevocable thing to let me know for always that I was the only one. Along with the terrible hurt I could not help but feel a great gladness and exaltation. I knew that he would have wanted me to. (*Cast the First Stone*, 302)

In his autobiography—far from echoing his novel's triumphant finale—Himes reduced the effect prison had had on him personally to one brutal insight:

It is nonsense, even falsehood, to say that serving seven and a half years in one of the most violent prisons on earth will have no effect on a human being. But as far as I could determine at the time, and for a long time afterward, the only effect it had on me was to convince me that people will do anything—white people, black people, all people. Why should I be surprised when white men cut out some poor black man's nuts, or when black men eat the tasty palms of white explorers? (*The Quality of Hurt*, 65–66)

But the big novel in which Chester Himes isolated and anatomized his prison experience said something much more positive. It demonstrated that human beings can fulfill their potential, for good or evil, can achieve maturity and wholeness in even the most negative and hostile environments. Though it deals, exhaustively, with aberrations in the behavior of caged men *Cast the First Stone*, at times a very funny book, is always a very hopeful one.

IV The Primitive

In 1948, when the Knopf company declined to respond to the negative criticism of *Lonely Crusade*,[19] Chester Himes decided "to leave the United States forever if I got the chance" (*The Quality of Hurt*, 103). But "the chance," the necessary funds and some encouragement from abroad, was long in coming. In May and June, 1948, he was one of many guest artists at the Yaddo foundation, but that establishment's carefully nurtured and sumptuous solitude merely triggered a dangerous spasm of alcoholic despair in Himes.[20] With the summer's end he solved the pressing problem of supporting himself and his wife Jean by taking a job as live-in caretaker at an abandoned resort in New Jersey. The only significant writing he accomplished there was the three-act play version of *If He Hollers Let Him Go*.[21] In the summer of 1949, he worked as a bellhop at a rural hotel, with no time for writing at all, and in the winter he found another job as a caretaker, at a country club. After that he and Jean were joint caretakers, and housekeepers, at a New York lawyer's plush farm in Connecticut. In June 1950, this string of menial jobs, this pattern of humiliation, degradation, and despair, was briefly broken when he was invited to his brother Joe's college in Durham, North Carolina, to give a two-week seminar in creative writing. False hope that *Cast the First Stone* was about to be published, however, then lured the Himeses into jubilant, and unwise, spending, and they had to take refuge as guests for the winter with friends in Vermont. Then, in the first three months of 1951, the year his marriage finally collapsed, Chester Himes was a porter at the YMCA in White Plains, New York (*The Quality of Hurt*, 103–33).

Somehow during these jumbled, hopeless, confused years—

19. See p. 133, this volume.
20. See pp. 68–69, this volume.
21. See p. 83, this volume.

"a hodgepodge.... a period of recurring blackouts" (*The Quality of Hurt*, 115)—Himes had managed to write the early drafts of *The Third Generation* and to bring *Cast the First Stone* into publishable form, and late in 1951 money from publishers' advances, the one form of encouragement he most desperately needed, was again a factor in his life, and he emerged from his self-enforced seclusion, from what had been an almost total disappearance: "It's simply that I'm like an animal—when I'm hurt and lonely I want to go off alone in my hole and lick my wounds" (p. 132). He began then a long love affair with a white woman. He had met her years before when he was completing *If He Hollers Let Him Go* with help from a Julius Rosenwald fellowship, and she had been acting administrator of fellowships for the Rosenwald Foundation. In 1951 she was a junior executive for another, similar foundation in New York City, and she had a posh midtown apartment, where, for some eighteen months, Chester Himes sought vainly to shake off his sense of futility and failure in frantic lovemaking and hard drinking. This mutually destructive affair skidded to a half-halt toward the end of 1952, "All the hurts of all my life seemed to come up into me and I went into a trance and kept on slapping her compulsively until suddenly the sight of her swollen face jarred me back to sanity" (p. 136). He retreated again to his friends in Vermont, but when his father died his erstwhile mistress sent the money he needed to attend the funeral, and she would join him for a short time in Paris a few months later, but Himes had finally realized how dangerous the relationship had become, to him personally, and, once he was completely disengaged, he would devote his third autobiographical novel, *The Primitive*, to exorcizing her decidedly sinister spell.

In 1951 he began also his long correspondence and friendship with Yves Malartic, a French writer with influential contacts throughout the French publishing world. *If He Hollers Let Him Go* had been translated into French, principally by Marcel Duhamel, in 1948, as *S'il braille, lâche-le...*, and Malartic was working on a translation of *Lonely Crusade*, to be entitled *La Croisade de Lee Gordon*. He urged Himes to try his luck in Paris, where he was already well known (*The Quality of Hurt*, 140).

In 1953, after *La Croisade de Lee Gordon* had received enthusiastic reviews in Paris, *Cast the First Stone* had been published in New York, and substantial advances had been paid for *The Third Generation*, then well into the editing process, Himes decided that his "chance" to leave America had finally arrived. He booked passage on a French steamer and sailed on April 3, 1953, arriving in Paris on April 10.

On the crossing, under the idyllic and improbable circumstances of a typical shipboard romance, he met a forlorn white woman named Alva, the highly polished product of a wealthy Philadelphia family unhappily married to a Hollander, on the verge of divorce and possible nervous collapse. He found her innocent and good—"In my own way I was as innocent as she was. The difference was that she was a good woman, and I have never been a good man"—"gallant" and "elegant" (*The Quality of Hurt*, 162, 243, 167). Quite simply, they fell in love, and committed themselves to a long affair. Within a few weeks, after Himes's earlier affair had been definitively terminated, Alva separated herself from her family in Holland and came to live with Himes, first in Paris, then in a villa owned by Yves Malartic in Arcachon on the coast south of Bordeaux. There Himes completed the final rewrites of *The Third Generation*, "trying to dramatize the ending," as his editors had suggested (p. 235), and Alva resumed work on the manuscript of a long-neglected autobiographical novel of her own, tentatively entitled *The Golden Chalice*, a Henry Jamesian account of an innocent though cultured American heiress hopelessly enmeshed in the unfathomable complexities of a corrupt and sophisticated European society (pp. 235, 263–65).[22] His own immediate writing projects concluded, Himes decided to help Alva with her book, eventually becoming something somewhere between a full coauthor and a creative editor, "Alva would write the first draft . . . and I would rework it into chapters" (p. 264). They decided life might be simpler in England, where both could speak the language and Himes would not have to rely on Alva's excellent French for his every social contact, and they left Arcachon in July 1953, to spend

22. The manuscript's title is given as *The Silver Altar* in Himes's interview with John A. Williams, "My Man Himes," p. 31.

the next six months in London. There, amid grinding poverty, miserable cold, nagging hints of racial prejudice, and invincible domestic bliss, they worked steadily at *The Golden Chalice* and finished it by December, though they never succeeded in finding a publisher for the manuscript. Throughout this period Himes was productive and happy as never before, but the hardships of a British winter began to tell on Alva, and in January 1954, they left London for Majorca.

During their stay in Majorca, where they lived for almost a year in a series of ramshackle rented villas, Himes wrote the novel he first entitled *The End of a Primitive*, then simply *The Primitive*. The surroundings were turbulent, his love affair was souring rapidly, sinking irredeemably into mutual pity, and he relied heavily on tranquilizers; but he was nevertheless convinced that he had at last found optimal conditions for writing:

> My tranquilizers sealed me inside of my thoughts so that I was almost completely unaware of the peasants and the flies and the movement in the distant street and could only experience the sweet, sensual, almost overwhelming scent of the lemon blossoms and the nearly unbearable beauty of the blossoming day far in the back of my mind. I wrote slowly, savoring each word, sometimes taking an hour to fashion one sentence to my liking. Sometimes leaning back in my seat and laughing hysterically at the sentence I had fashioned, getting as much satisfaction from the creation of this book as from an exquisite act of love. That was the first time in my life I enjoyed writing; before I had always written from compulsion. . . . for once I was almost doing what I wanted to with a story, without being influenced by the imagined reactions of editors, publishers, critics, readers, or anyone. By then I had reduced myself to the fundamental writer, and nothing else mattered. (*The Quality of Hurt*, 302)

Alva read every page as it was completed, fascinated by this account of Himes's earlier love affair, and she typed the manuscript and offered suggestions, encouragement, and admiration, and, though "she didn't share in the writing" (p. 300), she was certainly a prime factor in Himes's unprecedented productivity.

But the exotic Mediterranean island itself, the very foreignness of their surroundings, was perhaps an even more significant factor. Himes had found in travel, in the contemplation of the new and strange, a remarkably potent source of relief from all his tensions. In his racist homeland he had been a borderline alcoholic, compulsively embracing the degradation of menial jobs to eke out a precarious living; abroad, he was a completely functional, generally dead broke, moderately happy, working writer. Majorca, as much as Alva, played muse to *The Primitive*:

> We went . . . by ourselves in the early morning, returning late at night in the bright moonlight to the scent of the lemon blossoms and undressing in the warm, dark, impossible house and making love. There couldn't have been a house so primitive, nor sunsets so enchanting. Neither the pink mountains nor the swarms of flies in the dusty city could possibly be real, I thought. Only my book was real. (*The Quality of Hurt*, 305)

The Primitive, first published by the New American Library in paperback in 1955, is precisely the type of impeccably structured and elaborately stylized book that one might expect to emerge from such relatively ideal circumstances. It is a very short novel, less than seventy thousand words, but it is as richly packed and complex a book as the sprawling *Lonely Crusade*. It is the most intricately patterned piece of fiction Himes ever produced. The narrative approach is officially third-person omniscient, but the anonymous, all-knowing narrator is far more than an expedient technical device, the most convenient way to bring a variety of facts before the reader. The narrator is as much a presence in the early chapters as the book's two main characters, bringing to the recitation something very like the "immortal pity, over the lot of man" of the Christ figure that appeared at the end of Himes's first novella, "Prison Mass"[23]—and a cynically morbid deadpan humor as well. The novel begins as a chronicle of despair and disillusion, violence and degradation, told with a variety of hysterically funny comic flourishes. But as the book progresses the narrator becomes less and less visible, as long, unbroken stretches of dialogue and straightforward reportage of action come

23. See p. 38, this volume.

to dominate. The book is overflowing with "symbols"; the characters live surrounded by things, crowded on all sides by objects of every kind, objects that seem to exist solely for the sake of the resonances they create in the minds of the protagonists, their mysterious capacity to jar loose vagrant fragments of almost forgotten memories or to inspire vague premonitions of dread, a sense of malevolent forces at work beneath the surface of things.

Like *If He Hollers Let Him Go*, *The Primitive* relates a story that is confined to the events of a single week and it too is structured very much like a play. In fact, the novel's basic organization is precisely that of a play in three acts of four scenes each. Each of the novel's twelve chapters corresponds to a specific scene in a dramatic structure. The two protagonists, Jesse Robinson, the black man, and Kristina Cummings, the white woman, participants in a violently destructive interracial love affair, have each in their own way reached the final stages of a long series of personal defeats. At the story's beginning both are about to arrive at the particular point at which death seems the only possible release, and here their parallel courses converge. They are drawn, more by mutual despair than desire, into a brief, passionate sexual episode, an emotional storm for two whose steadily mounting tensions can only culminate in murderous violence. The action of the novel's first four chapters, or its "Act I," takes place on a Tuesday early in April 1952 in New York City. It is a classic "exposition." Jesse and Kriss are introduced, their personal histories recorded, and the private abysses of loneliness both inhabit are exhaustively explored. On that Tuesday evening Jesse phones Kriss, both recall their first meeting and brief love many years before, and they make a date to have dinner together Thursday evening. The second "act" embraces both the Thursday evening dinner and the events that follow on Friday, after they have spent the night together. On this fatal Friday both experience ultimate defeat. The novel that Jesse had thought he had sold is unexpectedly rejected at the last moment, and the one man Kriss had wanted to marry, Dave, visits her for what he makes very clear is the last time. As Friday ends both Kriss and Jesse have lost themselves, separately, in alcoholic stupors. In the climactic third act, beginning on Saturday afternoon when

Jesse shows up at Kriss's apartment with food and liquor, and continuing on through Sunday and into Monday morning on a monstrous, nonstop weekend binge, Jesse and Kriss savagely claw at one another—and at a series of guests who show up and leave—trying to escape the intolerable sense of hurt each feels by inflicting hurt on someone, anyone, and, in the end, in the early hours of Monday when both are so drunk that the real and the unreal have ceased to be separate, identifiable entities, he kills her.

In the short general summary statement Himes wrote on June 6, 1971, for the dust cover of *The Quality of Hurt*, he described himself as basically "a black man who pitied white women." The characterization of Kriss in *The Primitive* is the most complete exposition he gave in his writing of his conviction that the hurts of the white woman are at least comparable to those of the black man, and that she endures a roughly similar, and equally pitiable, minority status. This conviction was the product of his experience with two white mistresses, amplified and reinforced by the months he had spent collaborating with Alva on the lugubrious "woman's story" manuscript novel, *The Golden Chalice*. Kriss epitomizes "the female condition," as Himes saw it, the unique quality of defeat a sadistic society has reserved for its women: "Not defeated like a man in battle, but like a woman who is defeated by her sex, by the outraged indignity of childbearing, menstrual periods, long hair and skirts."[24] Kriss's minority status, the dues she has paid for a place in the foremost ranks of the outraged and insulted, is a prime factor in maintaining and insistently stressing the parallelism of the novel's two central characterizations. Both Kriss and Jesse are first presented to the reader at their moments of greatest vulnerability, as they literally pull themselves together out of drunken or drugged sleep early on Tuesday morning. Within an hour after awakening Kriss will be a redoubtable and formidable figure, still a beautiful woman at thirty-seven, a striking blonde executive, dressed in expensive and stylish clothes, possessed of both a brilliant creative mind and a sure sense of office routine. But

24. Himes, *The Primitive*, p. 6.

at the moment of awakening Kriss is a flabby and terrified derelict, agonizingly aware of her outcast status, her absolute isolation in a totally indifferent universe:

> When it came as her first conscious realization of the day, she found the aloneness terrifying. . . . She had always been lonely with Ronny, throughout the ten years of their marriage. . . . But there had been the security of his presence, his being there, his heart pulse at her side, assuring her that she was not alone, that her desires and emotions, her living and breathing, were joined with another's, linked in the chain of the larger whole, if only temporarily. (*The Primitive*, 5)

It has been Kriss's ill luck, or perhaps her ineluctable fate, to be thrown always with people, mostly men, whose only possible relationships with others were based on exploitation and manipulation. Kriss has been "used," repeatedly, and repeatedly discarded, and as she moves toward middle age she can see clearly the moment of her final abandonment, and beyond that a future of unbroken aloneness. When he has killed her Jesse will pray for her: "Forgive her God . . . she was a good girl, God . . . we were the bastards" (p. 157). In the beginning Kriss had trusted men, trusted society, the world, given of herself freely and generously, but at the time the novel opens she has been hurt so many times by so many men that she can tolerate no other relationship. She must seek out pain, seek to hurt and be hurt, to twist all offered warmth into enmity. She has little to say to the men who pass her way that is not calculatedly vicious. She is a victim by vocation, but she has acquired something of the same delight in the destructiveness of her relationships that characterized the monstrous white Madge of *If He Hollers Let Him Go*. In her intimate social contacts Kriss is now scarcely distinguishable from the long line of predatory males in her own past: her alcoholic father, "the last soured dregs of a line of German nobility" (p. 5), or Ronny, her bisexual former husband, or Ted or Harold or Jesse, her unsentimentally lustful black lovers, or Fuller, the aging, perverted white admirer whose relationship to her is openly that of patron to prostitute. The narrator insists heavily on the paradox of

Kriss's beauty, "as handsome as four peacocks" (p. 11), her talent, her prestigious job, and opulently furnished New York apartment, and her pathetic sense of total defeat:

> She began to cry, her full matronly face stretching and puckering in the ugly grimace of the little towheaded girl called "Dutch" crying because her mother had slapped her drunken father the day he lost his grocery store in a little village in North Dakota. "You ruined me, you louse!" And in that moment of emotional torture, she couldn't have said whom she meant by this last louse. (*The Primitive*, 81)

On awakening—"at this moment of emotional helplessness when the mind is not fully detached from the body, when thoughts are still vaguely orgastic, to a large degree physiological, sleep-stupid and defenseless; when the feminine mind suffers its one brief period of honesty" (p. 6)—Kriss feebly draws a few fitful glimmerings of strength from the "things" that are extensions of her being—"a modern room with a stunning decor, the facing walls done in soft pastel shades of gray and pink, the floor in rose-colored carpet . . . floor-length drapes of a deep maroon color" (p. 10). She swallows a blue-gray pill, prescribed for "states of mental and emotional distress," washing it down with a shot of Scotch, the first installment on her daily quota of one quart. She switches on her television set. The TV is authentic solace. She is an avid, "hooked" listener-viewer, needing the sounds and flickering images to fill the menacing emptiness of her vaguely cavelike apartment, "situated as it was on the first floor rear, entombed by the concrete cliffs of other buildings" (p. 6). The program that seems always, inevitably "there," all through the novel, features a suave, perpetually smiling moderator who conducts interviews with a prophetic talking chimpanzee. In the novel's most patently surrealistic twist, the electronic pseudomiracle of a chimpanzee that talks is complemented by the authentic miracle of genuine, precise, detailed prophecy. In April 1952, the TV chimpanzee predicts such assorted unlikely events as Richard Nixon's speech in the fall of 1952 explaining and defending the sources of his vice-presidential campaign funds, the 1954 Supreme Court school desegregation decision, and Jesse Robinson's trial and sentencing for the murder of Kristina Cummings. Nobody who "listens," however, neither Kriss nor Jesse, pays the slightest attention nor understands a word the simian Cassandra pronounces. Like the Fool in *King Lear*, a very ancient Briton who explains with miraculous wisdom, "This prophecy Merlin shall make, for I live before his time" (III, ii), Himes's chatty and omniscient chimpanzee seems to have been created primarily to remind the reader, and perhaps the writer, that fictional worlds are at best only pale copies of an awesomely mysterious reality, and, again like Shakespeare's Fool, the chimpanzee, with his clear view through the fictional fabric to the greater outside, is totally unable to communicate with the other characters in the work, each one lost in his own private rut, surrounded by impenetrable walls. The chimpanzee is also, however, perhaps a bit too obviously, an element in Himes's satire of the highly "advanced," consumer culture that produced Kriss and all her lamentable sisters and stranded them in the meaningless void of a social order whose only positive value is material productivity. Determined to make absolutely clear the pointless "thinginess" of Kriss's world, the narrator relentlessly catalogs every item she touches, even to describing and identifying each individual key on her key ring (p. 17).

Once Kriss has struggled into her girdle, felt her pill take hold, and emerged from her decidedly unearthly apartment, she is caught by the excitement of the giant city, her one totally effective escape; and her own strong side—indispensable in a character intended to be authentically tragic—routinely asserts itself:

> She continued down Twenty-first Street to Fourth Avenue, turned north to the subway entrance at Twenty-second Street. There was a smile on her lips. She felt very happy. Passers-by, even the surly printers and warehousemen of the neighborhood, noticed her happiness and smiled at her. She smiled in return, suddenly recalling the Harlem saying she had often heard at Maud's: *I'd rather be a doggy lamppost in New York City than Governor General of the State of Mississippi. (The Primitive, 18–19)*

At her office Kriss radiates calm, effortlessly soothing the ruffled feathers of prim, neurotic, mannish Dorothy Stone, outraged for the umpteenth time by the insufferable Mr. Watson's insistence on using the one bathroom on the floor at the very moment she is making coffee there. Kriss's high-powered skills are in trim working order, and she races through the typed copies of her own summaries of foundation applications, earning her handsome salary in short order, with time left over to read the newspaper: "She was an expert proofreader with a complete command of punctuation and grammatical construction. . . . Her sentences were always concise and to the point, never ambiguous and were phrased with amazing simplicity and conclusiveness and in perfect logical sequence. Men would never believe a woman wrote such prose" (p. 39).

But when Jesse phones that evening and she hears, first, "a little catch on the other end, not quite a laugh nor a sigh, a sort of blowing from the mouth and nostrils all the vanities behind which people hide themselves" (pp. 48–49), followed by the sound of his "soft slurred voice with its faint, almost indistinguishable lisp" (p. 49), she is instantly venomous, the hurt hurter with claws at the ready. When he begins to talk about the new book he believes he has just sold, she cuts him short: "I hope it's nothing like that last thing you wrote. . . . I'm tired of listening to you Negroes whining. I've got enough worries of my own" (p. 50). But she does make a date for two nights later, and giggles delightedly when she hangs up, in anticipation of the renewal of their long-ago amours.

Their dinner Thursday evening is an occasion for disquieting reappraisals and small shocks for both. Jesse is vaguely surprised to find little trace of "the daredevil girl whom he'd once liked" in the heavy, rapidly aging Kriss, who, like the Jackie Forks of *Lonely Crusade*, had once had a distinctly sexual enthusiasm for the love of poetry of John Donne (pp. 52, 64);[25] Kriss notes, with a mixture of sympathy and grim satisfaction, the marks that long sieges of bad luck have left on Jesse: "This man before her, in the old trench coat she recognized immediately, was dead; hurt had settled so deep inside of him it had become a part of his metabolism" (p. 52). They had first met, toward the end of World War II, when both had been deeply involved in the Civil Rights movement and related black politics, and they share now a sense of

25. See p. 119, this volume.

being outcasts, rejects, "both now ostracized from the only exciting life they had ever known" (p. 55).

They share uncomfortable, almost obsessive, memories of Maud, the powerful black woman who had been the center of the group they had both belonged to:

> "What a bitch!" he thought. "A great woman, really. Greater than anybody'll ever know!" Many times he'd considered writing a novel about her. But he'd never been able to get the handle to the story. "Great Madame, actually. Worked with her tools. Besides which she was a cheat, liar, thief, master of intrigue, without conscience or scruples, and respectable too. That was the lick—the respectability." He felt a cynical amusement. "Son, that's the trick. Here's a whore who's friend of the mighty, lunches with the mayor's wife, entertains the rich, the very rich, on all kinds of interracial committees, a great Negro social leader. While you, you with your so-called integrity, are just a pest and a nuisance." (*The Primitive*, 46)

Himes alludes only briefly to that particular period of his life in *The Quality of Hurt*: "Harlem at the end of the war . . . the company of high-society blacks whom I had met during the short time I lived with my cousin Henry Moon and his wife Molly" (pp. 75, 76, 178).[26] But he had already brought it into his fiction in a few vagrant pages of *Lonely Crusade*,[27] in which Lee Gordon quite inexplicably leaves Los Angeles for a brief stay in New York City. This incident is so disconnected from the rest of the novel and so foreign to the basic character of Lee Gordon that it seemed to have been inserted into the novel solely to permit Himes to stake a claim to that particular block of literary material. Later, he would center one detective novel, *The Crazy Kill* (1959), and his long satiric novel *Pinktoes* (1961), around the character he calls Maud in *The Primitive* and "Mamie" in the rest of her nu-

---

26. In his interview with Hoyt Fuller, Himes specifically identified Molly Moon as the model for a later literary character: "*Pinktoes* was first published in France as *Mamie Mason*, and the story was a take-off on Molly. I was living with Molly Moon and Henry up on 157th and St. Nicholas Ave. during the time that *If He Hollers* . . . was published" (Fuller, "Interview with Chester Himes," p. 12).

27. Himes, *Lonely Crusade*, pp. 48, 49, 95.

merous appearances in his writing. Himes, like Jesse, apparently had to work very hard "to get the handle to the story," and to the character Maud-Mamie-Molly. Kriss's memories of Maud have an even sharper edge, more pain in them, than Jesse's, a fact that bursts into the open almost immediately when she and Jesse begin to discuss Maud:

> "God, that woman hurt me!" the hurt coming through in her voice. "I lived with them when I first came to New York."
> "I didn't know."
> "I practically paid their rent and liquor bills. I had that little sitting room where you stayed. . . . Then when I broke off with Ted, Maud practically threw me out. And we'd been just like sisters for years." (*The Primitive*, 54)

On Sunday, when Jesse and her other drunken black guests are beginning to prove unmanageably turbulent, the memory of Maud thrusts through again, and Kriss lashes out, "I'm not going to have you niggers break up this apartment. Maud hacked my dining room table to pieces with a kitchen knife" (p. 127). The casual, tired efforts of Kriss and Jesse to rekindle a lost love represent for both of them a drastic plunge back into a past neither has been able to master, a past dominated by the exasperating figure of Maud, who had lived at ease, obscenely flourished, in the midst of circumstances and conditions they had found ultimately unacceptable. The memory of Maud, shameless, ever victorious, insufferable, and lovable, is the emblem of their own defeats, in a world that is both intransigent and absurd.

As Kriss repeatedly cuts at Jesse with a dozen assorted insults during their few days together, he responds first with indifference, then by punching her to the floor with his fists, and, finally, with full insight: " 'Woman's sick,' Jesse said from a sudden subconscious realization. 'Really sick . . . Negroes hurt her . . . really hurt her' " (p. 118). But Kriss's hurts, though always in full view, are far from being the sum total of this truly complex characterization. In *Cast the First Stone* the first-person narrator, every bit as compassionate—and as patronizing—as Jesse, remarks of Duke Dido: "Poor little kid . . . too bad he wasn't a woman. He had a woman's fascinating temperament, with a man's anatomy" (p. 262). Himes endowed Kriss too with "a woman's fascinating temperament," and this involved the same elements of perversity, cruelty, vulnerability, confusion, and childishness that he had given Dido. The "fascination," however, is primarily a function of the childishness. Among her intimates Kriss lets drop completely every trace of her professional manner and is, at these moments, equally free of poise and pretense. At home, with friends, she has a child's complete spontaneity and artlessness. Most of her tirades end when she suddenly perceives her own pomposity and breaks into uncontrollable giggles. She has an unexpected, improbable, impish love of play. When they awake together on Friday morning, she begins to give Jesse a series of orders in a tone that can only be used with servants, but he, knowing her well, is for once sufficiently free of tension to enter into the game:

> "Did you do what I told you to do?" she asked, laughing up at him with childish humor, and he knew then she'd done it to annoy him.
> He pulled the covers from her and in the soft pink light her nude body resembled one of Van Dyke's nudes. Sitting slantwise on the bed he tickled her until she was nearly hysterical, then said, "That's what you get for being so mean," and left her to get the paper and make the coffee and toast. (*The Primitive*, 66–67)

A few minutes later they are exchanging reasonably sophisticated banter at the breakfast table:

> "That's what I'll do! I'll write a book about chimpanzees," Jesse exclaimed. Then hastened to ask, "There isn't any chimpanzee problem is there?"
> "Not that I know of," Kriss said. "All of those I've seen —mostly at the zoo—seem to be well satisfied."
> "I guess you're right at that," Jesse said. "I've never heard of a chimpanzee being lynched for raping a white woman and so far none have been cited as communists."

"No-o-o," Kriss said thoughtfully. "But I once saw a chimpanzee in the zoo leer at me."

"Damn!" Jesse said. "That lets them out. Leering at a white woman is considered rape in some states." (*The Primitive*, 68–69)

Kriss also has the straightforward, uncomplicated sensuality of a child, a frank joy in fine food, good liquor, sex, and her own eminently satisfactory body. She can't pass a mirror without stopping to admire herself: "She loved her legs with such ecstasy that for several minutes she stood there voluptuously caressing them" (p. 108). Yet, like Dido, whose entire life is a prelude to his inevitable suicide, Kriss is driven by hidden compulsive forces within her, of which she is only dimly aware. There is a rampant death wish, possibly completely unconscious, that drives her to provoke dangerous situations and to toy tenaciously with the threats she precipitates:

She turned on him in a flurry of rage. "Jesse, if you ever sleep with your wife while you're sleeping with me. . . ."

"That I'd like to see," he thought, but when she persisted, "I'm not going to have some black bitch after me with a knife," he also flew into such a violent rage the room turned white-hot in his vision. "This bitch wants me to kill her," he thought, gripping the sofa for control. (*The Primitive*, 112)

When Dave, her last fiancé, drops her, immediately after Jesse's first visit, Kriss reacts by frantically trying to swallow the contents of an entire bottle of sleeping pills but is too drunk either to succeed or remember the attempt later. She finds the pills on the floor the next day and assumes the bottle fell.

Kriss's remarkably sturdy physical constitution permits her to plunge deep into vice and dissipation with relative impunity, triumphantly healthy to the end, and, similarly, her common sense and bubbly humor, her bouncy sense of fun, permit her, for a long time, to play fast and loose with the demons of her own psyche. She is monumentally unhappy but suffers from no obvious debilitating mental illness. Yet, she has acquired the vocation of murderee, a half-mischievous urge to provoke men to violence against her, to incite them beyond the limits of their control, and she represents an enormous danger to any man with difficult-to-control murderous impulses.

The character of Jesse, the potential murderer who is set on a collision course with Kriss, is a portrait not so much of Himes himself, the man he believed he had really been, but rather of the man he believed he might easily have become had the sequence of misfortunes that overwhelmed him been just a little bit worse, if the screws had been tightened, ever so slightly, just a few notches more. Jesse is a violent man, almost powerless to control an ever more pressing urge toward overt, lethal expression of his destructive impulses. And the final rejection of his manuscript novel cuts fatally deep into his already badly eroded reserves of control.

> At nine o'clock he awakened. . . . His face was swollen and had the smooth greasy sheen of overdrinking; his eyes were glassy, almost senseless. . . . For five full minutes he stood and stared at the paper-wrapped manuscript. . . . Without being conscious of his reason for doing so, he picked up his big clasp knife, opened it, then stood with the naked blade and stared at his manuscript for another two minutes. Abruptly, with a cry of stricken rage, an animal sound, half howl, half scream, he stabbed the manuscript with all his force. The strong forged blade went deep into the pages without breaking. Then all of a sudden thought surged back into his mind.
>
> He grunted a laugh and said aloud, "Really protest now!" (*The Primitive*, 102)

In his sleep he lashes out with his fists, screaming aloud, "I'll kill you!," again and again, night after night. He dreams "countless horrible scenes of murder and savage fights and apoplectic arguments, all of which had been blasted from memory at the moment of awakening" (p. 124). On Sunday, on entering Kriss's kitchen, he finds that some time the night before, blind drunk, he had stabbed her carving knife into the kitchen door with such force that it remained inflexibly embedded in the centerboard: "For an instant he was shocked out of his nice sensation of deranged normality and felt a tremor of fear. 'I ought to get the hell out of here!' he thought, but quickly drowned it with a drink" (pp. 126–27, cf. p. 144).

In his autobiography, however, Himes firmly contradicts the assumption, on the part of his friend Richard Wright, himself a very active fount of literary violence, that the creator of the likes of Bob Jones and Luther McGregor must be expected to be a fairly dangerous man: "He knew of my prison record and he had known Jean, and he suspected I had lived a life of wild and raging fury. I think I am one of the tamest men he ever knew, but he never came to know me well enough to know this" (*The Quality of Hurt*, 178).

Aside from the intensity of their respective penchants toward violence, however, it is very difficult to find traits that clearly distinguish Chester Himes from the fictional author Jesse Robinson, his avowed "rather exact" self-portrait. Jesse is renting one tiny room in a crowded apartment in Harlem, at 142nd Street and Convent Avenue, found just three weeks before, "directly after . . . he'd quit his porter's job in White Plains" (pp. 24, 31). Chester Himes, during the period this autobiographical novel covers, had just quit a porter's job in White Plains, where, he notes with some faint pride, "the director said I had been one of the best porters they had ever had and he hated to see me leave" (*The Quality of Hurt*, 132), and he then went "back to Harlem and took a room on Convent Avenue": "I had always been something of a snob, and a snob I have remained, despite the record of my life. . . . But most of the feeling of superiority was knocked out of me during that lonely period in Harlem, rooming in a household of perverts" (p. 133). Jesse's Harlem, however—and this is perhaps a major difference—is a locale fondly remembered from a villa in Majorca, a picturesque version of the great ghetto conjured up by an author who knows he will never again have to go back there to live. Jesse Robinson's Harlem, far from knocking things out of him, is a vastly amusing place, filled with the rhythms and excitement of life when it is lived recklessly and fully, the tremendous metropolis of black Americans, a courageous, creative, and magnificent people. Jesse must go downtown, to Kriss's apartment near Gramercy Park, to play out his tragedy, and he must reach into his own memory for its sources. In Harlem the fountains of life spout inexhaustibly, and though Jesse may sag with the weight of the alcohol he consumes he cannot manage to be a tragic figure in this ambiance:

> Outside was a soft warm night and the Harlem folk were crowded in the street. Jesse walked through the milling crowds, jostling and being jostled. The neon-lighted bars were jumping and the red buses bullied through the tight stream of traffic. Here and there a big braying voice pushed from the bubble of noise. The unforgettable scent of smoking marijuana pierced the gaseous mixture of motor fumes, cheap colognes, alcohol, foul breath, sweat stink, dust, and smoke that passed for air. "Going to float to heaven in a dream," Jesse thought.
>
> He went down to Seventh Avenue and stood for a moment watching the fat black boys with their bright gold babes glide past in their shiny Cadillacs. "Can't beat that, son," he said. . . .
>
> The next thing he knew he was in the balcony of the Apollo theatre watching a gangster picture on the screen. Weird faces in graduated rows appeared dimly in a thick blue haze of marijuana smoke like grim trophies of a ravenous cannibal. . . .
>
> He found himself getting a marijuana jag from inhaling the smoke and the black and white film began taking on patches of brilliant technicolor. . . .
>
> Then he was walking north on Seventh Avenue beneath a bright purple sky and the dingy smoke-blackened tenements were new brick red with yellow windows and green sills and the lights of the bars and greasy spoons slanting across the dirty walk burned like phosphorescent fires. "No wonder the cats smoke gage," he thought, then said aloud, "Every man his own Nero."
>
> "What?" a feminine voice asked.
>
> He looked about and found a woman on his arm. "Hello," he said.
>
> "Hello," she said thinking he was teasing. He had been buying her drinks at Small's bar for the past hour and now she was taking him home. "I'm here, baby," she said, steering him toward the entrance to a violet-colored apartment

house. He gave her a good look then and saw a pretty brown-skinned woman in a soft blue suit. Her full-lipped mouth was a deep purple like a lamb kidney and her black eyes shiny as twin cockroaches. "Is it good?" he asked. (*The Primitive*, 97–98)

The Harlem of *The Primitive*, evoked with bittersweet nostalgia and a marvelous, completely original, laughter-filled lyricism, was to be Himes's major subject throughout the European phase of his writing career, carried through the long series of detective novels and on into *Pinktoes*. In his enchanted garden in Majorca Himes found within himself the gifts of a great humorous prose poet, whose destined and unique subject was to be Harlem, the great, crowded black metropolis, more a continuing explosion of human energy than a city. He was soon to win a whole new circle of readers, as the chronicler, the poet, of Harlem, Harlem seen as only Chester Himes could describe it.

Even the "household of perverts" in the apartment house on Convent Avenue, which sounds such a sordid note in *The Quality of Hurt*, is distinctly mythologized in *The Primitive*. Leroy, the leader of the homosexual claque Jesse finds himself rooming with, rather inexplicably—" 'Jesus Christ, how'd I get mixed up with these birdmen?' Jesse asked himself" (p. 31)—is a broadly comic characterization, genuinely funny despite persistent attempts to attach weighty symbolic labels to him. He is an enormous, powerfully built black man, with a gigantic belly and hands of monstrous size and roughness, who affects the voice and mannerisms of a tiny Victorian gentlewoman. His huge apartment, in addition to housing a number of dubious roomers, including that alcoholic scribbler Jesse Robinson, serves as a kind of warehouse for the incredible quantities of hand-me-down bric-a-brac he has acquired from grateful white employers through his long years as a chauffeur and house servant. Numbered among these second-hand possessions are two effeminate male Pomeranians that spend almost all of their time yapping and nipping at Jesse's heels, or soiling his bedroom, despite Leroy's frantic attempts to seriously scold them into more sedate behavior:

But now Leroy called sharply, "Napoleon! Napoleon! You nasty thing! You come back here and let Mr. Robinson alone." He raised his lidded lecherous look to Jesse's face. "He likes you," he said with double-entendre; "Those are just little love bites. He takes after his Papa." (*The Primitive*, 30)

Some of Jesse's smoldering violence is harmlessly discharged in pursuing Napoleon, the more active of the two Pomeranians, belt in hand, in and out among the bric-a-brac, whenever Leroy is out. It is Jesse himself, though, his writer's mind feverishly and incessantly grinding away, rather than the narrator, who attempts to place Leroy in clear symbolic context, finding in his clumsy clownishness disturbing evidence of the lamentable degeneracy of modern society that extends even into the quality of its buffoons. Paraphrasing Hamlet's address to Yorick's skull, Jesse ponderously orates, in a melodramatic aside to his own psyche: "*Here hung those lips that I have kiss'd I know not how oft. But now his place hath been taken by uncouthness, a mean and sordid fellow without humor and refinement. How I despise this lowborn prole. But methinks, fair friends, that he is here to stay, a way of life, for a thousand years to come*" (p. 79). Similar symbolic significance, a value as testimony to the overwhelming triumph of vulgarity, in America in general and black America in particular, is attached to the two heavy-drinking, tipsy black men who show up briefly at Kriss's apartment during Jesse's long weekend there. Harold and Walter are slightly shopworn leftovers from the great days at Maud's, failing kingpins of black society and the Civil Rights movement. Harold, almost a national hero not long before as a glamorous and dramatic black sociologist, drops his thin veneer of worldly sophistication with a thunderous crash when incessant bickering between Jesse and Kriss abruptly veers toward violence: " 'Don't cut her, man, don't cut her!' Harold said in alarm . . . 'Hit her with your fist but don't cut her' " (p. 147). Walter, one of the editors of the black bourgeoisie's most successful picture magazine, master of the secrets of effective and profitable interracial relationships, plunges all the way to the gutter in one startling instant, under the goad of Jesse's open disdain:

"Listen, son . . ." Jesse began in a patronizing tone, and before he'd finished Walter leaped to his feet and snapped open a switch-blade knife. "I'll cut your yellow throat!" he threatened dangerously. (*The Primitive*, 146)

Jesse's only reaction is to stare coolly, and calmly, "as if he were watching with impersonal interest some vaguely valid but not very novel exhibition of idiocy, like a Hollywood treatment of a Negro theme" (p. 146). Walter, incidentally, the editor of an *Ebony*-like magazine, has an irritating habit of repeating, with dull, clownish persistence, the line "It's time you niggers count your blessings" (p. 144), a rough paraphrase of a line in *Ebony's* brutal, cutting editorial on Himes's *Lonely Crusade*, an editorial righteously entitled "Time to Count Our Blessings."[28]

The symbolic thrust of such episodes, however, in spite of very explicit narrative comments, is never very firmly established in *The Primitive*, possibly because the "refinement" extolled by contrast is never concretely exemplified or even defined, or possibly because the rampant energy held up to condemnation is inevitably depicted with what seems to be smiling good humor. An effective satirist should not so evidently enjoy his subjects' foolish behavior, nor offer such open sympathy.

On the other hand, the tragic character of Jesse himself, in contrast to the basic ambiguity of the Rabelaisian backdrop provided, is solidly established from the first with unerring stark simplicity. Jesse is forty-one, with the hard muscular body of a man accustomed to physical labor, but his face is worn and haggard: "Only his face ever showed his age; now it was swollen from heavy drinking and had the smooth, dead, dull-eyed look of a Harlem pimp" (p. 25). He is haunted by tormenting memories that give him no peace: the memory of the "vile stoning" (p. 73) the critics gave his second novel—" 'Jesse Robinson,' he said aloud. . . . a reflex comment of a man whose name has been so beaten and reviled it's become anathema to himself" (p. 25)— and the memory of the failure of his marriage and the great love he had had for his wife Becky, his desperate need to shelter and protect her, to give her pride in himself and his work, and the memory of the mire of humiliation and despair he had dragged

28. Himes, *The Quality of Hurt*, p. 100; cf. p. 22, in *The Quality of Hurt*, for Himes's use of the phrase in connection with his father. See chap. 3, n. 16.

her into, his compulsive heavy drinking, and the "blanks," the periodic blackouts of awareness, memory losses in tiny chunks that had resulted from the drinking; and all the debasing jobs as porter, servant, and general handyman that string across the five years just past. The detailed accounts given of some particularly traumatic incidents in this flood of memories are the novel's most closely autobiographical sections. In fact, Himes later reused several of these passage from the novel, only slightly rewritten (and not identified as such) in his official autobiography *The Quality of Hurt*.[29] In one of these, a minor traffic accident in Bridgeport, Connecticut, Jesse-Chester is lodged temporarily in the local jail, guilty of being an indigent, uninsured black man whose car has been rammed by a prominent citizen with a flair for small white lies:

> The desk sergeant set his bail at twenty-five dollars. "But I'm a well-known American writer," he said. "You can release me on my own recognizance."
> The desk sergeant said the law didn't permit it.
> "Should have told him you were a porter, son," Jesse reproached himself. "All Americans trust Negro porters and black mammies—even with their children." (*The Primitive*, 75; cf. *The Quality of Hurt*, 112)

Jesse lives on the borderline where the real and the unreal merge. He has long, fantastically elaborate dreams, sometimes when he is not even asleep, that are reported by the narrator in full, scrupulously psychoanalytic detail: "He dreamed he was writing a soft, sweet, lyrical, and gently humorous account of his experiences as a cook on a big country estate somewhere, and as he completed each chapter it was being printed on pale green pages of stiff Irish linen, each page with an individual hand-painted border of various ancient Egyptian designs" (*The Primitive*, 148). He drinks constantly, mostly gin in small quantities, beginning at the moment he gets up in the morning. He is never quite sober, though seldom entirely drunk. His blackouts recur throughout the novel. He is constantly finding himself somewhere without quite knowing how he got there, or what he had been doing for

29. Cf. *The Primitive*, pp. 73 77, 142–43; *The Quality of Hurt*, pp. 110–15, 119–20.

the preceding few hours. Like the protagonist of Himes's 1948 short story "Da-Da-Dee,"[30] whenever he is really "blotto" Jesse hums, or shouts, his "private dirge" (p. 96), which he calls the Da-Da-Dee; "Its basic theme," the narrator notes, "was the melody of a popular song . . . sung by Ella Fitzgerald, with words that went, *I'll get by as long as I have you* . . . but he had never known this" (p. 60).[31] Jesse is ferociously aware of white oppression, the Negro Problem, his own status as victim, but, paradoxically, he seems to despise and dislike almost all of the black people he knows, feeling himself somehow an outsider, and he has an overwhelming need to make love to a white woman, any white woman, convinced beyond all logic that the act will somehow help to restore his shattered ego. It is this unlovely obsession that drives him to seek out Kriss, even to force himself on her, ignoring her every rebuff, "He knew . . . he didn't feel a thing for her; he just wanted to sleep with a white woman again" (p. 49). Jesse finds in Kriss, though, an easily recognizable soul mate. Even in his dreams and half-dreams he has known her wrenching sense of loneliness: "—Who's Jesse Robinson?—He de one wu't died uf lonesomeness. Say fust time in hist'ry uh nigger die frum lonesomeness. In all de newspapers" (p. 24).

All of Jesse's creative capacity has been channeled into an involuntary, nonstop effort to reduce his recent frustrating experiences to a simple, intelligible verbal formula, to think his way through it to a final, absolutely convincing "answer." He had, with sure faith, followed the path prescribed for dedicated idealists, and, inexplicably, the entire world had turned fierce and savage, apparently determined to rend him into pieces, or squash him like a bug. Even after he had definitively abandoned his self-conscious efforts to be "noble" (pp. 46, 72, 78), surrendered his self-appointed role of "Dark Avenging Angel with his pen dipped in gall" (p. 23)—"That guy once wrote for publication, *I consider it my duty to write the truth as I see it*" (p. 105)[32]—and made

30. See pp. 67–69, this volume.

31. The unhappy black girl, snubbed by white coworkers in a California shipyard, in Himes's story "The Song Says 'Keep on Smiling' " (*The Crisis,* April 1945, pp. 103–4) also sang "I'll Get By as Long as I Have You."

32. Cf. Chester Himes, "*If He Hollers Let Him Go,*" *Saturday Review* 29 (February 16, 1946), p. 13, for this line.

a "separate peace" (p. 50), figuratively "signed the paper" (p. 124), abandoning "protest" forever, acceptance had still been denied him. His manuscript novel *I Was Looking for a Street*, which he had considered innocuous and private, a blameless attempt to resolve his own bewilderment in literary form—"I'd just like to find some God-damned one-storied street of simple folk whom I could understand" (p. 116)—is brutally rejected with the routine formula: "the public is fed up with protest novels" (p. 93).[33] And now he seems doomed, like a character out of some ancient myth, to endlessly seek a simple explanation for the world's rejection of Jesse Robinson, "*Some goddamned reason for all the hate, the animosity, the gratuitous ill will*" (p. 22). At times the quest, though difficult and discouraging, seems perfectly reasonable: " 'Jesse Robinson,' he said in a voice of utter futility. 'Jesse Robinson. There must be some simple thing in this life that you don't know. Some little thing. Something every other person born knows but you' " (p. 71). But this inner quest, this process of "figuring it all out," continues inexorably even when he is drunk, with nightmarish intensity: " 'What you never knew, son, what you never knew. . . .' His head seemed to burst with the effort to catch that one simple thing he never knew which in moments of extreme drunkenness was always so close" (p. 116). This quest, this ultimately rational effort, is in fact the short road to madness: "What's your plan, Charlie Chan? . . . He felt the solution was contained in one sentence. In two words, perhaps. . . . He tried combinations of words. . . . Black-love . . . black-thin . . . white-right . . . white-light . . . repeat-defeat . . . change-same" (p. 101). In the end, when he awakens from a blackout to find he has murdered Kriss, the "answer" is there at last: " 'End product of the impact of Americanism on one Jesse Robinson— black man. Your answer, son. You've been searching for it. *Black man kills white woman.* All the proof you need now. Absolutely incontrovertible behaviorism of a male human being. . . . Human beings only species of animal life where males are known to kill their females. Proof beyond all doubt. Jesse Robinson joins the human race' " (p. 158).[34] The moment of discovery, when Jesse

33. See pp. 6–8, this volume.
34. In his interview with Hoyt Fuller, p. 14, Himes indicated that he

finds Kriss dead, is, in the novel's final drastic shift of tone, a
scene in Hell:

> Then, prodded by her continued silence, he turned on her
> furiously. . . . His voice stopped short when he clutched her
> naked shoulders. Her ice-cold flesh burned his hands.
>
> His next action of which he was aware occurred two and
> a half minutes later. He was kneeling on the bed, trying to
> make her breathe by means of artificial respiration; and see-
> ing his tears dripping on the purple-lipped knife wound over
> her heart, thought she was beginning to bleed again. He felt
> such a fury of frustration he began beating her senselessly
> about the face and shoulders, cursing in a sobbing voice,
> "Breathe, Goddamn it, breathe!" (*The Primitive*, 157)

In his final, long soliloquy, Jesse laboriously explains, to himself—or perhaps to God, for he cannot prevent himself from
praying—precisely why the term that most accurately describes
him is *primitive*. The true "human being," no longer a "primitive,"
has adjusted completely to a social order in which expediency is
the only recognized value:

> "Your trouble, son," his thoughts continued, "You tried too
> hard to please. Showed right there you were a primitive. A
> human being never tries to please. Not restricted by con-
> science like a primitive. Reason why he's human. All other
> animals restricted by conscience. Call it instinct but con-
> science all the same. Reason why your own life was so
> bitter, son. Had conscience. . . . But gone now. No more
> worrying about what's right and what's wrong. Just what's
> expedient. You're human now." (*The Primitive*, 158–59)

Some years later, Himes offered a second interpretation of the
title *The Primitive*, markedly different from the one he had provided in the novel itself, but not entirely contradictory:

> . . . I was trying to . . . say that white people who still re-
> garded the American black, burdened with all the vices,
> sophistries, and shams of their white enslavers, as primitives
> with greater morality than themselves, were themselves

---

might have taken the phrase "join the human race" from a Ralph Ellison
essay, about which he had once "kidded" his friend Ellison.

idiots. . . . Obviously and unavoidably, the American black man is the most neurotic, complicated, schizophrenic, unanalyzed, anthropologically advanced specimen of mankind in the history of the world. (*The Quality of Hurt*, 285)

The Primitive is not an easy book to evaluate. In conversations with John A. Williams, who had been so engrossed when he first read *The Primitive* that he missed his stop on the subway, Himes described this novel as his "favorite book": "I didn't have any distractions with *The Primitive*. I wrote that out of a completely free state of mind from beginning to end; where I saw all the nuances of every word I put down."[35] It would be equally easy to defend or attack the thesis that *The Primitive* is also Himes's best novel. The book has evident faults—constant shifts in tone, an uncomfortable density of texture, a narrator who philosophizes, often gratuitously, and an organizational structure that is stiff and symmetrical to a point of obvious artificiality— but each of these, according to the reader's individual tastes, might equally well be regarded as virtues. *The Primitive* is, however, beyond question, the autobiographical novel in which Himes achieved the greatest degree of control over his material, perhaps because the events covered had hurt him less, marked him less profoundly, than the memories of childhood, adolescence, and prison he had dealt with in the two earlier novels. Himes did succeed, as he had not quite succeeded with Charles Taylor and Jimmy Monroe, in making Jesse Robinson a purely novelistic creation, an effective vehicle for the expression of his own deepest insights into the human condition in general. *The Primitive* is, of the three autobiographical novels, the least dependent on autobiographical interest. Its hold on the imagination is that of a novel, a product of the creative imagination, rather than that of

35. Williams, "My Man Himes," pp. 73–74. The editing and publishing process for *The Primitive*, however, was, Himes told Hoyt Fuller, one of the most difficult he had experienced in his entire writing career, necessitating his return to New York to carry on the struggle with the editors at first hand (Fuller, "Interview with Chester Himes," pp. 10, 20). He also told Fuller (p. 20) that *The Primitive* was his "favorite" book, denying at the same time that he had ever said that *Blind Man with a Pistol* was his "most important" book. Cf. Chester Himes, "My Favorite Novel," *The New York Times Book Review* (June 4, 1967), p. 7.

an autobiography, a chronicle of facts, a simple act of self-revelation. Every reader is left free to find some aspect of the incredibly complex, multilayered Jesse Robinson, a compound of rage, despair, love, and hope, that he can personally identify with. As John A. Williams put it, *The Primitive* succeeds in "attacking the sensitivities on all levels."[36] Himes's French friend, Yves Malartic, immediately after reading the manuscript, jotted down his first reactions in a letter to Himes, reactions which are at the same time effusive personal compliments and perceptive criticisms, valid for the general reader:

> Jesse is not a colored man. He's an unsuccessful writer. White ones are just like him. I know it. I am one and don't need to be colored to understand his reactions. They are exactly like mine. I thought, "How does Chester know I am and think like that." (*The Quality of Hurt*, 315–16)

36. Williams, "My Man Himes," p. 74.

5

The Continental Entertainer
The Detective Novellas
Pinktoes

I Himes and the Translators

In 1958 Chester Himes was awarded a French literary prize, the *Grand Prix de Littérature policière*, for a detective novel entitled *La Reine des pommes*, published in 1958 in a French translation by Minnie Danzas by Marcel Duhamel's Série Noire. The title of Himes's English original, according to the French edition, was *The Five-Cornered Square*, but the work had been published in America the year before with the title *For Love of Imabelle* as a paperback original by Fawcett's Gold Medal Books. A few years later it was brought out again in English, with the title *A Rage in Harlem*, by Avon in New York and Panther Books in London. In 1971 it reappeared with its original title, *For Love of Imabelle*, as a Dell paperback. Like many of the devious characters whose deeds they chronicle, Himes's detective novels tended to have a number of aliases.

The publication of *La Reine des pommes*, a book written to be translated, at the specific suggestion of a French publisher, marked Himes's entry into an entirely new publishing market, and an essentially new writing career. He was to write, in all, eleven books—more properly *novellas* than *novels*, both in their length of about fifty thousand words and in their general lightness of touch—that would be aimed primarily at readers who would read them in translation. And translations of Himes's works, his early serious novels as well as the lighter novellas, found a market, first in France, thanks to the publisher Marcel Duhamel, then throughout Europe, Latin America, and even Japan. Detective novels brought Himes not only his first significant literary award but his first experience with an open, thriving literary market as well.

Marcel Duhamel, one of the authentic geniuses in French publishing, had created a substantial demand for American detective novels in France with his Série Noire, launched shortly after the second World War. The Série Noire editions of American detective stories in translation were attractive in format, inexpensive, and usually sold between forty and fifty thousand copies. In addition, Duhamel paid both his authors and his translators, if not handsomely, at least moderately well, and regularly. For Chester Himes, who had spent some years learning exactly how small the demand was for protest and autobiographical novels by serious and ambitious black American authors, the prospect of writing both for a substantial readership and for adequate pay was overwhelmingly attractive, though the money was the decisive factor. "That's why I began writing these detective stories," Himes told John A. Williams. "The Série Noire was the best-paid series in France. So they started off paying me a thousand-dollar advance, which was the same as the Americans were paying, and they went up to fifteen hundred dollars, which was more."[1]

Marcel Duhamel, in a preface to the translated edition of one of Himes's later detective novels, provided a brief vignette of the beginning, as he remembered it:

> . . . that day in 1954 when he [Chester Himes] came to see me at #5 Sébastien-Bottin Street, handsome, rather frail in appearance, elegant, distant, and not at all at ease, the rugged, bony face lit by eyes as soft as velvet. He was looking for a solution to a very simple problem, which was becoming a bit pressing: his books were selling as badly in France as they had in the U.S., and he had to live.
>
> "Have you ever thought about writing thrillers?" I asked him.
>
> "Never," he replied. "And I would be absolutely incapable of doing it."
>
> "You're wrong, there's nothing to it," I told him, affecting an optimism which, on the basis of past experience, I was

1. John A. Williams, "My Man Himes: An Interview with Chester Himes," p. 32; cf. Hoyt Fuller, "Traveler on the Long, Rough, Lonely Old Road: An Interview with Chester Himes," p. 11.

very far from feeling. "You have the backgrounds, characters as colorful as anyone could wish, imagination. . . ."

"But don't you have to invent plots?"

"No. There's plenty going on in Harlem all the time, more than enough to take care of any problems along that line. Start with a simple street incident, a crime, or a scene in a police station. . . ."

Chester agreed to try.

Less than two weeks later he returned with a first version of *Four Cornered Square*, which was to become *La Reine des pommes*. There was enough material in it for three *Série Noire* novels. I took the liberty of offering a few suggestions on necessary cuts and, perhaps, a reworked ending.

Well, not only did he assume an attentive air, but something like a week later he came back with the finished novel, complete with a set of two or three alternative endings, all equally astonishing, and believable.

Imagination he had, an abundant surplus of it. His series of detective novels proves it.[2]

By the 1950s, when Chester Himes entered the field, the detective novel was already a rigidly defined literary subgenre. In America, half a dozen highly gifted writers, led by Dashiell Hammett and Raymond Chandler, had left it with both a distinctive atmosphere and a prescribed set of character types and standard plot structures; in France and Western Europe the awesome figure of Georges Simenon had lifted it all the way to full literary respectability. Himes had, however, few illusions as to the depth and range of literary opportunities offered by this already senescent subgenre. "It's just plain and simple violence in narrative form, you know," he remarked to John A. Williams, offering a working writer's laconic thumbnail definition, which he then proceeded to elaborate: "When I went into it, into the detective story field, I was just imitating all the other American detective story writers, other than the fact that I introduced various new angles which were my own. . . . the detective story originally

2. Marcel Duhamel, "Preface," in Chester Himes, *L'Aveugle au pistolet*, trans. Henri Robillot (Paris: Gallimard, 1970), pp. 15–16 (my translation). The original title of *La Reine des pommes* was *The Five-Cornered Square*. In his interview with Hoyt Fuller, p. 11, Himes stated that he began to write his detective stories in 1957.

in the plain narrative form—straightforward violence—is an American product. So I haven't created anything whatsoever; I just made the faces black, that's all."[3]

The heart of the subgenre, however, as Marcel Duhamel insists, is a firm contact with reality, "a point of departure that is really believable, if not actually lived,"[4] and Himes's background, his intimate contacts with every form of violence, the scores of criminals he had come to know well in prison and in the black ghettoes of Cleveland, Los Angeles, and New York, had provided him with a unique training, an almost unmatchable set of qualifications for the subgenre. In discussing his detective novels with John A. Williams, Himes insisted heavily on the vital role "memory," both voluntary and involuntary, had played:

> I began writing these series because I realized that I was a black American, and there's no way of escaping forty some odd years of experience, so I would put it to use in writing. . . .
>
> Well, then, I went back—as a matter of fact, it's like a sort of pure homesickness—I went back, I was very happy, I was living there, and it's true. I began creating also all the black scenes of my memory and my actual knowledge. I was very happy writing these detective stories, especially the first one.[5]

He chose Harlem as his scene, as Marcel Duhamel had suggested, the most glamorous and the most famous of all the black ghettoes of America, and invented two black precinct detectives, already dimly sketched in a story written long before,[6] as his counterparts to Dashiell Hammett's Sam Spade and Raymond Chandler's Philip Marlowe. Coffin Ed Johnson and Grave Digger

3. Williams, "My Man Himes," p. 49.

4. "Interview: Marcel Duhamel: le roman noir part toujours de la réalité," *Magazine littéraire* 20 (August 1968): 17 (my translation).

5. Williams, "My Man Himes," pp. 49–50.

6. See pp. 39–40, this volume. In an interview for *Publishers Weekly* in 1972, Himes suggested a slightly different origin: "The two cops, Coffin Ed Johnson and Grave-Digger [sic] Jones, are roughly based on a black lieutenant and his sergeant partner who worked the Central Avenue ghetto in L.A. back in the 1940s. My cops are just as tough, but somewhat more humane. The original pair were pitiless bastards." *Publishers Weekly* 201 (April 3, 1972): 20–21.

Jones were their names—Ed Cercueil and Fossoyeur in the French translations—and they soon won him an enormous circle of fanatically devoted readers. In all, he wrote eight novels featuring Coffin Ed and Grave Digger, between 1957 and 1969, and varied the formula slightly in another violent tale, *Run Man Run* (1959, 1966), and in the Harlem satire *Pinktoes* (1961).

It was not a simple decision to make, however, not in any way an easy choice, this total commitment to the detective novel. It meant turning aside from the high ambitions, the lofty dedication, that had kept him going for so long, but his head had been pretty thoroughly battered and he was ready for a rest. The most important aspect of the decision, however, was the fact that it meant that he would have to concentrate exclusively on the most violent and sordid aspects of black life in America. He would have to limit himself almost entirely to describing black criminals, black crime, black poverty, and black violence. It could not have been a comfortable prospect. Yet he had never been anything even remotely resembling an apologist for his people. In *The Quality of Hurt* he flatly states: "The black [American] is a new man—complex, intriguing, and not particularly likable. I find it very difficult to like American blacks myself."[7] His role, as he had seen it, had been to force his readers to an awareness of the complexity, the superior complexity, of the black American—and not at all to win sympathy and affection for the Brother—and this was a function he could continue to fulfill as he explored and exposed what went on under assorted rocks in Harlem.

Writing detective stories also meant, however, openly extolling violence—the established subgenre involved a definite ethos as well as a mythos—and this was a really substantial problem for a writer whose memories included a professionally efficient beating in a Chicago police station and many a tap from the clubs of prison guards. It could be solved only by the creation of a fictional world in which violence would be unambiguously laudable. Even so, the novel in the Coffin Ed–Grave Digger series he most enjoyed writing was the first one, *For Love of Imabelle* (*La Reine des pommes*), the only one in which Digger and Ed, the men of violence, men similar to the Sergeant Cody of *Cast the First*

7. Himes, *The Quality of Hurt*, p. 285.

Stone,[8] are still really secondary characters, and the protagonist is a fat little pacifist.

Grave Digger and Coffin Ed, with their big fists and shiny pistols, did bring Himes a measure of prosperity, small enough, but more than welcome. He wrote easily and traveled freely during the years he was writing these stories. He was constantly on the move, shifting his residence from one European city to another, with an occasional trip back to America, before he finally settled in Spain. Even John A. Williams, a firm friend, fan, and correspondent of long-standing, found it hard to keep track of the peripatetic Himes during these years, as he notes in the preface to his interview with Himes:

> Although he had won the Grand Prix for detective novels . . .
> he was still living pretty much from hand to mouth. I man-
> aged to see him once in Paris, but most often I saw him here
> [in New York City] after he arrived on the *France*. He stays
> at the Hotel Albert on 10th Street and University Place
> when he comes. In Europe I missed him often enough, for he
> would move frequently to avoid having his work disturbed
> by other expatriate Brothers. Then he would undergo peri-
> odic fits of disgust with the Parisians and go to Scandinavia
> or Holland. Sometimes . . . he went to La Ciotat near the
> Riviera to be isolated and to work.[9]

During these years Himes's financial success was to some extent contingent upon the quality of the translations his work received, and by a typically Himesian paradox, the translations were seldom more than adequate, and often much less. His writing, with its strong emphasis on content rather than niceties of style, presented only one major problem to the translator—the generous use of slang in his dialogue, the very special and subtle slang of the black American—but his translators were usually more concerned with speed than problem solving. An additional problem was that many of the translators were, of course, not only working with detective novels, a form that normally commanded little respect, but with rough typescript versions as well,

8. See pp. 167–68, this volume.
9. Williams, "My Man Himes," pp. 27–28; cf. Fuller, "Interview with Chester Himes," pp. 4, 12.

unedited first drafts of works that had not yet been published in English. Yet, even in the case of Himes's major published works, his occasional stylistic experiments were often ignored or fumbled by the translators, and the special problems involved in his choice of idiom were seldom given the attention they deserved.

In the French translation of *If He Hollers Let Him Go*, by Marcel Duhamel himself and Renée Vavasseur, Himes's first novel and his first work to be translated, there was a determined, and largely successful, effort on the part of the translators to capture that novel's major stylistic feature, identified by Duhamel as "the intensity with which the author expresses the sentiments, the personalities, and the actions and reactions of his characters, as though he were writing under intolerable pressure."[10] Unfortunately the translators' choice of a slang typical of an average French factory worker—with its connotations of membership in a debased and largely uneducated social class—as the normal speech for Bob Jones, the novel's protagonist and first-person narrator, effects an important dislocation in the machinery of the novel. Bob Jones, a former college student who still entertains hopes of an eventual law career, is distinctly middle class. Despite his fondness for black slang, he both acts and sounds like a man with a university background. His tragedy is precisely that his color makes both his education and his exceptional abilities invisible to his white employers and coworkers. "If it had come down to a point where I had to hit a paddy I'd have hit him without any thought," ruminates Bob Jones in the novel, maintaining both his cool and his impeccable grasp of grammar,[11] but in his French incarnation he seems to spit the line out through clenched teeth and lips twisted into a perpetual gutter sneer, saying, in effect, "If it had come down to a point where I had to break a prick's yap I did it without fuss."[12] In France, where the barriers between the major social classes were both rigid and highly visible, by mutual choice, the combination of a factory milieu

10. Duhamel, "Preface," in *L'Aveugle au pistolet*, p. 10 (my translation).
11. Himes, *If He Hollers Let Him Go*, p. 7.
12. Himes, *S'il braille, lâche-le . . .*, trans. Renée Vavasseur and Marcel Duhamel (Paris: Gallimard, 1972), p. 10. The line is, in French: "*Si j'en arrivais au point où il fallait que je casse la guele à un con, je le faisais sans histoire.*"

and speech patterns suited to the university or the upper bourgeoisie was, quite simply, inconceivable. But the entire tragedy of Bob Jones, black American, lay in that combination.

Margarita Garcia, Himes's principal Spanish translator, failed to respect even the most easily translatable of Himes's stylistic devices, his deliberate use of repetition. In *The Third Generation* Himes uses the phrase "the short black man" to designate Fess Taylor ten times within two pages at the beginning of Chapter 2 without any variations, but in the Spanish translation the phrase is arbitrarily varied from "*el negro bajito*" to "*el hombrecito negro.*"[13] In *The Primitive* Himes repeated verbatim the two long sentences that begin Chapter 1 at the beginning of Chapter 6 but in the Spanish translation the second sentence begins to change about halfway through in Chapter 6.[14] More seriously, even relatively banal slang is often mistranslated in the Spanish versions. For example, Jesse Robinson's comment in *The Primitive*, "No wonder the cats smoke gage," emerges in Spanish as, literally, an observation on the behavior of that ever-mysterious animal, the cat.[15]

Himes's detective novels, however, did not suffer in the translation process, particularly in France, nearly as much as his earlier, more serious work, not because the translators were any more scrupulous or any less heavy-handed but because the works themselves were deliberately unsubtle, frankly and skillfully written for a popular commercial market. There were no delicate distinctions to be blurred, no fragile nuances of meaning to be lost.

13. Himes, *La tercera generación*, translated by Margarita Garcia (Mexico City: Editorial Grijalbo, S. A., 1967), pp. 27–30; cf. Himes, *The Third Generation*, pp. 19–21.

14. Himes, *El Primitivo*, translated by Margarita Garcia (Mexico City: Editorial Grijalbo, S. A., 1967), pp. 5, 104; cf. Himes, *The Primitive*, pp. 5, 64. Yves Malartic, Himes's close friend, made a similar change in the French edition in *La fin d'un primitif*, translated by Yves Malartic (Paris: Gallimard, 1956), pp. 11, 131.

15. *El Primitivo*, p. 160; cf. Himes, *The Primitive*, p. 98. The line is, in Spanish: "*No me sorprende que hasta los gatos fumen verdal.*" In the French version (p. 197), Yves Malartic rendered the line with his usual heavy clarity, mercilessly eradicating all traces of ambiguity, intentional or otherwise: "*On comprend que dans un décor pareil les petits mecs du quartier fument du kief.*"

Like almost everything written for the subgenre, Himes's detective novels read as though they had been written with a possible film adaptation in mind. Nothing is attempted that could
not easily be accomplished in a low-budget "action" film. The
texture of the fiction is as close to that of "the movies" as any
printed flow of words can possibly get. The stories are told
almost entirely through long, uninterrupted passages of dialogue,
intermixed with short snatches of purely physical description. The
anonymous third-person narrator—the narrative technique used
in all of these works—is kept firmly in the background, rigidly
restrained from gratuitous philosophizing. There are, of course,
occasional hints of "protest" but nothing more along that line
than what a film camera can easily manage with its panning
lens, embracing scenes of white prosperity and black misery in
one short swing that creates an unmistakably clear "visual metaphor." Psychological analysis never goes much deeper than suggesting the presence or absence of sincerity, again an "in-depth"
element that any film director, working with competent professional actors, can state clearly in his own peculiar image-language
with no difficulty whatsoever. For the most part, the reader is
told nothing about Himes's Harlem characters beyond what they
look like, what they say, and what they do.

Even so, Himes's detective novels—written "to order" for the
Duhamel organization—did not pass through the translation
process entirely unscathed. Marcel Duhamel's Série Noire had
developed a definite style all its own—though Duhamel vigorously denies it in interviews[16]—and the works of all the authors fed
through the company's translation mill came out with a marked
family resemblance. The detective story genre lent itself readily
to Série Noire techniques of standardization, like the routine use
of a purely literary tough-guy vernacular that never passed out
of fashion, featuring words like *mec*, *flic*, *pétard*, etc., for *man*,
detective, and *gun*—an idiom precisely similar to that Himes had
used in the crime stories he had written while he was still in
prison a quarter of a century before.[17] In his mature detective
stories Himes had steered clear of the subgenre's notorious clichés,

16. "Interview: Marcel Duhamel," *Magazine littéraire*, p. 17.
17. See p. 19, this volume.

had kept the characters real and the language authentic, but his work invariably emerged from translation refashioned to suit the tastes of European readers who had never seen Harlem, never spoken to a black American, and who sought only amusement in its most elemental forms. Himes's detective novels remain readable and powerful in translation, but it is nevertheless almost always rather painful to compare a passage in Himes's original prose with a corresponding translated passage. The master pimp in Himes's *Blind Man with a Pistol*, for example, sounds very much like someone he probably knew: "Listen whore, that's your problem. . . . I expect you to score. How you do it is your business. If you can't collar a whitey John with them all about, I'll get myself another whore."[18] In Henri Robillot's French translation the same pimp sounds like someone you could only meet in a second-rate detective story:—*Écoute, pute, ça, ça te regarde. . . . Moi je veux que tu marques des points. T'as qu'à bien faire ton boulot. Si t'es pas de taille à te faire un miché blanc avec toutes ces souris dans le secteur, je me trouverai une autre nana.*[19]

II A World for Heroes

In *The Primitive* Himes's fictional novelist Jesse Robinson amuses himself in a random moment by composing in his mind a "typical" naturalistic black protest novel, condensed to sentence length, which he imagines himself presenting to a "liberal" white publisher, just for the sheer bitter fun of it:

> He blew laughter from his nostrils. "The nigger woke, sat up, scratched at the lice, stood up, made a wind, natured, gargled, harked, spat, sat down, ate a dishpan of stewed chitterlings, drank a gallon of lightning, hated the white folks for an hour, went out and stole some chickens, raped a white woman, got lynched by a mob, scratched his kinky head and said, Boss, Ah's tahd uh gittin' lynched." (*The Primitive*, 44)

18. Himes, *Hot Day, Hot Night*, first published as *Blind Man with a Pistol*, p. 70 (hereafter cited as *Blind*).
19. Himes, *L'Aveugle au pistolet*, p. 115.

A similar parody-condensation of a typical Chester Himes Harlem detective novel, featuring the black detectives Grave Digger Jones and Coffin Ed Johnson, might read something like this: An assorted group of sinister Harlem characters are searching for Object X. Most of them don't actually know what Object X is (it could very well turn out to be Dashiell Hammett's Maltese falcon), but they assume it's valuable, or otherwise the other people looking for it wouldn't be looking for it, and they proceed to kill everyone who gets in their way. This makes for an awful lot of killing, all over Harlem: bodies, bodies, bodies! Coffin Ed and Grave Digger join the search, either because they need one of the searchers as a witness to clear them of brutality charges or simply because it's their duty as precinct detectives to retrieve Object X, and they dash all over Harlem in their tiny, battered, black sedan, for the day or two the action lasts, thrashing and choking information out of likely suspects and innocent bystanders alike with impartial zeal and stumbling all the time over bodies, bodies, bodies. Along the way, with their extra large, extra shiny pistols, they kill off any killers who haven't already killed each other off, grab Object X (which always turns out to be the subject of a really big surprise), triumphantly clear themselves of all charges, and go home to their wives and families in their respective little white cottages in a peaceful Long Island suburb, thoroughly tired out from all that chasing around, shooting and pistol whipping, and usually more than a little battered or shot up themselves.

In *For Love of Imabelle* (1957) Object X is a padlocked trunk full of ore samples, supposedly almost pure gold, but actually all absolutely pure fool's gold. Imabelle had stolen the trunk from her philandering husband, a dangerous con man whose gang, a thoroughly vicious lot of black hoodlums, had used the trunk as part of an elaborate scheme to peddle fake gold mine stock certificates throughout the length and breadth of black America. In *The Big Gold Dream* (1959) Object X is simply a bundle of money, a black maid's winnings from playing the numbers concealed somewhere in the hand-me-down antique furniture that fills her apartment to overflowing, but it has a "double," a second bundle of money, Confederate money, concealed by somebody else in one of the ancient sofas a full century before. In *All Shot Up* (1960) Object X is once again a bundle of money, an envelope filled with campaign funds that a crooked Harlem politician has arranged to have stolen from him in a very public robbery, a robbery that develops into a savage street gun battle in the course of which the envelope mysteriously vanishes. In *The Heat's On* (1961) Object X is a string of five Hudson River eels, stuffed with about three million dollars' worth of smuggled heroin in small plastic sacks, which a dimwitted, gigantic albino janitor's helper finally throws into the furnace because "they didn't even look fit to eat."[20] In *Cotton Comes to Harlem* (1965) Object X is a bale of cotton into which a fanatic white Alabama colonel has stuffed $87,000. The "colonel" had come to Harlem to fight a resurgence of the Back-to-Africa movement—which he considered clearly "un-American," even "un-Alabamian"—and he had taken the money at gunpoint in a robbery of a fund-raising rally of the Back-to-Africa movement, only to lose both bale and money during his getaway. Why did the white-whiskered white colonel stuff the bundle of stolen money into a bale of white cotton in the first place? Possibly because "it was a symbol,"[21] suggests Lieutenant Anderson, the black detectives' erudite, tweedy, pipe-smoking white superior, who functions as a kind of resident literary critic within the novels, pointing out implausible motivations and highly unlikely coincidences whenever Coffin Ed and Grave Digger attempt to explain exactly what has been going on.

In *The Real Cool Killers* (1958) Himes switched from the Maltese falcon gambit, his favorite, to a Perry Mason type murder mystery. Coffin Ed and Grave Digger have to find out exactly which one out of a crowd of people with ample motives actually killed Ulysses Galen, the big Greek, a wealthy white sex pervert whose targets of choice were very young black girls. And in *The Crazy Kill* (1959) Himes turned to another time-honored formula: murder in the midst of a social function of the very rich and elegant. The social function is the wake of Big Joe Pul-

20. Himes, *The Heat's On*, p. 191 (hereafter referred to as *Heat*).
21. Himes, *Cotton Comes to Harlem*, p. 221 (hereafter referred to as *Cotton*).

len, gambler and dining-car chef on the Pennsylvania Railroad, who choked to death when he fell asleep and swallowed his own cigar. The wake is a wild Harlem drinking party presided over by Mamie Pullen, Joe's formidable widow; a large selection of the ghetto's well-heeled gamblers and their fast, sleek women are in attendance. The French translation of *The Crazy Kill*, by H. Robillot and J. Hérisson, is a wildly hilarious—and mildly vicious —parody of the traditional Agatha Christie murder-among-the-gentry mystery, but in Himes's original the parody is amazingly gentle and in the end manages to undercut itself. In English the characters sound just a shade less ridiculous, and that shade is important. Mamie Pullen is much older than the other Harlem hostesses who bear that name in Himes's fiction.[22] She is thin, religious, and coolly commanding. Though the preacher presiding at the wake comments, when she passes out on the maroon rug, "She ain't nothing but a whore, O Lord,"[23] she is an authentic great lady, courageous and compassionate. "She looked as though she had been washed with all waters and had come out still clean," the narrator notes (p. 9). And her stepson Johnny Perry, the principal suspect in the mystery of the murdered guest, has the physical attributes of Luther McGregor: ". . . his six-foot height lost impressiveness in his slanting shoulders and long arms. . . . In the center of his forehead was a puffed, bluish scar with ridges pronging off like immobilized octopus tentacles" (*Crazy*, 28–29).[24] Yet this frightening figure, in spite of an uncontrollable temper and an alarming capacity for murderous violence, manages to demonstrate in the course of the story that he is in fact a very sensitive and gallant gentleman. "I'm just trying to tell you that these people are not so simple as you think." (p. 31). Coffin Ed rasps angrily to Brody, the white detective from Homicide who is officially in charge of the case, and Chester Himes's intentions toward his readers in *The Crazy Kill* seem to be along very much the same lines.

In *Blind Man with a Pistol* (1969), written years after the other novels in the series in a definite anti-novel mood, bits and pieces

22. See pp. 191–92, this volume.
23. Himes, *The Crazy Kill*, p. 24 (hereafter referred to as *Crazy*).
24. See pp. 47, 49, 123, this volume.

of earlier plots are stirred together into a bafflingly thick ragout. There is both an Object X—a Gladstone bag containing the life savings of a hundred-year-old Harlem pimp—and a white pervert who is mysteriously murdered in Harlem.

Whether they are parodied or straight, however, or some ingeniously subtle or willfully perverse combination of the two, the plots of Himes's detective novels were quite obviously not constructed to bear heavy weight or to hold a reader's interest even for the very short time required to read one of these slim little books. Speed and surprise were the elements he relied on, the surprise generated by fantastic, almost-impossible-to-believe incidents, crowding in one after the other in a headlong rush, and the speed of a breakneck narrative pace that never lets up. The narrator seems obsessed with time—he takes note of it rather too often, always giving the exact hour, the precise minute, and he remarks frequently that time is running out fast, too fast, for Grave Digger and Coffin Ed—but he has in fact no respect whatsoever for chronology. The narrative line jumps back and forth in time with complete freedom. It can leap from what one set of characters is doing at one particular time to what another set of characters is doing a few hours earlier, or a few hours later, or at the same time, without so much as shifting tense. The action unfolds in perpetual, and very elastic, present time. Whenever the narrative line shifts, and it shifts drastically every five or six pages, the move is always to the point of maximum contrast, without regard to chronology.

The fantastic incidents create an atmosphere that is a blend of humor, fantasy, reluctant horror, and the exaggerated earnestness typical of the you-ain't-heard-nothing-yet brand of roadside raconteur, a dim but glittering figure out of a nation's almost forgotten past. However sturdy, muscular, and infinitely flexible his own imagination may be, the reader who longs for surprises is never disappointed, but, though credibility takes many a severe beating, it is never allowed to fall by the wayside. The narrator's ever-ready special plea, his favorite rickety rationalization, is that the milieu itself is truly extraordinary—"It was Harlem, where anything might happen" (Blind, 50)—but, in fact, nothing does happen in Himes's Harlem, however fantastic it may seem, that is not at least a remote possibility in the truly extraordinary world we all live in. One often has the uncomfortable feeling that the author might well have read of the incident in some unlikely place, perhaps in the files of a defunct newspaper during his years as a WPA researcher, or in some obscure medical journal gathering dust in a doctor's waiting room, or that he might even have seen it happen himself or talked to a man who had seen it. . . .

Grave Digger and Coffin Ed are pursuing a thief fleeing on a motorcycle, dangerously gunning their little black car over the frozen, icy surface of one of the highways that leads out of Harlem. The motorcycle driver swerves past a truck carrying sheet metal, the edge of the metal extending a bit to the side, to form a kind of "blade": "He was hitting more than fifty-five miles an hour, and the blade severed his head from his body as though he had been guillotined. His head rolled halfway up the sheets of metal while his body kept astride the seat and his hands gripped the handlebars."[25] The headless motorcycle driver continues on his way, as his body "gradually . . . spewed out its blood and the muscles went limp," turns off the highway back into the streets of Harlem, and finally crashes into a jewelry store sign that reads: "*We Will Give Credit to the Dead.*"

A Harlem hoodlum is stabbed in the head and walks away from it: "But for the bone knife-handle sticking from one temple and two inches of blade from the other, he looked like the usual drunk" (*Shot*, 127). He is scolded by a few passersby, who think it's all a bad joke, but finally winds up in the hospital, to be operated on by unbelieving doctors, who decide to leave the knife in place "until an encystment had formed about it in the brain": "There was no record of such an operation being successful, and brain specialists all over the country had been alerted to the case" (p. 152).

Big Smiley, a gigantic Harlem bartender, is slashed by a little old man with a knife; he severs the knifeman's arm with one blow of a huge axe he keeps concealed behind the bar:

25. Himes, *All Shot Up*, p. 84 (hereafter referred to as *Shot*).

The little knifeman . . . . was too drunk to realize the full impact. He saw that the lower part of his arm had been chopped off. . . . He thought Big Smiley was going to chop at him again.

"Wait a minute, you big mother-raper, till Ah finds my arm!" he yelled. "It got my knife in his hand."

He dropped to his knees and began scrambling about the floor with his one hand, searching for his severed arm. Blood spouted from his jerking stub as though from the nozzle of a hose.[26]

When a car strikes a pedestrian in Himes's Harlem he is apt to fly "through the air like an over-inflated football" (*Cotton*, 12), sometimes winding up stuck fast to a distant wall (*Shot*, 7, 44). Not all of the fantastic incidents are sanguinary, however. Sometimes the surprise is the harmless outcome of an apparent disaster, like a man hurtling to the street from a tenement window, only to land safely in a massive basket of very soft bread:

Time passed.

Slowly the surface of the bread began to stir. A loaf rose and dropped over the side of the basket to the sidewalk as though the bread had begun to boil. Another squashed loaf followed.

Slowly, the man began erupting from the basket like a zombie rising from the grave. His head and shoulders came up first. He gripped the edges of the basket, and his torso straightened. He put a leg over the side and felt for the sidewalk with his foot. The sidewalk was still there. He put a little weight on his foot to test the sidewalk. The sidewalk was steady. (*Crazy*, 7)

And the unceasing effort of every Harlemite to outwit every other Harlemite may produce a bit of humor, to go along with the surprise:

To one side of the entrance to the movie theater an old man had a portable barbecue pit made out of a perforated washtub attached to the chassis of a baby carriage. The grill was covered with sizzling pork ribs. . . .

Another old man, clad in his undershirt, had crawled onto

26. Himes, *The Real Cool Killers*, p. 8 (hereafter referred to as *Killers*).

the marquee of the movie, equipped with a fishing pole, line, sinker and hook and was fishing for ribs as though they were fish. (*Blind*, 95–96)

However, fantasy and realism must cohabit, albeit reluctantly, and a body that has been improbably catapulted into a wall by a speeding hit-and-run car is still an appalling sight, and completely real, as real as the sober, grim men who have to move it:

> Grave Digger clutched one arm, Coffin Ed the other; the two detectives from Homicide took a leg apiece. The body was stiff as a plaster cast. They tried to move it gently, but the face was firmly stuck. They tugged, and suddenly the body fell.
>
> They laid the corpse on its back. The black skin of the cheeks framing the cockscomb of frozen blood had turned a strange powdery gray. Drops of frozen blood clung to the staring eyeballs.
>
> "My God!" one of the Homicide detectives muttered, stepped to the curb and vomited.
>
> The others swallowed hard. (*Shot*, 44)

Death is always real, always unlovely in these oddly antic tales of mayhem. The shocking reality of the murders described is perhaps the most important of the "new angles" Himes felt he had introduced into the subgenre.[27] "He didn't fall like they do in the motion pictures; he just collapsed," explains a homosexual bartender who has just seen his former boy friend shot to death on the street outside the bar, and even Coffin Ed and Grave Digger are moved by his grief:

> "What in the hell were you doing then? Hiding when it was all over?"
>
> The bartender lowered his eyes. When his voice came it was so low they had to lean forward to hear it. "I was crying," he confessed.
>
> For a moment neither Grave Digger nor Coffin Ed had anywhere to look.
>
> Then Grave Digger asked, in a voice unnecessarily harsh, "Did you see the license of the Buick, by any chance?" (*Shot*, 37)

27. See p. 209, this volume.

Their capacity for suffering humanizes all of the strange figures who surface briefly in the savage, funny, and bloody world of Himes's detectives.

The central core of reality, as solid as bedrock within all of these stories, the firm foundation in which all of the fantasy is securely anchored, is Harlem itself. Himes had lived in Harlem for only a very few relatively short periods during the years immediately preceding his departure for Europe in 1953, but he knew this city within a city as only a compulsive walker, a tireless observer, can come to know a dense, crowded modern city. He knew it in meticulous detail, street by street, block by block, in spots almost house by house, as Dickens had known London and Joyce had known Dublin. To be sure, the Harlem of the novels, like Dickens's fictional London and Joyce's fictional Dublin, owed as much to exaggeration and imagination as it did to firsthand observation, but it never ceased to be immediately recognizable, totally real, albeit a bit heightened, a trifle retouched, here and there. The essential recognizability of Himes's Harlem, his "big turbulent sea of black humanity" (*Cotton*, 113) persists even when a few random details from Cleveland intrude—like the names of the players in the dice game in *For Love of Imabelle*[28]—or when the sheer density of unleashed violence displayed irresistibly calls to mind the closed, claustrophobic, and viciously turbulent society that was the prison of *Cast the First Stone*. Himes's Harlem, with its colorful, picturesque, and suffering people, the people who "had been forced to live there, in all the filth and degradation, until their lives had been warped to fit" (*Blind*, 233), is even more dangerous a place than Jimmy Monroe's prison at the height of the riots that followed the great fire:

> Even at past two in the morning, "The Valley," that flat lowland of Harlem east of Seventh Avenue, was like the frying pan of hell. Heat was coming out of the pavement, bubbling from the asphalt; and the atmospheric pressure was pushing it back to earth like the lid on a pan.
> Colored people were cooking in their overcrowded, over-

28. *The Quality of Hurt*, p. 36. Himes, *For Love of Imabelle*, p. 25 (hereafter referred to as *Imabelle*).

priced tenements; cooking in the streets, in the after-hours joints, in the brothels; seasoned with vice, disease and crime.

An effluvium of hot stinks arose from the frying pan and hung in the hot motionless air, no higher than the rooftops— the smell of sizzling barbecue, fried hair, exhaust fumes, rotting garbage, cheap perfumes, unwashed bodies, decayed buildings, dog-rat-and-cat offal, whiskey and vomit, and all the old dried-up odors of poverty.

Half-nude people sat in open windows, crowded on the fire escapes, shuffled up and down the sidewalks, prowled up and down the streets in dilapidated cars.

It was too hot to sleep. Everyone was too evil to love. And it was too noisy to relax and dream of cool swimming holes and the shade of chinaberry trees. The night was filled with the blare of countless radios, the frenetic blasting of spasm cats playing in the streets, hysterical laughter, automobile horns, strident curses, loudmouthed arguments, the screams of knife fights. (*Heat*, 25)

Lieutenant Anderson, who is as much out of place in Harlem as Coffin Ed and Grave Digger are thoroughly at home—"Anderson's face was too sensitive for police work" (*Blind*, 138)—often finds that just reading the reports that come into his pleasant little office can be a bit much:

[Anderson] then looked from one detective to the other. "What the hell's going on today? It's only ten o'clock in the evening and judging from the reports it's been going on like this since morning." He leafed through the reports, reading charges: "Man kills his wife with an ax for burning his breakfast pork chop . . . man shoots another man demonstrating a recent shooting he had witnessed . . . man stabs another man for spilling beer on his new suit . . . man kills self in a bar playing Russian roulette with a .32 revolver . . . woman stabs man in stomach fourteen times, no reason given . . . woman scalds neighboring woman with pot of boiling water for speaking to her husband . . . man arrested for threatening to blow up subway train because he entered wrong station and couldn't get his token back—"

"All colored citizens," Coffin Ed interrupted.

Anderson ignored it. "Man sees stranger wearing his own new suit, slashes him with a razor," he read on. (*Cotton*, 19)

Even for the two tough black detectives, just possibly the two toughest men alive, some aspects of Himes's city of the damned, the outcast and the abused, can prove too severe a test for casual equanimity, or even ice-cold ghetto "cool":

> Children ran down the street, the dirty street littered with rotting vegetables, uncollected garbage, battered garbage cans, broken glass, dog offal—always running, ducking and dodging. God help them if they got caught. Listless mothers stood in the dark entrances of tenements and swapped talk about their men, their jobs, their poverty, their hunger, their debts, their Gods, their religions, their preachers, their children, their aches and pains, their bad luck with the numbers and the evilness of white people. Workingmen staggered down the sidewalks filled with aimless resentment, muttering curses, hating to go to their hotbox hovels but having nowhere else to go.
> "All I wish is that I was God for just one mother-raping second," Grave Digger said, his voice cotton-dry with rage.
> "I know," Coffin Ed said. "You'd concrete the face of the mother-raping earth and turn white folks into hogs."
> "But I ain't God," Grave Digger said, pushing into the bar. (*Cotton*, 47–48)

But Himes's Harlem has many faces, and a fair number of them are passably seductive. The bars and nightclubs are enough to make Job, boils and blisters and all, scream for joy and join the dancers:

> The jukebox was giving out with a stomp version of "Big-Legged Woman." Saxophones were pleading; the horns were teasing; the bass was patting; the drums were chatting; the piano was catting, laying and playing the jive, and a husky female voice was shouting:
> "*. . . you can feel my thigh*
> *But don't you feel up high.*"
> Happy-tail women were bouncing out of their dresses on the high bar stools. (*Killers*, 55–56)

There are even a few luxury buildings and apartments that are, literally, staggeringly ornate: "there wasn't anything serene in that violently colored room. The overstuffed pea green furniture garnished with pieces of blonde wood fought it out with the bright red carpet, but the eyes that had to look at it were the losers" (*Crazy*, 86). Himes's concern for local color even goes so far as reproducing a complete "soul food" restaurant menu, and giving detailed instructions on how to play the card game called Georgia Skin (*Crazy*, 59–60, 109).

In his conversations with John A. Williams, Himes expressed strong dissatisfaction with the first attempts to make a screen version of one of his Harlem detective stories. "Are you pleased with the present screenplay of *Cotton Comes to Harlem?*" queried Williams. "Well, no one could be pleased with that," fired back Himes, "But I don't know enough about screenplays to know what it'll be like when it's finished."[29] His principal source of dissatisfaction was with the perfunctory treatment accorded Coffin Ed and Grave Digger:

> ... the main purpose of Goldwyn [Samuel Goldwn, Jr., the producer] is to make a series of movies of Coffin Ed Smith [*sic*, for Johnson] and Grave Digger Jones; he wants to keep them alive. But if this is the purpose of the first movie, they are dead because they are of no consequence in the movie. He has to bring them out stronger if he wants to keep them.[30]

As it turned out, in the film itself, this proved to be no problem at all. The actors chosen for the roles—Godfrey Cambridge as Digger and Raymond St. Jacques as Coffin Ed—had built their careers on their ability to dominate the films they appeared in with no dependence at all on strongly written parts. Both had developed stage presence that went far beyond charismatic, all the way to hypnotic, and they managed to upstage the film's heady combination of erotic nude scenes and noisy gunfights with little more than exchanges of sidelong glances. Himes's criticism, however, might be applied with equal justice to the novels as he had written them. The little books devoted to the adventures of Coffin Ed and Grave Digger add up to a total of more than half a million words, but the two detectives remain to the end, in many ways, shadowy and elusive figures, more adumbrated than defined. Though the reader can form, by as-

29. Williams, "My Man Himes," p. 54.
30. Ibid., p. 55.

siduously collecting all the details dropped along the way, reasonably clear impressions of what they look like, how they operate, and why, there remain unresolved a number of contradictions and inconsistencies, and more than a few omissions.

The most obvious apparent contradiction involves what would seem to be the least complex aspect of any literary characterization: physical appearance. We are told, in every novel, that like all good detectives Coffin Ed and Grave Digger are basically unremarkable in appearance and that they are so definitely of the same type they are almost indistinguishable. In fact there is a mildly depressing sameness in the capsule physical descriptions of the pair that are routinely given on the occasion of their first appearance in the various novels. In *For Love of Imabelle* (1957), the first novel in the series, the narrator sets the pattern: "Both were tall, loose-jointed, sloppily dressed, ordinary-looking dark-brown colored men" (p. 52). In the novels that follow there is practically no variation at all in the wording of these first-impression, general descriptions. In *The Real Cool Killers* (1958), the description, is "two tall, lanky, loose-jointed detectives," looking "like big-shouldered plowhands in Sunday suits" (p. 14), and in *The Crazy Kill* (1958), it is "two tall, lanky colored men dressed in black mohair suits that looked as though they'd been slept in" (p. 27), and in *The Heat's On* (1961), "two big loose-jointed colored men wearing dark battered felt hats and wrinkled black alpaca suits," who run "in identical flat-footed lopes" (p. 10). They are always first described as a pair, almost a unit, with heavy stress on their basic ordinariness and similarity. Yet, in the first novel of the series, *For Love of Imabelle*, a very drastic—and rather mechanical—point of difference between them was established with overwhelming emphasis, when a hoodlum threw a glassful of acid into Coffin Ed's face, leaving him permanently disfigured (p. 83). Despite the best efforts of the plastic surgeons, Coffin Ed's face remains something out of a nightmare:

> The acid scars had been covered by skin grafted from his thigh. But the new skin was a shade or so lighter than his natural face skin and it had been grafted on in pieces. The result was that Coffin Ed's face looked as though it had been

made up in Hollywood for the role of the Frankenstein monster. (*Shot*, 17)

Allusions to Ed's deformity—"His acid-burned face looked like a Mardi Gras masque to scare little children. . . . He looked like the dead killer in the play *Winterset*, coming up out of East River" (*Cotton*, 116–17)—are scattered throughout the novels, never very far from the passages that affirm the banal ordinariness and basic similarity of the two detectives' appearance. Sometimes, in fact, the rival notations reside peacefully in the same passage:

> [Grave Digger was] a big, rough, dangerous man in need of a shave, clad in a rumpled black suit and an old black hat, the bulge of a big pistol clearly visible on the heart side of his broad-shouldered frame.
>
> Coffin Ed looked the same; they could have been cast from the same mould with the exception of Coffin Ed's acid-burned face that was jerking with the tic that came whenever he was tense. (*Cotton*, 165–66)

It is hard to see how Coffin Ed, particularly when he is "tense," "the skin of his face jumping like a snake's belly over fire" (*Cotton*, 38), could really look very much like anybody else, but detective-story readers need a great deal of faith. Besides, Digger and Ed work the night shift, in a dark city of dark, battered people, and they are often almost invisible anyway, cruising silently in their nondescript, battered, souped-up, little black car:

> The car scarcely made a sound; for all its dilapidated appearance the motor was ticking almost silently. It passed along practically unseen, like a ghostly vehicle floating in the dark, its occupants invisible.
>
> This was due in part to the fact that both detectives were almost as dark as the night, and they were wearing lightweight black alpaca suits and black cotton shirts. (*Blind*, 41)

In fact, even their handkerchiefs are black, like the bandannas of Western gunmen (*Cotton*, 198).

Though the considerable solidity and depth that the characters of Digger and Ed gradually acquire stem almost entirely from the

dialogue and action of the novels, a few assorted items of background data do pop up from time to time, usually in the form
of random reminiscences, either their own or those of old friends
or acquaintances. When Mamie Pullen is brought to the station—
the 126th Street precinct—to answer questions about the murder
at Big Joe's wake, she proves to be a mine of information in this
regard:

> Then she looked up to see the face of the cop . . . and ex-
> claimed, "Lord bless my soul, you're little Digger Jones.
> I've known you ever since you were a little shavetailed kid
> on 116th Street. I didn't know you were the one they called
> Grave Digger."
> Grave Digger grinned sheepishly, like a little boy caught
> stealing apples.
> "I've grown up now, Aunt Mamie."
> "Doesn't time fly. As Big Joe always used to say; *Tempers
> fugits*. You must be all of thirty-five years old now."
> "Thirty-six. And here's Eddy Johnson, too. He's my part-
> ner."
> Coffin Ed stepped forward into the light. Mamie was
> stunned at sight of his face.
> "God in heaven!" she exclaimed involuntarily. "What
> hap—" then caught herself.
> "A hoodlum threw a glass of acid in my face." He
> shrugged. "Occupational hazard, Aunt Mamie. I'm a cop. I
> take my chances." (*Crazy*, 34–35)

The detectives' background, like their appearance, is presented as
essentially identical, and, in this case, the identity conceals no
gaping flaws. They are veterans of World War II, born about
1922 in New York City and raised in Harlem (*Cotton*, 44). They
attended a P.S. on 112th Street together, in "the late 1930s—the
'depression' years" (*Heat*, 161). Digger can still dance "the intricate steps of an old-time jitterbug with great abandon" (*Shot*,
103), and both are enthusiastic jazz buffs, able to pick out
the styles of favorite instrumentalists on juke-box records (*Heat*
161; *Cotton*, 142). They both spent some time in France while
they were in the Army and speak passable French (*Shot*, 49; *Cot-*

ton, 143). Their method of controlling crowds by shouting "Straighten up!" and "Count off!" suggests they may have been M.P.'s, but this is never made definite. They owe their promotions to the rank of detective, in the late 1950s, to their army records and "marks of eighty-five and eighty-seven percent in [their] civil service examinations," plus some political pull (*Shot*, 98). In the late 1960s, when the series ends, they are still awaiting a second promotion:

> After twelve years as first grade precinct detectives they hadn't been promoted. Their raises in salaries hadn't kept up with the rise of the cost of living. They hadn't finished paying for their houses. Their private cars had been bought on credit. (*Blind*, 124)

Their houses are only a few blocks apart, in either Astoria (*Heat*, 58) or Jamaica (*Killers*, 44) on Long Island, and their idea of fun on their days off is to go together "to the pistol range at headquarters and practice shooting" (*Cotton*, 159). They own matching pistols that look like they could "kill a rock,"[31] each a "long-barreled, nickel-plated, brass-lined .38 revolver on a .44 frame" (*Cotton*, 17), custom-made. Their wives, Molly Johnson and Stella Jones, are close friends and go shopping together (*Cotton*, 159). Coffin Ed has one daughter, Evelyn, born about 1942, who has a brief fling at delinquency at sixteen (*Killers*, pp. 36ff), and Digger has two daughters, slightly younger than Ed's and apparently much less trouble (*Cotton*, 158). Ed dresses with great care when not on duty (*Heat*, 114) and has at least one lady friend in Harlem (*Blind*, 186–91). He is more at ease with women than Digger and enjoys joking with them (*Shot*, 105, *Heat*, 31). Digger seems closer to his wife, who is always a bit "frightened and alarmed" when he goes on duty (*Cotton*, 164). He is a lot more solemn than Ed, but he unwinds rapidly at the wheel of a car, like a long-frustrated demolition derby racer (*Shot*, 64). They both enjoy "soul food," Digger usually ordering for Ed (*Cotton*, 141). They never quarrel, never argue, never even disagree. Their

31. *Imabelle*, 59; *Killers*, 49; see p. 20, this volume.

friendship is as absolute as their dependence on each other. Neither ever forgets for a moment just how dangerous their job is: "On duty all of [their] senses were constantly on the alert. Coffin Ed had once summed it up by saying, 'Blink once and you're dead.' To which Grave Digger had rejoined, 'Blink twice and you're buried' " (*Heat*, 57; cf. *Blind*, 9).

The most basic, and important, of the contradictions and inconsistencies in the characterizations of Digger and Ed involve their operating methods, the standard procedures they follow in preserving law and order, and putting down villainy, in Harlem. Justice could hardly be reached by more devious paths or more questionable methods. In order to maintain their massive network of "stool pigeons"—almost all of them very active con men and petty thieves—Digger and Ed routinely use their authority and influence to shield some of the choicest villains in Harlem from arrest and prosecution, in exchange for random bits of information about the few criminals they personally consider worth pursuing. They even have a private supplier of illegal drugs, their personal "pusher," who keeps the addicts among their stool pigeons well supplied and fully operative, and in *The Crazy Kill* they indignantly scold their pusher for excessive honesty:

> On the way out, [Coffin Ed] said to the old lady who'd let them in, "Cut down on Gigolo, Ma, he's getting so hopped he's going to blow his top one day."
> "Lawd, I ain't no doctor," she complained. "I don't know how much they needs. I just sells it if they got the money to pay for it. You know, I don't use that junk myself."
> "Well, cut down anyway," Grave Digger said harshly. "We're just letting you run because you keep our stool pigeons supplied."
> "If it wasn't for these stool pigeons you'd be out of business," she argued. "The cops ain't goin' to never find out nothing if don't nobody tell 'em."
> "Just put a little baking soda in that heroin, and don't give it to them straight," Grave Digger said. "We don't want these boys blind. And let us out this hole, we're in a hurry."
> (*Crazy*, 80–81)

Slapping, punching, pistol whipping, and worse are part of their standard approach toward witnesses, suspects, and even the general public. "I'm just trying to get your attention is all," Coffin Ed explains, when a witness complains about being slapped hard "a half-dozen times" (*Cotton*, 74). Ed, as a psychological aftereffect of his acid burns, tends to get carried away rather easily, and Digger often has to restrain him pretty vigorously to keep their witnesses in talking condition:

> "Easy, man, easy!" Grave Digger shouted, realizing instantly that Coffin Ed was sealed in such a fury he couldn't hear. He dropped the telephone and wheeled, hitting Coffin Ed across the back of the neck with the edge of his hand just a fraction of a second before he'd have crushed her windpipe. (*Cotton*, 39)

Digger, however, has a maniacal temper of his own, which he makes no effort to control, as an effeminate barman learns in *The Real Cool Killers* when he calls Digger "you mean rude grumpy man":

> The muscles in Grave Digger's face began to jump. . . . He stood up with his heels hooked into the rungs of the barstool and leaned over the bar. He caught the barman by the front of his red silk shirt as he was trying to dance away. The shirt ripped down the seam with a ragged sound but enough held for him to jerk the barman close to the bar.
> "You got too goddamned much to say, Tarbelle," he said in a thick cotton voice, and slapped the barman spinning across the circular enclosure with the palm of his open hand.
> "He didn't have to do that," the first woman said. (*Killers*, 64)

Even other policemen are not immune, when they have the bad taste to talk too much or say the wrong thing:

> "All I can say about it is it looks like hair," the lieutenant said.
> "Looks like real nigger hair," the flip cop said.
> "If you use that word again I'll kick your teeth down your throat," Coffin Ed said.
> The cop bristled. "Knock whose teeth—"

He never got to finish. Coffin Ed planted a left hook in his stomach and crossed an overhand right to the jaw. The cop went down on his hips; his head leaned slowly forward until it stopped between his knees.

No one said anything. (*Shot*, 42)

When Ed and Digger are dealing with genuine suspects, however, there is a suitable escalation in the level of violence, particularly if the two detectives happen to be a bit upset themselves. In *The Crazy Kill* they subject a cocky and insolent young gambler named Chink Charlie, in the police station's interrogation room, to a peculiarly sadistic procedure that Chester Himes himself had experienced, in 1928, in a Chicago police station after he had been arrested as a robbery suspect:

[Grave Digger] stopped talking and they waited for Chink to answer.

Chink didn't speak.

Suddenly, without warning, Coffin Ed stepped forward from the shadows and chopped Chink across the back of his neck with the edge of his hand. It knocked Chink forward, stunning him, and Coffin Ed grabbed him beneath the arms to keep him from falling on his face.

Grave Digger slid quickly from the desk and handcuffed Chink's ankles, drawing the bracelets tight just above the ankle bones. Then Coffin Ed handcuffed Chink's hands behind his back.

Without saying another word, they opened the door, lifted Chink from the chair and hung him upside down from the top of the door by his handcuffed ankles, so that the top part of the door split his legs down to his crotch. His back lay flat against the bottom edge, with the lock bolt sticking into him.

Then Grave Digger inserted his heel into Chink's left armpit and Coffin Ed did the same with his right, and they pushed down gradually.

Chink . . . tried to stand it. He tried to scream, but he had waited too late. All that came out was his tongue and he couldn't get it back. He began choking, and his eyes began to bulge. (*Crazy*, 122)[32]

32. See p. 22, this volume.

Like Himes himself, Chink agrees to talk. Coffin Ed and Digger are, just possibly, even more brutal with women. "I'll pistol-whip your face until no man ever looks at you again," Digger promises Imabelle and she sees at once that he means it, and talks (*Imabelle*, 158). In *The Heat's On*, Ed, believing for the moment that Digger has been shot to death by white syndicate gunmen, abandons all restraint. He strips a young black woman, a witness, of all her clothes and cuts a long shallow line across her throat with a knife. She faints.

> Then he slapped her until she came to.
> He knew that he had gone beyond the line . . . he knew that what he was doing was unforgivable. But he didn't want any more lies.
> She lay rigid, looking at him with hate and fear.
> "Next time I'll cut it to the bone," he said.
> A shudder ran over her body as though a foot had stepped on her grave.
> "All right, I'll tell you," she said. (*Heat*, 160)

In the same novel, a sleazy pimp named Red Johnny fares even worse when he defies the heartsick, grieving Coffin Ed: "He didn't see the motion of Coffin Ed's left hand at all as it came from the front with Grave Digger's pistol and smashed the barrel in a backhanded swing straight across his loose-lipped mouth. The whole front line of Red Johnny's teeth caved into his mouth, two of the bottom teeth flew out sidewise like corn popping, and Red Johnny spun over backward" (*Heat*, 124).

When they begin to pull the triggers of their oversized pistols, always with phenomenal accuracy, Coffin Ed and Grave Digger are even more terrifying. Grave Digger tracks down Hank, the black hoodlum who threw the acid into Ed's face, and shoots out both his eyes:

> Hank . . . swung up the black snout of his .38 automatic, knowing that he didn't have a chance.
> Before it had cleared his hip, Grave Digger shot him through the right eye with his own pistol held in his right hand. While Hank's body was jerking from the bullet in the brain, Grave Digger said, "For you, Ed," took dead aim with

Coffin Ed's pistol held in his left hand, and shot the dying
killer through the staring left eye. (*Imabelle*, 178–79)

Coffin Ed, suspended upside down from a tenement roof by
wires attached to his ankles, fires through a windowpane at
Sheik—a teenage hoodlum who is pressing a knife to the throat
of Ed's daughter—and places the bullet "in the exact center of
Sheik's forehead between his two startled yellow cat's eyes";
Sheik's knife drops harmlessly from his nerveless hand, clattering
across a nearby table. "They don't have any reflexes when you
shoot them in the head," Ed explains (*Killers*, 142–43). They can
also use their guns, though, on occasion, in a spirit of pure fun.
Ed playfully shoots the decorative chrome off a prominent black
racketeer's car, just to force him to pull over (*Killers*, 14). When
the Alabama colonel parades through Harlem, Grave Digger
sends the man's hat dancing down the street by repeatedly shooting holes in it and then shoots it out of his hand when he tries
to pick it up (*Cotton*, 162).

However, their rare displays of good humor and their official
alliance with the forces of justice and right are obviously not
enough to keep the reader's sympathy firmly on their side through
all this mayhem. They too must take lumps, must appear often
as underdogs, even victims. And so Ed is hideously scarred with
acid, and Digger is shot up so badly he needs six months to recover (*Cotton*, 16). And, fairly often, they run into someone who
is really, really tough, like the gigantic and virtuous black sailor
called Roman in *All Shot Up*, who, defending his ladylove from
questioning, grabs Ed and Digger by one leg each, lifts them in
the air and slams their heads into the ceiling (pp. 90–91).

The reader's immediate sympathy, however, is not really the
problem—the writer's skill and the artifices of the genre are
adequate to deal with any passing qualms—but Grave Digger's
and Coffin Ed's wanton brutality in the pursuit of justice also
raises some abstract questions as to the "statement" the novels
make, either intentionally or unintentionally. "Fascists!" screams
one witness-suspect, when he finally manages to clear his throat
after Coffin Ed has finished choking him (*Blind*, 117). And the
charge, at first glance, appears to carry some weight. Fascists, in
the most elemental terms, are simply those who believe there

are a great many bad people in the world and that violence should be used against them—and that certainly sounds like Grave Digger and Coffin Ed. Moreover, the two detectives spend a fair amount of time rationalizing and justifying their actions, in terms that are often rigidly authoritarian, if not totalitarian. They believe that society's principal problem is its war against "criminals" or "hoodlums," members of a dangerous subgroup who are easily distinguishable from the "innocent," i.e., the rest of us, by their violent, troublemaking tendencies. "Life could be great but there are hoodlums abroad" (p. 46), remarks Digger, in a characteristically sententious vein in *Cotton Comes to Harlem*. In *All Shot Up* Digger answers an indignant Harlem citizen's sputtering protests—"You p'licemens . . . whippin' innocent folkses' heads with your big pistols"—with a firm and dignified "Not if they're innocent" (p. 19). In *The Real Cool Killers*, a novel in which Coffin Ed shoots a teenager to death for facetiously tossing some perfume on him—a practical joke that was obviously in very poor taste—Digger confidently defends his partner before the police commissioner's inquiry board with the same calm affirmation, "He was never rough on anybody in the right" (p. 149). In *The Heat's On*, when both Digger and Ed are brought before the commissioner to answer brutality charges—Digger had punched a dwarf, a criminal dwarf, in the stomach, just once, while Ed was holding the dwarf's arms pinioned behind him, and the criminal dwarf, quite unexpectedly, died—Digger can scarcely control his indignation at the officials' mealy mouthed hypocrisy, "You think you can have a peaceful city letting criminals run loose?" (p. 59). Coffin Ed, looking down at the body of an innocent young man killed in a robbery in *Cotton Comes to Harlem*, mournfully and angrily intones: "This is what happens when cops get soft on hoodlums" (p. 31). When Digger, in a momentary lapse, is tactless enough to suggest that Ed may be treating an obvious criminal type just a little bit too roughly, Ed solemnly reminds his partner: "The law was made to protect the innocent" (*Cotton*, 136).

The two detectives' moral judgments are simplistic and unsubtle, confidently, even smugly, righteous. Yet they are neither simple nor insensitive men. Coffin Ed goes out in the hall and cries when his feelings are hurt in *The Crazy Kill* (p. 104), and in *The Heat's On* he faints when he is told that radio reports of Digger's death were false, a hoax, an artful stratagem by white detectives. Digger, in *The Big Gold Dream*, is severely shaken when an intern emphatically suggests that his insistence on questioning an injured witness is "heartless": " 'Heartless,' he repeated to himself as though it worried him."[33] And, several times, Digger brings literary allusions into their conversations, apt and accurate references to Gorki's *Bystander* (*Shot*, 101)—a work that also preoccupied Jesse Robinson in *The Primitive*[34]—and to Hemingway's *For Whom the Bell Tolls* (*Heat*, 85). Their response to music, particularly the "jungle" of jazz, is sophisticated, even philosophical:

> . . . the two saxes started swapping fours with the rhythm always in the back. "Somewhere in that jungle is the solution to the world," Coffin Ed said. "If we could only find it."
> "Yeah, it's like the sidewalks trying to speak in a language never heard. But they can't spell it either."
> "Naw," Coffin Ed said. "Unless there's an alphabet for emotion." (*Cotton*, 45)

But, in their moral outlook, they belong to a simpler, more brutally direct age. They are throwbacks to Americans of the past, earnest and upright men with rigid, uncomplicated ethical codes, who sometimes found lynch law both necessary and natural. Chester Himes's own mother, whose reaction to the crimes he committed in adolescence was unequivocally moral—"she did not excuse me . . . she felt I should be punished" (*The Quality of Hurt*, 42)—would not have found Grave Digger's and Coffin Ed's moralistic rationalizations very difficult to understand or accept.

But Digger and Ed are heroes. If they lived in the real world, it might be more accurate to call them fascists, thugs, or vigilantes, but they live instead in the very special world of literary heroes, a world of the imagination, in which the forces of right and the forces of evil finally have it out, tooth and claw, and the forces of

33. Himes, *The Big Gold Dream*, p. 148 (hereafter referred to as *Gold*).
34. Himes, *The Primitive*, pp. 22, 23; cf. Maxim Gorki, *Bystander*, trans. Bernard G. Guerney (New York: The Literary Guild, 1930), pp. 103, 113, 114, 134, 304, 435, 505, 556, 718.

right, represented by the heroes, inevitably triumph. The detective-story reader is never unduly disturbed by the horrendous roughness of detective heroes because he knows that in the end all will be well. Object X will be retrieved, the villains will be caught and punished—usually both at the same time—and it will turn out that every one of the people the detectives had to hurt along the way richly deserved it. And Digger and Ed do come up with some uniquely satisfying resolutions to the problems they wrestle with. In *The Real Cool Killers* Digger decides to shield from prosecution the real killer of the white sex pervert, when he discovers that it was one of the young black girls the murdered man had tortured. He threatens to resign if the police commissioner does not accept his conclusion that the big Greek was killed by a young hoodlum testing his zip gun, a zip gun the ballistics lab says could not possibly have fired the .32 caliber bullet found in the victim, and he even checks to make sure the pathetic young murderess—who still believes that it was the zip gun that actually killed the Greek—has properly disposed of the murder weapon, a .32 caliber revolver she had stolen from her uncle (pp. 153–56). In *The Big Gold Dream*, the two detectives are delighted when a vindictive victim succeeds in "framing" a master villain—who had managed to remain technically innocent, and legally untouchable—for several unsolved murders (p. 156). In *All Shot Up* Digger and Ed easily find the corrupt politician's missing campaign funds, but they decide not to tell anybody and instead donate the money to "the New York Herald Tribune Fresh Air Fund, which sends New York City boys of all races and creeds on vacations in the country during the summer" (p. 160). In *Cotton Comes to Harlem* the detectives are not able to retrieve the missing $87,000, which hundreds of poor black citizens of Harlem had invested in the Back-to-Africa movement, because a lucky junk dealer had found it first and had used it to go back to Africa. They solve the problem by selling the eccentric and wealthy white Alabama colonel, who stole the money in the first place and was involved in several murders in Harlem, twenty-four hours of getaway time in return for $87,000 of his own money. "Is it because they are nigras and you're nigras too?" queries the colonel, nonplussed, but relieved, as he quickly accepts the deal (p. 214). He makes it home to Alabama, and safety —"the State of Alabama refused to extradite . . . on the grounds that killing a Negro did not constitute murder under Alabama law" (*Cotton*, 220)—and Digger and Ed are given an outdoor testimonial barbecue dinner in a vacant lot in Harlem by the grateful Back-to-Africa families, happy to have their money back under any conditions.

In *Blind Man with a Pistol*, however, published in 1969, Himes rudely jerked the rug out from beneath his two heroes and roughly catapulted them into a reasonable facsimile of the real world, a world in which detectives almost never succeed in solving crimes, a world in fact in which nothing at all ever seems to make very much sense. In *Blind Man with a Pistol* Digger and Ed resolutely thrash witnesses and threaten everybody in sight with their big pistols, but to no avail. In this unique, almost formless antinovel, they are totally ineffective figures, clumsy and clownish, unable even to understand the seething Harlem of the era of the great ghetto riots. Object X disappears without a trace never to reappear; their star witness, who really doesn't know anything anyway, is knifed to death in a senseless street fight. Riots and demonstrations erupt in every direction, and they are dragged into them, losing every trace of their "case" and its already nebulous outlines in the boiling chaos. They are badly beaten by rioters, because they have orders not to use their guns—"They couldn't have drawn them anyway, in the rain of fists showering over them" (p. 134). A Molotov cocktail comes out of nowhere and sets their little black car and their wrinkled black suits on fire, and they have to scramble to safety, shedding their clothes as they go: "They looked like two idiots standing in the glare of the blazing car, one in his coat, shirt and tie, and purple shorts above gartered sox and big feet and the other in shirtsleeves and empty shoulder holster with his pistol stuck in his belt" (p. 177). As if this version weren't enough, a young Black Muslim minister, who bears a remarkable resemblance to Lee Gordon of *Lonely Crusade*—"he looked young and immature and very vulnerable: like a young man who could be easily hurt" (p. 219)[35]—solemnly tells them, "you don't really count in the overall pattern" (p. 218).

35. See p. 105, this volume.

Worst of all, when they try to justify themselves, and their role in maintaining monstrously unjust social patterns, the two detectives, obviously aging—"Their short-cropped hair was salted with gray and they were thicker around their middles" (pp. 123–24)—sound more than a little like a black radical's caricature version of Uncle Tom:

> "Them Doctor Toms," a youth said contemptuously. "They're all on whitey's side."
> "Go on home," Grave Digger said, pushing them away, ignoring the flashing knife blades. "Go home and grow up. You'll find out there ain't any other side." (*Blind*, 175)

It was rather a rude trick for Himes to play on his two grizzled old campaigners, but they manage to float through, indestructibly tough to the end. "It's a job," Coffin Ed remarks, "enigmatically," when he's pointedly asked by a police official whether or not he "likes" the new order of things in the precinct (p. 121). The world of *Blind Man with a Pistol* differs basically from that of the other novels in the series only in the inability of Grave Digger and Coffin Ed to control events, and by the novel's end they have adjusted completely and are placidly blasting away with their pistols at rats that are running from a building that is being demolished by wreckers (pp. 234–35), as happy and contented as they would be on their day off in the target range at police headquarters. Moreover, by an odd twist of fate—perhaps it is only poetic justice, reaching this time all the way to the author himself—*Blind Man with a Pistol* is also the novel in which Himes's expatriate memory tricks him the most often into factual errors and anachronisms in his description of Harlem; not only is the 125th St. ferry still running, but conked hair is in evidence everywhere in the Harlem of the riots (pp. 29, 46).

Though Grave Digger and Coffin Ed are responsible for whatever shape the novels have—when they have a shape—the two detectives are nevertheless only one component in a remarkably complex fictional world. The Harlem of Chester Himes's detective stories is seen almost exclusively through the distorting lens of crime, but the spectrum of characters included is astonishingly full and varied. Almost all of these characters are representative types rather than idiosyncratic individuals, of interest more for the light they shed on the anatomy and mores of the ghetto than for depth of personality, but they are all vigorously alive. They function as caricatures and symbols but also as viable literary characters. The axis about which they orient themselves is crime, either adherence to crime as a way of life or a passionate (though not exactly uncompromising) rejection of crime in all its forms. They are either innocent or guilty, in the terms of Grave Digger and Coffin Ed, but, more fundamentally, they are either "squares" or "sharpies," an equally absolute distinction. "He wasn't a square, but he wasn't sharp, neither," remarks gambler Four Ace Johnny Perry of *The Crazy Kill's* murder victim, Valentine Haines, a rare, almost unclassifiable type: "He didn't have any racket, he couldn't gamble, he couldn't even be a pimp. But I liked to have him around. He was funny" (pp. 53–54). The sharpies are always comfortably committed to some kind of lucrative illegal activity, and the squares have back-breaking jobs that bring in almost no money, but the most essential point of demarcation is the question of gullibility. Squares will believe literally anything, and sharpies are fanatically cynical. "[My] father was senile but he wasn't a square" (p. 90), insists the son of an elderly Harlem racketeer in *Blind Man with a Pistol*, refusing even to consider the possibility that his father could have been victimized by a con man.

The greatest square of them all, the perfectly gullible man, is Jackson, Imabelle's long-suffering lover in *For Love of Imabelle*. Jackson has the most unpleasant underpaid job imaginable. He works for the undertaker-tycoon H. Exodus Clay, "He drove the limousines for the funerals, brought in the dead in the pickup hearse, cleaned the chapel, washed the bodies and swept out the embalming room, hauled away the garbage cans of clotted blood, trimmed meat and rotten guts" (p. 7). Jackson had attended "a Negro college in the South" (p. 9), doubtless one quite similar to Fess Taylor's Mississippi school, but he readily believes that one of Imabelle's "friends" can turn ten-dollar bills into hundred-dollar bills by rolling them in "chemically treated paper" (p. 6) and heating them in the oven. When the oven explodes it never occurs to him to doubt that his life savings, in ten-dollar bills, were actually in the oven at the time, and he sets out to find more ten-dollar bills, to be "raised" in a more reliable oven. He believes that the shiny rocks in Imabelle's trunk are half pure gold. He believes that his twin brother Goldy, a notorious con man, female impersonator and drug addict, will help him to find the missing Imabelle out of brotherly loyalty, even after Goldy has repeatedly drugged him and locked him in a basement room. After all, they are twins, two short, fat black men, who had been called the Gold Dust Twins during their boyhood years in the South (p. 34), after the advertising trademark of a popular brand of soap, a "funny" picture of inky black children with enormous eyes. Goldy is, however, enough like his brother to believe in Imabelle's trunk of gold as earnestly as Jackson. Above all, Jackson believes that the beautiful, sensuous, and slightly sinister Imabelle loves him as truly, deeply, and faithfully, as he loves her and that he will be able to find her again when she vanishes, hiding somewhere in the huge ghetto. Himes's squares, however, always have an extraordinary amount of "dumb luck," as is only right; Jackson does find Imabelle, and she does love him. "Jackson. That mother-raping tarball. How the hell could he find out where she's at?" exclaims one of Imabelle's dangerous sharpie friends (p. 122), when the indefatigable Jackson unexpectedly turns up. Jackson is even able to help Coffin Ed and Grave Digger apprehend the villains, even though the particular villain the detectives arrange for him to trick is instantly suspicious: "Jackson looked too much like a square to be a real square. . . . He decided to go slow" (p. 69). Jackson's authenticity, however, could never be in doubt for very long:

"You shouldn't talk that way to women," Jackson protested.
The man looked at Jackson queerly. "What can you call a two-bit whore but a whore, friend?"
"They were good enough for Jesus to save," Jackson said.
The man grinned with relief. Jackson was his boy. (*Imabelle*, 70)

In his desperate search for Imabelle, Jackson does bend a few rules and commandments, even "borrows" a few ten-dollar bills from his boss's till, but he never falls behind on his prayers for forgiveness: " 'Lord, you just have to forgive me in this emergency,' he said silently" (p. 13). And he is willing to forgive God's own small, but evident, errors, as readily as he expects forgiveness: "As evil a woman as God ever made," he remarks of his landlady, who keeps fussing over the exploded stove, "He must have made her by mistake" (p. 16). Aside from his limitless gullibility, moreover, Jackson has as ready a wit as his slippery brother Goldy, and he delivers some of the most imaginative and colorful lines in all of Himes's fiction. "I feel low enough to be buried in whalebones, and they're on the bottom of the sea" (p. 27), he moans, after losing all of his tens in a dice game he had thought sure the Lord, in view of the emergency, would let him win. And, like many of Himes's simple black characters, he is able to outwit white police officers at every turn simply by exaggerating his own natural innocence. Jackson dominates *For Love of Imabelle*, upstaging Coffin Ed and Grave Digger on their first time out, and he is one of the few characters that turns up for brief reappearances in later novels (*Gold*, 13; *Shot*, 113; *Cotton*, 221), one of the rare recurrent characters that help to justify the label "the Balzac of Harlem" that French critics pinned, half seriously, on Chester Himes. None of the lovelorn young squares of the later novels, not Roman of *All Shot Up*, who can believe that a freshly gilded car has a solid gold body, nor Sonny, of *The Real Cool Killers*, who believes that the fact that he fired a pistol that he knows can only shoot blanks has made him a valid murder suspect and proceeds to elude a police dragnet, hopelessly fuzzing the investigation, have quite the class of Jackson the quintessential square. Jackson's panicky flight in a hearse through the Harlem produce market is an unmatchable high point of the series:

> All he could do was try to put the hearse through whatever opening he saw. It was like trying to thread a fine needle with a heavy piece of string.
> He bent to the right to avoid the truck, hit a stack of egg crates, saw a molten stream of yellow yolks filled with splinters splash past his far window.
> The right wheels of the hearse had gone up over the curb and plowed through crates of vegetables, showering the

fleeing men and the store fronts with smashed cabbages, flakes of spinach, squashed potatoes and bananas. Onions peppered the air like cannon shot.

"Runaway hearse! Runaway hearse!" voices screamed. (*Imabelle*, 163)

Among the much larger number of sharpies there are two that stand out: Casper Holmes, the crooked black politician of *All Shot Up*, and Deke, the con man and Back-to-Africa minister of *Cotton Comes to Harlem*. Casper Holmes is a completely admirable sharpie. He is first seen lying unconscious on a freezing cold sidewalk, but even under these circumstances he radiates dignity, well-being, control: "He had a broad, smooth-shaven face with a square aggressive-looking chin. The black skin had a creamy massaged look, and the short, carefully clipped kinky hair was snow-white. His appearance was impressive" (*Shot*, 23). In the hospital, swathed in bandages, he has the air of "an African potentate" (*Shot*, 93). The tidy little robbery he had planned, to help him make away with a sizable chunk of his party's campaign funds, had gone awry and people had been killed, but he faces down suspicious police questioners, including Grave Digger and Coffin Ed, with the cold, steely confidence of a highly successful "vote-getting politician" (*Shot*, 108). His marriage is a disaster and he is secretly a homosexual, but the front he presents to the world is magnificent, unblemished. And Casper is tough. He has contacts throughout the Harlem underworld, firm, warmly cordial, working relationships based on mutual distrust. When he is kidnapped by the hoodlums he had imported to rob him, men simple enough to permit themselves to be tricked, double-crossed, by a man as notoriously wily as Casper, he stands up to the torture they inflict on him with unflinching disdain. They slit his eyelids, his tongue and his nostrils with a knife, without getting any information, or even a grunt, out of Casper, and when he is rescued by Digger and Ed he promptly shoots his chief tormentor. "He is a great man," Grave Digger tells Lieutenant Anderson, "According to our standards" (*Shot*, 156). The money he tried to steal had belonged to rich whites, not poor blacks, and, partly because he likes to play God (*Shot*, 151), he personally makes sure that the one poor black who was victimized in the "caper" gets his money back (*Shot*, 152). He is rather like a wealthy crooked gambler whose victims are other, equally wealthy, and even more crooked gamblers. Deke, of *Cotton Comes to Harlem*, is, on the other hand, a despicable sharpie. Digger and Ed put more passion, more pure, boiling righteous indignation, into the beating they give him than they display in any of their other vigilante exercises. In fact, the anger Deke elicits in them frightens even the two detectives: "Coffin Ed turned and walked into the shadow. He slapped the wall with the palm of his hand so hard it sounded like a shot. It was all Grave Digger could do to keep from breaking Deke's jaw. His neck swelled and veins sprouted like ropes along his temples" (p. 136). Yet, on the face of it, Deke is in many ways very much like Casper. He too depends on his ability to sway people as a public speaker. Like Casper, he even arranges to have himself robbed and is later kidnapped by his own hired hoodlums and rescued in the nick of time by Digger and Ed. In the hands of the kidnappers he pleads a bit too much, yet he stands up well under the really terrible beating given him by Digger and Ed, grating through clenched teeth, "You're hurting me, . . . but you ain't killing me. And that's all that counts" (p. 136). But the money he tries to steal does belong to poor blacks, and the forum he chooses for his deceitful demagoguery is the church pulpit, not the political platform, Casper's more normally seamy, and more sporting, medium. Deke is the arch traitor, the epitome of all the men with golden voices who have made impossible promises to the poor, downtrodden black American, in the name of hope and brotherhood, and then taken the money and run. He is the king of liars, this "young Communist Christian preacher who's going to take our folks back to Africa" (p. 9).

The preachers, God's men in Himes's Harlem, are not all outright ruffians like Deke, but they are all sharpies, never squares, and at times they may generate enough mystery around their persons to puzzle even the omniscient narrator. They are the most surprising people in Himes's startling city. Sweet Prophet Brown, the fabulously wealthy black evangelist of *The Big Gold Dream*, is a dazzling figure—"Sweet Prophet sat on a throne of red roses. . . . Over his head was a sunshade of gold tinsel made in the shape of a halo. . . . His tremendous bulk was impressive in a bright purple robe lined with yellow silk and trimmed with mink" (pp. 5, 7)—but he is not above using hypnotic suggestion to filch the cached money of a poor, devout, hard-working black maid. In *The Crazy Kill*, where the solution to the neatly traditional murder mystery turns out to be not "the butler did it" but "the preacher did it," Grave Digger declares at the outset, "folks in Harlem do things for reasons nobody else in the world would think of" (pp. 55, 154), and the Reverend Short—murderer, alcoholic, visionary, and prophet—proves him right. He is minister of the First Holy Roller Church of Harlem, and his preaching style is something else: "Reverend Short was jumping up and down on the flimsy pulpit like some devil with the hotfoot dancing on red-and-white-hot flames. His bony face was quivering with religious fervor and streaming with rivers of sweat that overflowed his high cellluloid collar and soaked into the jacket of his black woolen suit" (p. 64). When his congregation responds the toughest men in Harlem don't dare leave their seats until the rolling, threshing, wrestling, and screaming have finished (p. 66). The Lord speaks to Reverend Short fairly frequently, and as often as not the Lord instructs him to knife some sinner:

> "Val saw me right away and said, I thought you went back upstairs to the wake, Reverend. I said, no, I've been waiting for you. He said, waiting for me for what. I said, waiting to kill you in the name of the Lord, and I leaned down and stabbed him in the heart."
>
> Sergeant Brody exchanged glances with the two colored detectives.
>
> "Well, that wraps it up," he said, then, turning back to Reverend Short, he remarked cynically, "I suppose you'll cop a plea of insanity."
>
> "I'm not insane," Reverend Short said serenely. "I'm holy." (*Crazy*, 154)

Preacher Ham, of *Blind Man with a Pistol*, however, makes both Reverend Short and Sweet Prophet Brown seem a bit banal. Ham holds forth in the Temple of Black Jesus, "beneath the feet of a gigantic black plaster of paris image of Jesus Christ, hanging by his neck from the rotting white ceiling. . . . an expression of teeth-bared rage on Christ's black face. . . . his fists balled, his toes curled. Black blood dripped from red nail holes. The legend underneath read, THEY LYNCHED ME" (p. 94). Ham is a "short, fat, black man with a harelip" (p. 94), who sprays spit and whose hair looks artificial. He may or may not be connected with the bald, short, fat, black man with a harelip, who sprays spit and is apparently feeble-minded, who appears in the novel's first chapter, a nightmare evocation of a black communal family living in inconceivable squalor in a condemned, abandoned Harlem tenement. Ham is all mystery. He rejects all familiar labels:

> "Don't call me a Prophet," he said. He had a sort of rumbling lisp and a tendency to slobber when angry. He was angry now. . . .
> "Neither am I a latterday Moses," he went on. "First of all, Moses was white. I'm black. . . . he led them into the wilderness to starve and eat roots. Moses was a square." (*Blind*, 97)

Ham has a simple program: "We're gonna march with the statue of the Black Jesus until Whitey pukes" (p. 100). Inexplicable and unexplained, in fact needing no explanation, Ham leads his followers into the monster tangle at the center of *Blind Man with a Pistol* and is lost to sight.

The violent hoodlums of the novels are, like the preachers, far removed from the squares but too much a prey to unrestrained emotion to be really sharp. Casper Holmes's unruly pet hooligan in *All Shot Up*, a young white Southerner, is, if not the most distinguished, at least the most remarkable of the brethren. His crimes are immediately recognizable because "there is something specially vicious about" them (p. 52).[36] Even his physical appearance is frightening: "Thick, coarse, straight black hair was plastered back from a forehead as low as that of the Missing Link. The blue-white face with its beetle-brows, high cheekbones, coarse features and wide, thin-lipped mouth looked part Indian" (p. 126). With a knife, a gun, or a garrote, he is "lightning fast" (p. 148). Shot in the elbow and kneecap by Grave Digger, helpless and in great pain, he still intimidates, "like a wounded tiger, si-

---

36. Cf. p. 19, this volume.

lent, crippled, but still as dangerous a killer as the jungle ever saw" (p. 149). The murderous thugs of detective fiction are there principally to be shot by the heroes at the proper time, not to be analyzed, but it is all to the good if they manage to generate some genuine terror along the way, suggest a vision of the abysmal brute, and Himes's thugs almost always succeed in this secondary function.

In each of Himes's detective novels there is also at least one stunningly attractive black woman among the major characters, but the function of these women is possibly even more limited and precise than that of the gunsels and pistoleros, and they vary only minutely from novel to novel. Imabelle was the prototype, and those who followed resembled her far more closely than Jackson resembled his errant twin, physically and psychologically. Imabelle is "a cushioned-lipped, hot-bodied, banana-skin chick with the speckled-brown eyes of a teaser and the high-arched, ball-bearing hips of a natural-born *amante*" (p. 6). Iris, Deke's woman in *Cotton Comes to Harlem*, is "a hard-bodied high-yellow woman with a perfect figure. . . . and her jiggling buttocks gave all men amorous ideas" (p. 38). Ginny, of *The Heat's On*, has "the high sharp hips of a cotton chopper . . . the big loaded breasts of a wet nurse," and a "big, wide, cushion-lipped mouth" (p. 19). Leila, Casper Holmes's sultry, sullen, and conniving wife in *All Shot Up*, blatantly underscores her share of the natural endowments common to all these Afro-American Aphrodites with a sure clothes sense and a spectacular wardrobe:

> She was rather short and busty, with a pear-shaped bottom and slender legs. She had short wavy hair, a heart-shaped face, and long lashed, expressive brown eyes; and her mouth was like a red carnation.
> She wore gold lamé slacks which fitted so tight that every quiver of a muscle showed. Her waist was drawn in by a black leather belt, four inches wide, decorated with gilt figures. Her breasts stuck out from a turtleneck blue jersey-silk pullover as though taking dead aim at any man in front of her. (*Shot*, 103–4)

None of these women are squares; innocence is apparently the exclusive province of young males in Himes's Harlem, but, with a few exceptions—most notably Leila Holmes and Sister Heavenly, the aging ex-whore, faith healer, and drug dealer of *The Heat's On*—they lack the willpower to actively manipulate events. They are all madly in love with one man, though not at all indifferent to other attractive males who pass their way. They are virtuoso sexual athletes, aggressive and demanding:

> She went limp for a moment and looked up at him with burning black challenging eyes. An effluvium of hot-bodied woman and dime-store perfume came up from her in a blast. It filled his mouth with tongue floating in a hot spring of saliva. Her lips were swollen, and her throat was corded. He could feel the hardness of her nipples through his leather jacket and woolen shirt.
> "Take it and you can have it," she said. (*Shot*, 78)

They have extraordinary physical courage—Iris punches Coffin Ed in the nose after he finishes choking her, and Imabelle so effectively defends herself against a huge man who grabs her in the street, slashing him with a knife, that sadistic onlookers comment on his "leaky veins" (*Cotton*, 40; *Imabelle*, 137–42)[37]—but when they are faced with an overpowering threat they lapse into terror and promise sexual delights in return for safety. "You'll want me when you've had me," Ginny babbles at the inexorable, terrifying Coffin Ed, determined to wring information out of her at any cost: "You won't be able to get enough of me. I can make you scream with joy. I can do it in ways you never dreamed of" (*Heat*, 160).[38] The function of these women in the novels is, quite simply, to be desired and to be frightened. They offer literary thrills that have obvious and direct affiliations with the realms of sex and sadism. "I hate to see people tearing at one another like rapacious animals," Lieutenant Anderson sadly remarks to Grave Digger and Coffin Ed, after the two detectives have succeeded in frightening Iris into betraying her man, the despicable Deke. "As long as there are jungles there'll be rapacious animals," retorts Grave Digger, with calm authority (*Cotton*, 139). The world of detective fiction is, in effect, a stalking

37. Cf. *Killers*, 36; *Crazy*, 90.
38. Cf. *Imabelle*, 173; *Shot*, 147.

ground for primeval predators, and the picture would hardly be complete without a generous sprinkling of succulent victims.

Himes was resolutely faithful to his basic concept of the detective story—"just plain and simple violence in narrative form"[39]—throughout the Grave Digger and Coffin Ed stories, but the importance of his personal contributions went far beyond the modest claim made in his interview with John A. Williams: "I just made the faces black, that's all."[40] He made the themes and the atmosphere black as well. He introduced major elements of black folk art into the subgenre. His remarkable combinations of humor, pathos, sex, horror, and just plain home truths are very similar to those of the bitter and beautiful blues lyrics and to the traditional black humor that is essentially laughter at black degradation, laughter curiously close to tears or to howling rage. He kept intact all the paraphernalia of the detective subgenre—complicated intrigues, heroes and villains, shaggy monsters and interesting victims, horrendous acts of violence. He managed at the same time, with the sense of lived reality he infuses throughout these novels, to suggest very clearly what the quality of life must be in a huge black urban ghetto, a vast area within a modern city that is literally a jungle filled with rapacious animals, thanks to the impenetrable indifference of established authority to everything that goes on there. The peculiar strength of Himes's position was that he could write popular tales of mayhem and make them both thrilling and amusing, without ever pushing exaggeration to a point where it would seriously interfere with his habitually scrupulous naturalistic style. The sordidly violent atmosphere of the real ghettoes that Himes had lived in proved remarkably compatible with the luridly violent fantasy world of detective fiction. The striking originality of Himes's detective tales is the ring of truth and the edge of protest that come through at almost every turn. In the final analysis, the concessions made to popular taste, and to the traditions of the subgenre, are never so extensive that they blunt the impact of the basic message of protest and outrage. However, it must be added that there are innumerable passages throughout these novels in which Himes's tone suggests that he

39. See p. 209, this volume.
40. Ibid.

was not entirely at ease with many of the concessions made, most particularly with the convention that identifies the police officer and his every act with unchallengeable right. After all, Coffin Ed's most strenuously moralistic pronouncement—"Is everybody crooked on this mother-raping earth? . . . You think because I'm a cop I've got a price. But you're making a mistake. You've got only one thing I want. The truth" (*Heat*, 160)—is blurted out, "like a cry of agony torn out of him," at the very moment he is torturing Ginny.

III Cruel World

A young black man stands at the window of his rented room in Harlem, staring at the park across the street, looking for the white man he knows is there, the white man who is trying to kill him. "What did a man do when he knew someone was going to kill him?" he asks himself. "Kill the killer first? That was what men did in the western movies. But this wasn't a movie. Not even a gangster film. This was real life."[41] This is the basic situation of Chester Himes's *Run Man Run* (1959, 1966), a Harlem murder story in which Grave Digger and Coffin Ed do not figure, a story that Himes had determined to make as real as he possibly could, drawing upon every resource of skill and knowledge at his command, an experiment he would attempt again, within the Grave Digger-Coffin Ed series itself, with *Blind Man with a Pistol*.

The story of *Run Man Run* moves at the rapid pace of the typical thriller, because it is the basic situation itself rather than the characters or the atmosphere that is the center of interest. The situation was rooted deep in Himes's own private terrors, his unshakable conviction that official indifference makes it possible for a white man to kill a black man in America with complete impunity, the conviction that blacks in effect stand outside the protection of the laws. "White cops were always shooting some Negro in Harlem. This was a violent city, these were violent people. Read any newspaper any day. What protection did he have?" (p. 85), wonders Jimmy Johnson, the young black man of

41. Himes, *Run Man Run*, p. 91 (hereafter referred to as *Run*).

Run Man Run, icy with terror in the knowledge that the white man who is methodically stalking him with a gun, Matt Walker, is himself a New York City policeman, a first-grade detective.

There is absolutely no one Jimmy Johnson can turn to for help. He had seen Matt Walker, with a gun in his hand, in the early hours of the morning, moving through the empty midtown Manhattan luncheonette where Jimmy works as a night porter, moving like a man in the grip of some kind of strange frenzy, of hysteria, drunkenness, or madness, only a few minutes after the luncheonette's two other black night porters, Luke and Fat Sam, had been shot to death. Walker had then turned his gun against Jimmy, wounding him lightly three times, but was unable to bring him down as Jimmy fled in panic down an underground corridor that linked the basements of the buildings in the area. But Matt Walker had had no motive to kill the other two porters, and he had seemed calm enough when other police had arrived at the scene, and his service revolver had not been fired, and police authorities had refused to credit Jimmy's story. Jimmy was sent to a city hospital for psychiatric examination, bound in a strait jacket, then transferred to a jail cell and held without charges until the lawyers of the luncheonette chain secured his release. After he is freed, Jimmy sees Matt Walker wherever he goes, lurking, following him, waiting for the opportune moment to silence the man who stubbornly insists on accusing him of murder. Matt Walker is under temporary suspension because of Jimmy's accusations, but the detective in the homicide division who is in charge of the investigation, Sergeant Brock, is Matt's brother-in-law. He is determined to protect Matt, convinced that black people are shiftless and unreliable, not to be believed.

Even Jimmy's girl Linda, a blues singer in a Harlem nightclub, cannot believe Jimmy's story. Matt Walker is too boyish, logical, likable, handsome, with his long, light blond hair and his sharp, even, hawklike features, to be the homicidal maniac Jimmy claims he is: " 'I mean if he looked vicious,' she said defensively. 'Like some of those Negro-hating sheriffs in the South. It'd make more sense. But he doesn't act as if he's got any prejudice at all' " (p. 132). She finds much more plausible the story Walker tells, that the killer of the two porters was a professional gunman and the midtown luncheonette was being used in some kind of racket in which the other porters and Jimmy, perhaps innocently, must have been involved. Linda, believing without question that Walker is shadowing Jimmy only to protect him, even permits herself to be seduced by the handsome and persuasive young detective, and Jimmy finds himself, not only menaced with death, but humiliated in his very manhood as well, by his implacable white foe.[42] Convinced that it must be Walker's silken yellow hair that has attracted Linda, Jimmy, in desperation, has his own hair burned and straightened with lye in a Harlem barbershop:

> The operation had required two hours.
> He stood and looked at himself in the mirror. Having straight hair gave him a strange feeling. He felt that he was handsomer, but he was vaguely ashamed, as though he'd turned traitor to his race.
> The barber stood smiling, waiting for a compliment, but Jimmy couldn't meet his gaze. He tipped him a dollar from a sense of guilt, paid his check at the cashier's cage, and hurried from the shop. (*Run*, 155)

Jimmy is in many ways similar to Bob Jones of *If He Hollers Let Him Go*. He is six feet tall, powerfully built, and extremely strong even for a man of his size and build. He is a graduate of the excellent black college in Durham, North Carolina, where Chester Himes once conducted a creative-writing workshop under the sponsorship of his brother Joseph.[43] Though he works nights as a porter, he is also studying law at Columbia University. He is "quick-tempered," unwilling to give an inch when his rights are challenged by whites: "He just wanted to be treated like a man, was all" (p. 28).[44] He is literate and articulate, at his best when

---

42. Himes, in an open letter to his publishers (Dell), published in *Negro Digest*, protested the lurid cover design and "descriptive copy" of the Dell paperback of *Run Man Run*, stating that they "cast virulent and offensive calumnies on the morals of my black heroine Linda Lou," and adding that Linda Lou's affair with Matt was motivated by her love for Jimmy, "whose life she hopes to save by sleeping with a white policeman." *Negro Digest* (May 1969): 98.

43. See p. 180, this volume.

44. Cf. p. 183, this volume.

he is learnedly explaining Matt Walker's murky motivations to the protesting Linda:

> "But no one can think of any reason for him to have done it."
>
> "He had a reason. He's a schizophrene. Do you know what a schizophrene is?"
>
> "Somebody with two personalities, one good and one evil."
>
> "No. A schizophrene doesn't have any personality. He's out of contact with reality, with morality too. He could kill you in cold-blood murder and smile while he did it." (*Run*, 133)

Jimmy's intelligence and physical power are of no use to him against Matt Walker, however, and he procures an illegal gun for the inevitable showdown, in full knowledge of how slim his chances are against his deadly adversary, even after he is assured that his twenty-dollar pistol will "kill a rock" (p. 157).[45]

Himes, rather paradoxically, put a great deal of himself into Matt Walker, in his efforts to make the character completely credible. Walker suffers from alcoholic blackouts precisely similar to those of Jesse Robinson, and Himes himself, and the scene in which Walker compulsively slaps his mistress exactly parallels an incident reported in Himes's autobiography:

> He began slapping her with his right hand; her left cheek with his open palm, her right cheek with the back of his hand. He slapped her steadily, as though in a dream; with an expression of detachment he watched her terror-stricken face pivot back and forth, as though it might have been a punching bag. (*Run*, 116)[46]

Walker is drunk when he blunders into the lunchroom, just emerging from a short mental blackout and in a fury because he has misplaced his car and thinks the porters have stolen it. He soon realizes that he is mistaken, "but he decided to scare the Negroes anyway" (p. 12). He is carrying an extra gun that he has stolen from the police museum, a pistol with a silencer that had

45. Cf. p. 231, this volume.
46. Cf. p. 181, this volume.

been used in a famous gang murder, a gun whose ballistic description had been removed from all police and FBI files. He doesn't know the gun has a hair trigger and he accidentally shoots one porter while he is waving it at him menacingly and cursing him. This sobers him up at once, and he finishes off the wounded porter with a bullet in the brain and then quickly kills the second porter, after explaining to him in detail, in his affable and boyish way, exactly why he has to do it even though he doesn't want to. By this time Jimmy has arrived on the scene, coming up the basement steps, and it is only by a series of miracles that Walker, a crack shot, fails to kill him.

Despite the element of accident involved, however, parts of the complex pattern of Walker's motivations are never hauled completely out into the light. He is a crooked vice squad detective, adept at extortion and bribery, but no logical reason is given for his carrying a bizarre illegal gun. His background is absolutely normal, even exemplary: born and raised in the suburbs of New York City, a graduate of New York's City College, a guard of all-star caliber on its basketball team, two years in the armed forces, five years as a uniformed police patrolman, an honor graduate of the school for detectives, and two years "in plainclothes . . . on the Times Square beat, the really big time" (p. 24). "These mother-raping people with all their chances" (p. 24), thinks Luke, the second porter, as Matt earnestly tells him all this, just before he shoots him between the eyes. Even Jimmy, with all the confidence of the reasonably well educated, is at a loss to account for Matt's apparent psychotic breakdown: "Maybe he was all right when he first went on the force. Maybe something happened to him since he's been a detective. Some of them can't take it. There are men who go crazy from the power it gives them to carry a gun. And he's on the vice squad too. There's no telling what might happen to a man's mind who constantly associates with criminals and prostitutes" (pp. 133–34). Only Fat Sam, the first porter killed, approaches full insight into the workings of Matt's twisted mind:

> Fat Sam had never seen a white man go insane like this. He had never realized that the thought of Negroes could send a white man out his head. He wouldn't have believed

it. He had thought it was all put on. And now this sight of violence unleashed because of race terrified him as though he had come face to face with the devil, whom he'd never believed in either. (*Run*, 16)

Jimmy is helpless because not one of those who might help him, the city's white police authorities, can grasp the key element in Walker's motivation, a psychotic hatred of the black man that only a very few black men, the chosen victims, have experienced at first hand. Jimmy is a victim, not only of white indifference to black suffering but of the white man's willful ignorance of the depth of his own secret hatred of the black man. What menaces Jimmy, basically, is not one sick young man in a privileged position, but the national psychosis of racism, fully exposed. Matt, at times the typical sentimental "nice guy," is, almost subconsciously, acting out a deadly, hidden, national impulse toward black genocide: "Those poor colored people; they had a hard life, he thought. They'd be better off dead if they only knew it. Hitler had the right idea" (p. 112).

The sharpest goad in the flying barrage of social criticism that Himes built into his breakneck thriller, however, is the character of Sergeant Brock, Matt's brother-in-law, who shoots him to death in the end, but only after Matt has put several more bullets into Jimmy, bringing him almost to death's door. Brock, "physically . . . a tremendous man built like a telephone booth and about the same size" (p. 65), had talked to the grieving, outraged wives of the two dead porters, he had seen the eight young children one of them had left behind, he had seen the battered faces of two women Matt had compulsively beaten, and he had listened to Jimmy Johnson's tale of terror, but he had decided that all this was much less important than protecting his own son and daughter from the knowledge that their uncle was a psychopathic murderer. At the very beginning of his investigation he had stumbled on evidence linking Matt to the gun used in the murder, but he kept it to himself, hoping that Matt would dispose of the gun, come to his senses, and leave off his murdering ways (p. 189). Brock, who bears the ancient name of a vicious predator, and not Coffin Ed or Grave Digger, is Himes's definitive portrait of the police officer in a violent and racist society, the society in which Jimmy Johnson lives out his terrifying ordeal, a conscienceless society that Jimmy condemns with passionate anger and eloquence:

> "You're telling me it's hard to believe? In this violent city? The papers are filled with stories of senseless murders every day. What's one more murder in a city like this? If they ever caught all the murderers in this one city alone they wouldn't have space in the jails for them. These people look on a killing like a circus performance." (*Run*, 100)[47]

IV Satire

"Chester Himes finally got a piece of what he deserves through the American publication of *Pinktoes*,"[48] remarked John A. Williams, prefacing a discussion of the generally meager financial rewards Chester Himes had received for his long efforts as a writer. "What is the most you ever made on an advance of a book?" Williams had asked, and, after a few moments' thought, and some hesitation, Himes had replied: "Putnam paid a ten thousand-dollar advance for *Pinktoes*. Walter Minton was buying up Girodias' [Olympia Press] books. He had been successful with *Lolita* and *Candy* and he was anxious to get *Pinktoes*."[49] But Girodias's Olympia Press, one of the earliest of the publishers and promoters

47. In the earlier version of the story, which was the basis of the French translation *Dare-dare*, Brock was a strongly sympathetic character. The transformation of this character into a semivillain was very probably a deliberate feature of the rewriting that converted the work from a fanciful mystery novel, with comic touches, into a completely realistic protest novel, though it might also have been an accidental result of Himes's decision to have Jimmy denounce Walker, to a willfully unbelieving white world, early in the novel, instead of discovering late in the novel, as in *Dare-dare*, that the mysterious white drunk who had shot at him was actually one of the detectives investigating the case. The extensive rewriting of the earlier version also involved radical transformations in the characters of the murdered men's wives (from comic customers of H. Exodus Clay to pathetic survivors) and some alteration in the character of Jimmy himself, with a strong new emphasis on the seriousness of his law studies, his intellectualism, and his sensitivity (e.g., in *Dare-dare* Jimmy has his hair conked simply to pass the time, p. 189).

48. Williams, "My Man Himes," p. 28.

49. Ibid., pp. 32, 33.

of *Pinktoes* (1961), though its books were almost always of high literary quality, was principally known for pushing works that had gained the reputation—rightly or wrongly of "pornographic classics," and the advertising campaigns that made *Pinktoes* so extraordinarily successful, and profitable, had frankly stressed epithets such as *bawdy, ribald,* and *Rabelaisian,* terms that suggest *pornographic* to many potential reader-buyers. Yet Chester Himes has categorically and repeatedly labeled himself a "puritan," "repelled by . . . any form of obscenity":

> I must have been a puritan all my life. Then as now, I consider the sexual act private. I do not want my sexual experiences to be made public. I do not care for women who discuss the sexual behavior of men in public, or vice versa. I don't want to hear about it. (*The Quality of Hurt,* 134)

Is this the final Himesian paradox, the puritan pornographer? No. Despite the gleefully salacious tone of both the advertising copy and the general critical reaction to *Pinktoes,* the novel is not pornography, but something quite different: it is satire.

Satire is a much simpler genre than realistic fiction. It has a very selective and limited aim: to move the reader to derisive laughter and strong disapproval of the people and behavior brought before him. Himes had not been particularly successful in his earlier attempts at satire—most notably the treatment of Alice's family in *If He Hollers Let Him Go* and of Kriss's drunken black guests in *The Primitive*[50]—because he had not sufficiently flattened the characters he was attempting to satirize. He had allowed them either a disturbingly real capacity for suffering or an unchallengeably admirable vigor. In *Pinktoes,* however, every one of the novel's phenomenally large cast of characters has been reduced to just a few very definite and very memorable traits, a technique that makes it possible both to keep them separate and distinct throughout the action and to aim the satire with absolute accuracy. Further, the single basis of the novel's satire has the thoroughly unsubtle force of a hammer striking a finger. The people of *Pinktoes* purport to be crusaders, leaders in the sacred fight against the demon racism, but in reality they are totally,

50. See pp. 90, 91, 200, this volume.

exclusively, preoccupied with the sex act. When they are not doing it, they are talking about it. The laughter essential to satire is guaranteed by the rollicking good humor with which their sexual antics and acrobatics are described. It is easy to see how such an approach might lead the casual reviewer to confuse the book's tone and content with those of pornography, but to a puritan, any puritan, but most particularly to a puritan for whom the fight against racism is the most deadly serious business of all, the satire is unmistakable.[51]

Pinktoes is set in Harlem, a very funny Harlem, a city within a city where there is "more fun to be had than in any other city in the world":[52]

> ... there are more liquor stores, more churches, more whore-houses, more lying, more laughter, more screwing, fighting and footracing, more numbers players, more freeloaders, more sports, more bars, more jukeboxes, more jazz, more crime, more chitterlings eaten, more singing and dancing, more knife-toting and loud-mouthing, more praying and shouting, more credit-buying, more ducking and dodging the collectors. . . .
> ... laughing. Not only laughing at what is considered funny, but laughing at all the things considered unfunny, laughing at the white people and laughing at themselves, laughing at the strange forms injustice takes and the ofttimes ridiculousness of righteousness. (*Pinktoes*, 21)

Digger and Coffin Ed would have a hard time recognizing the place. The central figure in this fictional Harlem, this screamingly funny ghetto, is Mamie Mason, "Harlem's most famous hostess," the "Hostess with the Mostess" (pp. 58, 23). Mamie is "of a color termed 'yellow' by other Negroes and 'tan' by white people" (p.

51. According to Himes himself, however, in an interview, many of the novel's frankest passages were added at the insistence of Maurice Giro-dias: "When Editor Maurice Girodias first looked over the manuscript," Himes recalls, "he was not entirely satisfied. 'If you incorporate eight sex scenes,' Girodias told me, 'I'll publish it.' 'Okay,' I said. I went to work and put in so many sex scenes that Girodias had to censor it!" Rudolph Chelminski, "The hard-bitten old pro who wrote 'Cotton,'" *Life* 69:1 (July 4, 1970): 61. Himes told Hoyt Fuller that he wrote the first draft of *Pinktoes* in 1956 (Fuller, "An Interview with Chester Himes," p. 11).
52. Himes, *Pinktoes*, p. 21.

24), "a thirty-nine-year-old, big-boned, hard-drinking, ambitious, energetic woman with the instincts of a lecherous glutton" (pp. 24–25), who has to diet with savage dedication to struggle into her fashionable, size-twelve sheath dresses. The strain of dieting, "her constant hunger" (p. 24), keeps her in a "constant state of evil," but she is a consummate actress, "Few persons outside of her husband had ever seen Mamie when she was neither smiling nor laughing, both of which she could perform convincingly while in a state of raging fury" (p. 24). Whenever her will falters, and gluttony takes precedence over lechery, she devours whole turkeys and hams and bloats up alarmingly in the midsection, like a woman in the final stages of a monstrously abnormal pregnancy: "She looked as though she had been putting off her children's birth to allow them to grow up" (p. 190). But Mamie's slips are few, and her crash-dieting comebacks heroically rapid. Nothing ever interferes for very long with the endless succession of interracial drinking parties she gives in her large and elegant apartment on Harlem's Edgecombe Drive, nor with her assiduous infidelities to her husband Joe, a "consultant on interracial relations for the national committee of a major political party" (p. 64), whom she invariably deceives with prominent white "friends of the Negro." The avowed "purpose" of Mamie's wide-open, anything-goes parties is to "inspire such an abundance of interracial loving as to solve the Negro Problem—if not solve it, at least tire it out" (p. 23). The emcee at her gigantic Masked Ball in the Savoy Ballroom, the novel's climactic event, tipsily attempts to proclaim the ball an occasion for "interracial love from the hearts of us all" and "friendly ties between the races," but it comes out a plea for more "interracial loving" from the "private parts of us all" and more "frenzied ties between the races" (p. 218). Mamie suffers from a similar inability to manage the subtle distinctions between the various meanings of the word *love*, and in her practical mind it all comes down, triumphantly, to sex.

The novel's third-person narrator, who hastily records the highlights of the parties as well as the private peccadillos of everyone involved, a massive task, comes across, as every good master of the revels should, as a garrulous, pun-happy satyr with a perpetual drunken leer. His fondness for double entendre, as dubious as it is obvious, is inexhaustible. He is particularly obsessed with the word *faith*, which he insists on defining, as it pertains to Mamie Mason and her cohorts, at every turn. Jesse Robinson, the disconsolate black writer of *The Primitive*, had also puzzled over *faith*, in his quest for an "ultimate answer":

> There'd been a line in a piece he'd written for a white daily newspaper years ago, which all Negroes had objected to: *"Just a pure and simple faith in the white folks and the days. . . ."* For ten years he'd forgotten it; now it came back to mind. "Your trouble, son. You got no faith." . . .
>
> "How do these people do it, son? The white man is fouling on them too, and the days don't know them either. How is it they keep their wives, bring up children, get along? Why can't you believe too? . . . How come you have to be the only one to act a fool? And think you're being noble too." (*The Primitive*, 71–72)

For the *Pinktoes* narrator, *faith*, in something like Jesse Robinson's bitter sense of the word, i.e., the refusal to recognize their own futility that keeps most people functional, is in evidence everywhere in Mamie Mason's Harlem. Mamie's inevitable returns to her punishing diet after each lamentable lapse are marks of faith. Her inexorable pursuit of distinguished guests, ignoring every rebuff, is a sure sign of her inextinguishable faith. Every disappointed seducer who takes out after a fresh quarry is demonstrating faith. In the happy, happy Harlem of *Pinktoes*, where nobody is fouling on anybody, or if they are nobody minds, faith is the most readily available commodity of all:

> The inhabitants of Harlem have faith. They believe in the Lord and they believe in the Jew and they believe in the dollar. The Lord and the Jews they have, but the dollar they have not; but this does not diminish their faith in it. In fact, more than any other people in the world, they believe that the dollar, like the great whore of legend, will give them everything. (*Pinktoes*, 19–20)

When the satire is functioning, however, this omnipresent and inexhaustible "faith" has a very sour taste. It is a confidence in the permanence of aimless debauchery, the confidence of Sisyphus that his rock and his hill will always be there, an unresisting acceptance of the status quo, grounded in the inability to imagine a better world. The jovial narrator's *faith* is in fact a synonym for *hopelessness*.

There is, of course, a plotline of sorts running through the marathon lovemaking of *Pinktoes*—which is, by the way, about as pornographic as a speeded-up film of a rabbit hutch during mating season—and the meandering and fuzzy philosophizing and lewd joking of the narrator. The plot revolves around Mamie Mason's attempts to get even with Wallace Wright for not bringing his wife Juanita to her parties: "He always came alone, just as though she ran a whorehouse. She considered that a damn insult" (p. 113). Wallace Wright is a "great Negro race leader," who claims "only one-sixty-fourth Negro blood" (p. 30): ". . . a small blond man with a small blond mustache [who] looked so much like a white man that his white friends found it extremely difficult, in fact downright irritating, to have to remember he was colored" (p. 82). He is "Executive Chairman of the National Negro Political Society, NNPS" (p. 69). Juanita Wright is ostentatiously faithful to her husband, and Mamie will not be satisfied until she has maneuvered Juanita into a very public interracial love affair. Mamie picks Art Wills as the Don Juan for the job. He is a white magazine editor who is for the moment without a publication, though he has a black picture magazine in the planning stage. Art is handsome and promiscuous, and his sexual endowments are famous throughout Harlem, but he is so drunk, literally all the time, that Mamie can't get his attention long enough to blackmail him into cooperating. Fortunately, the power of suggestion alone is enough to launch Art on the trail, where the seduction of black women is concerned. Then, by passing out a great deal of misinformation over the telephone about who is going to be where, her standard technique for luring people to her parties, Mamie arranges for Wallace to run into Peggy, his white mistress, at the apartment of Patty Pearson who lives several floors below Mamie. Patty, a conniving, thoroughly amoral malicious young black woman, happens to be "the best friend" of both Mamie Mason and Juanita Wright. Just a few moments after Wallace meets Peggy at Patty's—Mamie's timing is phenomenally precise—Juanita, escorted by Art, who claims he's trying to arrange a family interview, also arrives at Patty's apartment.

> It goes without saying that Juanita was speechless with fury. She turned about to leave but Wallace, like a fool, tried to restrain her.
> "This is not at all as it appears," he said. "There is a very simple explanation."
> Everyone looked at him expectantly. But Wallace made the grave mistake of not presenting his simple explanation with the urgency the situation demanded, no doubt because he hadn't thought of one. (*Pinktoes*, 127)

Juanita succumbs to Art's advances, the Wrights' famously happy marriage slides into limbo, and Mamie Mason's revenge is complete. Unfortunately, there are a number of unexpected spin-off events, grave repercussions from the scandal that shake up the entire city. The news that Wallace Wright's white mistress has split Wallace loose from his black wife drives all of the black women of Harlem to band together in black women's defense organizations, Be-Happy-That-You-Are-Nappy clubs (p. 137). And the news that a black woman has come between Art Wills and his freckly white wife starts a similar panic among the white women of New York. They embark on a "dinge binge" (p. 182), buying up skin darkeners and strange new hair products, "Burr Maker and Kink Filler, advertised to make the straightest of hair kinky" (p. 184). The most drastic event of all is a move afoot among the white women to boycott Mamie Mason's upcoming, fabulous, interracial Masked Ball:

> How could the Negro Problem be served if only Negroes sat down to eat? Who was to serve it? Who was to eat it? . . . Who were to be the guests of honor? Who were to occupy the reserved seats? Who were to shake the hands of the black toadies? Who were to delight in the wit and vivaciousness of the darker brother? Who were to marvel at their laughter and appreciate the lovely colors of their skin, the crispy crinkle of their hair and the pearly whiteness of their teeth, if no white people were there? There was no telling what might happen to the Negro Problem. (*Pinktoes*, 189)

The much abused term *the Negro Problem* is, like *faith*, another of the subtle semantic word games the narrator is fond of throwing out to the reader. In Himes's view, *the Negro Problem* is apparently, as Dr. Johnson once wrote of *patriotism*, "the last refuge of a scoundrel," a slogan that grants instant significance to all that mouth it, loudly and earnestly enough. Mamie Mason's dedication to the Negro Problem—and her own Masked Ball—is such, however, that she immediately sets out to undo all the harm she has done to the Wallace Wrights. She sends Mike Riddick, a young black preacher whose specialty is wrestling sin out of the bodies of pretty women—and whose physical endowments are even more celebrated than those of Art Wills—to see Peggy, Wallace's white mistress. Riddick stays with Peggy three days and three nights, wrestling all the while, and in the end they decide to get married. The news of Riddick's triumph sends Art Wills scampering home to protect his own wife, and Juanita and Wallace are reunited. "So now . . . Mamie had reconciled that great Negro leader Wallace Wright with his droopy drawered wife, and reunited Debbie Wills with her luck-changing husband" (p. 195). The resolution of the novel's main plot, a kind of lighthearted exercise in musical chairs, or marriage beds, is thus about as difficult, and engrossing, as the average party game.

There is also a whole gnat swarm of equally ephemeral secondary plots. There is the story of Moe Miller, the distinguished black journalist, who drags himself reluctantly away from Mamie's parties from time to time to take up once again the fight against the giant rat that infests his home in Brooklyn, a rat so diabolically clever that it moves the traps Moe sets to places where they break Moe's own toes, and so big that it can grasp Moe's hunting knife in its teeth, and charge Moe with it, sending him fleeing out into the street in a blind panic, reduced to telegraphing his wife: "RAT . . . IN POSSESSION OF HOUSE STOP I AM DROPPING THE NEGRO PROBLEM UNTIL RAT IS CAUGHT" (p. 109). Then there is the story of Julius Mason, Mamie's young in-law who lives in the small guest bedroom in Mamie and Joe's apartment, having left his wife Judy temporarily behind in California—an arrangement identical to that Chester Himes had with his cousins Henry and Molly Moon when he went to New York from California during the war for the publication of *If He Hollers Let Him Go*.[53] If Julius were not seen only in very rare moments, in passing as it were, *Pinktoes* might be considered a fourth autobiographical novel. Julius is an amiable, heavy-drinking woman chaser, a determined party crasher, and of course a black writer:

> . . . Julius pushed into the apartment unperturbed and left the two white men to fight it out.
> "Who's he?" Lou [the white host] asked.
> "He's a writer too."
> "My God, another one. Who's going to be left to chop the cotton and sing 'Old Man River'?"
> Art chuckled. "You and me." (*Pinktoes*, 33)

Julius is the classic country cousin, a bumpkin so inept that he can barely manage an amatory conquest in a room that is normally swarming with prowling nymphomaniacs, which is to say, Mamie Mason's own living room. He is *"a five-cornered square,"*[54] an arcane term the narrator helpfully defines as "a square so square as to have an extra corner . . . a square's square," and it is only thanks to his uniquely interesting "sad eyes" (pp. 44, 85) that Julius finally obtains his due share of "pinktoes," another arcane expression that is quickly defined by the hovering narrator: "a term of indulgent affection applied to white women by Negro men, and . . . by Negro women to white men" (p. 7), or, in other words, white bedmates. There is, too, the story of poor little Merto Gordey, the nymphomaniac's nymphomaniac, whose intimacy with Mamie and possession of a homosexual husband give her more than a passing resemblance to the Kriss Cummings of *The Primitive*.[55] Merto is methodically giving her all for the Negro Problem, which simply delights swishy Maurice Gordey, so long as Merto tells him all about it, in detail. Merto knits replicas of the private parts of all the black men she sleeps with, being careful to get the size and color just right, and in

53. See pp. 70, 191, 192, note 26 in Chapter 4, this volume.
54. See notes 2, 28, p. 201, this volume.
55. See pp. 187, 191, 192, this volume.

the novel's climax she appears at Mamie's Masked Ball as Eve, wearing a very tiny fig leaf and a necklace of her knitted mementos (pp. 92, 216).

Needless to say, the white celebrants among "all those frantic white and colored people all mixed up together at those drunken orgies that took place at Mamie Mason's" (p. 140) are far more prone to genuinely distasteful behavior than their black playmates. And the most distasteful of all are *"The Distinguished White Doctors"* (p. 202), three awesomely dignified, patriarchal white heads of huge black foundations and colleges who share Mamie Mason as "their common colored mistress" (p. 213). In telephone conversations among themselves they differentiate between black people and "our species" (p. 156), and, sure enough, alone and unclothed with Mamie, they do turn out to be of other species:

> "It's no use undressing," she said adamantly. "I've lost mine."
> Silently he completed disrobing and when she looked into his old liquid eyes she realized it was not Dr. Garrett at all, but an old hairy salacious billy goat.
> "But I've found mine," the old billy goat, er, ah, Dr. Garrett said.
> With which he tore off her robe with one hand and with the other drew from his pile of clothing a bullwhip. (*Pinktoes*, 212)

The exact time period to which the events of *Pinktoes* belong is left, apparently deliberately, completely unspecified. However, remarks like "God bless our fighting men" and "Of course we must campaign for him" (pp. 85, 78), and the fact that authors' books are publicized by radio—not TV—interviews indicate that it takes place in the 1940s, the period when Chester Himes was living with his New York cousins and observing the inner workings of the Civil Rights movement and Roosevelt's campaign for a fourth term. Allusions to "reformed Communists" and references to the WPA as "twenty years previous" point just as definitely to the 1950s (pp. 69, 31). Inasmuch as so many of the book's characters are readily identifiable with actual historical figures, however, like Walter White and Henry and Molly Moon —and even Chester Himes's first editor, Bucklin Moon, the likeliest model for Art Wills—it would have been better, for the purposes of the satire itself, the impression of weight and authority it conveys, to have made the time period covered equally precise. It does not, for example, seem entirely fair to satirize, in a book published in the 1960s, the black leaders who laid the groundwork for the great Civil Rights breakthroughs of the 1950s on the basis of the lifestyles they may or may not have adopted while they were floundering in the frustrations of the 1940s, temporarily abandoned by their powerful "friends," and told to put off their demands, and their hopes, "for the duration."

The more general basis of the satire, moreover—the standing contrast between the characters' idealistic patter and their habitually lewd behavior—is itself a bit creaky. It seems to assume that lofty aims can only be achieved by the rigidly moral. It calls to mind H. L. Mencken's concept of a puritan as someone who is terribly afraid that there might be somebody somewhere who is having a good time. Himes's satire has the burning indignation, the *saeva indignatio* of Jonathan Swift's, the dean of satirists, but some of the fire and brimstone is wasted in broadsides futilely directed against the sheer complexity of reality, rather than its unnecessary component of avoidable injustice. He levels a thunderous protest at the carnival atmosphere generated by the more frivolous fellow travelers of the Civil Rights crusade, but he never comes to grips with the movement's deepest sources of strength and weakness, its long and ambiguous history of compromises, both necessary and unnecessary, and its motley array of allies, drawn to the banner by every conceivable motive, but always welcome. Too little distinguishes Himes's satire from unadulterated protest. "What is protest but satire?" Jesse Robinson demands of an imaginary editor in an argument he fantasizes in *The Primitive*, and is told: "Satire? Satire must be witty, ironic, sarcastic; it must appeal to the intellect. This dung is filth" (p. 45). *Pinktoes* is, in full measure, witty, ironic, and sarcastic. It is a marvelously funny book. But it does not bring into play any very complex analysis of the Civil Rights movement it satirizes. It is a cry of rage and disgust, the cry of a disillusioned zealot, an outraged and intransigent purist, and as such it merits respectful attention, but it falls short of truly great satire. Its appeal is not to the intellect, but to every man's capacity for righteous indignation.

6

The Summing Up
The Quality of Hurt
Recent Pieces from *Black on Black*

I The Quality of Hurt (and Une Affaire de viol)

Chester Himes's seventeenth and eighteenth books, *The Quality of Hurt* (1972) and *Black on Black* (1973), were published by Doubleday & Company, which had also published his first book *If He Hollers Let Him Go* in 1945. His first experience with the firm had left him with feelings of intense bitterness. The personnel and policies of companies change through the years, sometimes evolving in the direction of tolerance and maturity, but Chester Himes's recollections of significant ancient hurts seldom lost their sharpness of outline with the passage of time, and he reviewed the old controversy with Doubleday in *The Quality of Hurt*, "like a Dark Avenging Angel with his pen dipped in gall."[1]

The Quality of Hurt was a kind of summing up, a tying together of loose ends, more a casual "rap" about a few random segments of his past than a rigidly organized autobiography, primarily offering vivid sketches of the handful of characters and incidents important in his life that he had not already "used" in his three autobiographical novels. He had mixed feelings about probing into so many old sores, but his writer's instinct to get it all on paper was not to be denied:

> I hate exhibiting my wounds and scars and I don't know why I'm doing it now. I suppose I just want to get it on the record before it's too late.[2]

Like Sean O'Casey, William Butler Yeats, and W. E. B. Du Bois, Himes chose to limit the scope to his "struggling years" in his

---

1. Himes, *The Primitive*, p. 23; see pp. 71–72, this volume.
2. Himes, *The Quality of Hurt*, pp. 132–33.

first attempt at an official autobiography. *The Quality of Hurt* was labeled "Volume I" and covers the events of his life up to 1954. The events of the hectic and very full years that came after 1954 were to be treated in a volume—or volumes, if he should prove as tirelessly garrulous as Du Bois and the Irish autobiographers. In any case, the list of subjects reserved for future autobiographical writings was his long stay in France, his decisive shift to light fiction during that time, his connection with the film versions of some of his novels, his marriage to the lovely blonde Lesley, his residence in Spain, the severe stroke he suffered while traveling in Mexico in 1963, the second stroke in France in 1964, and his subsequent slow recovery and return to writing, producing some of his very best work later in the decade, and, in March 1972, the great tributes paid to him on the occasion of the publication of *The Quality of Hurt*, including a reception with "700 well-wishers gathered at New York City's United Nations Plaza," and a special issue of the prestigious magazine *Black World* devoted to his work.[3]

Much of the record of the pre-1954 years was already deeply eroded. Hurting memories had been defused, permanently robbed of their sting, and their reality, by the exhaustive treatment he had given them in the autobiographical novels, and they had become curiously remote, almost inaccessible, like very old and badly preserved snapshots:

> I knew that many aspects of prison life had made deep impressions on my subconscious, but now I cannot distinctly recall what they are or should have been. I find it necessary to read what I have written in the past about my prison experiences to recall any part of them. I have almost completely forgotten prison, what it was like and what I was like while there. (*The Quality of Hurt,* 3)

3. *Black World* (March 1972); *Black World* (June 1972): 92–94. The announced working title of the second volume of Himes's autobiography was "Writing for Life," see interview in *Publishers Weekly* 201 (April 3, 1972): 20. Ishmael Reed, in a long article on Himes in *Black World*, expressed the ultimate in reader anticipation concerning the forthcoming volume: "Another volume is on the way. Surely, that will be an additional monster destined to mind slam the reader." Ishmael Reed, "Chester Himes: Writer," p. 86.

He provided only very brief, almost perfunctory, accounts of the broad outlines of his personal history, in crisp and dispassionate little blocks of expository prose,[4] which served merely as connecting links between the lengthy and leisurely passages he devoted to the few selected people and episodes he had chosen to treat in elaborate, and frankly novelistic, detail.

Himes was too conscientious and professional a writer, however, to produce a book that is not united by a dominant, overall theme. The book's title, *The Quality of Hurt*, a variation of Shakespeare's phrase "the quality of mercy" (Portia's speech in *The Merchant of Venice*, IV, 1), a part of which is quoted in the opening pages of *The Quality of Hurt*, is itself a capsule statement of the autobiography's theme. Himes was determined to show that hurt, like mercy, has an almost inexhaustible variety of forms, all of which are rooted deep in the human heart. If mercy is a human quality that it behooves the race of masters to explore in depth—as Portia instructs her audience of Jew haters and unimaginatively legalistic bureaucrats—hurt is a quality that the oppressed, seldom through choice, invariably come to know in its full complexity. The autobiography of a talented man who is a member of an oppressed minority cannot help but be a valuable guide, a veritable textbook on the intricacies, the "quality," of this singularly unpleasant emotion. Himes was only too painfully aware that he was passing in review experiences and human relationships that had been damaged or destroyed, poisoned, embrued with a unique quality of hurt, by the racist pressures that had impinged at every point on his life. It is his unifying theme.

Himes devotes about 200 of the book's 351 pages to a relationship that began in April 1953. Three days out on his first sea voyage, bound for Europe on an ocean liner, Himes, miserably seasick and as lonesome as he had ever been in his life, wobbled down a long, narrow ship's passageway, headed for his cabin. Suddenly, a white American woman, the only other person in the corridor, chalky with terror and vertigo, trembling with near hysteria, clutched at him desperately, and cried, "Don't leave me! Please don't leave me!" (p. 153). Himes was intensely irritated but also strangely touched, and he rose to the occasion with

4. See p. 136, this volume.

strained, but genuine gallantry: "Like a cop I escorted her grimly to her cabin." He saw the woman many times in the next few days, in the lounge and on the deck, and they spent hours talking, trusting each other completely from the very first. She was "about forty, rather thin . . . with a mop of short brown hair . . . and a figure that wasn't bad at all" (p. 152). Long before the ship docked the sudden friendship of these two lonely people had become a love affair. Her name was Alva, and the description of their relationship in *The Quality of Hurt* forms one of the greatest love stories Chester Himes ever wrote.

In part, Himes was performing a rescue operation. His fondest fantasy had become tangible reality: " 'rescuing damsels in distress.' It's a holdover from the dreams of my childhood. I am completely blinded to my own welfare if there is a damsel in distress—and she doesn't really have to be a damsel, or even in real distress for that matter, just as long as I believe it" (p. 169). But Alva's distress was genuine enough. Tied to a European husband she feared, lacking the will to free herself, she had suffered three nervous breakdowns in the recent past. After the third she had fled in panic back to the United States, afraid that her husband might commit her permanently to a mental hospital. She was returning to Europe to complete divorce proceedings, still fearful, half convinced that she would never be able to resist her husband's dominant will and his opposition to the divorce. Himes was a bitter and distrustful man, with a sharp eye for human weaknesses and an ingrained suspicion of everybody and everything that was both white and American, but he never doubted for a moment that Alva was a person of great worth, and she fascinated him.

> She impressed me . . . as being good. I have never known why. Or how. I no longer remember. But I know the impression . . . never changed.
> But I thought then and now that she was a little crazy, too. She had been so very hurt by life. (*The Quality of Hurt*, 162)

His support and the love he so passionately offered gave her the strength she needed to free herself, confident in a better future, bound forever to Chester Himes. They met again in Paris a few weeks later, Alva fresh from her triumphant act of liberation, and they lived together for twenty months.[5]

The rescue operation was at first a very great success. Alva saw in Himes a man who had risen above hurts greater than any she had ever known or could even imagine. His blackness was an assurance of invincible strength, impregnable toughness, and a limitless capacity to understand, and share, the hurts of others: "What mattered to her was she had lost herself in the darkness of my race. She had hid from all her hurts and humiliations. In a strange and curious way, by becoming my mistress, the mistress of a man who'd never been entirely free, she had freed herself" (p. 219). But Alva did not know that Himes had never been free, that he reeled and staggered as helplessly as she did under the slings and arrows of outrageous fortune. "Tell me what to do. You're a writer. You should know" (p. 162), she demanded of him at the very start of their relationship, serenely confident in his special strength and wisdom. "You're the only complete person I've ever known" (p. 330), she had once told him, months later.

Himes valued this bullied and harried woman as no one ever had before, cherished qualities in her that she had considered beneath notice. He admired her poise, the casual, impressive poise of those born to lead lives of cultured ease, the moderately but solidly wealthy: "Alva arrived in a mink-dyed muskrat draped over a black evening gown, looking slightly anxious in a delectable sort of way. I felt immensely better. . . . I was very proud of her. She looked self-possessed and elegant" (p. 167). He was awe-struck at her skill in coping with the myriad difficulties of travel in Europe, all so new and forbiddingly strange to him, her sure and fluent command of French and German, and the trim and crisp efficiency with which she adjusted to, and made livable, the series of dilapidated houses and apartments they occupied. He delighted in her slightly hysterical gaiety during their best moments together, "her laugh . . . loud, mannish, raucous" (p. 155), her "whoop of . . . outrageous glee" (p. 256). And, though they were both "puritanical" (p. 229), their lovemaking was extraor-

5. See pp. 182–84, this volume.

dinarily successful: "We fused together in the hot passionate dark and became one, and the world didn't matter anymore . . . we overcame our loneliness and shed our regrets and grew strong together" (p. 219). Neither had "experienced such freedom of ecstasy before" (p. 219).

But it was not long before the rescue operation began to run into stormy weather. The manuscript novel, *The Golden Chalice*, which Alva had written with Himes's help, was rejected by publishers, and she had been totally unprepared to absorb the blow to her ego. Their funds, always limited, began to run very low, and finally scraped bottom. Alva was for the first time totally enveloped by Himes's world, the world of the black American, where the extremes of humiliation and poverty are familiar landmarks. She suddenly became very distant and remote, as though lost in some private realm of despair all her own.

> The rejection of our book coming so closely on top of our sudden, frightening destitution . . . had been too much for her. She had experienced many other hurts in her life but she had never experienced the hurt of helpless want, of suddenly finding herself in the world without money or friends. This happens to American blacks every day and we are accustomed to it, but it was shattering to a white woman of her class. I found it strange to see her trying to protect herself by her quiet withdrawal from the world that had hurt her. . . . I had never experienced the luxury of withdrawing from hurt. (*The Quality of Hurt*, 271)

The memory of her daughters, whom she had lost to her husband Jan, was a source of pain that no effort at withdrawal could still: "It became obvious that Alva was grieving for her own lost daughters. She grieved in public. Not that she cried—she was too well bred to cry in public—but she grieved. It was obvious" (p. 323). And it soon became equally obvious to Alva that Himes was not "complete" in the manner that she had thought, able to affront any crisis without being "touched" by it, his spirit and will, tempered in the fires of a thousand past hurts, remaining forever inviolably intact. In a minor, routine quarrel with one of their Majorca landlords Himes lost his head completely, threatening the man with a knife, precipitating a crisis that turned the whole village against them, a crisis he aggravated by attempting to knock down one of the landlord's supporters. Only the intervention of the Guardia Civil, somber men in absurd uniforms with a well earned reputation for lethal violence—perhaps the only police force in the real world in which Coffin Ed and Grave Digger would have been perfectly at home—made it possible for Himes and Alva to effect a hasty retreat to another town safely (pp. 308–17). The casual acceptance of violence was an aspect of Himes's strange, dark world that Alva found even more disconcerting, shocking, unacceptable, than grinding poverty and perpetual despair.

Slowly Himes came to grips with the realization that he had not saved Alva: "She had completely lost the harried, distraught look she had had when I had first seen her . . . it had been replaced by one of anxiety" (p. 316). His love and all the tenderness that he could muster were of no avail. Something had died in the woman he loved, perhaps the capacity for hope, and it could not be revived:

> I became afraid to leave her alone, as one dreads leaving alone a person who is likely to commit suicide. I could not trust her to keep herself alive. It hurt me terribly to see her hurt. I felt a sense of failure. I hate to fail. And I've failed as a thief, as a student, as a writer, even as a person, and now I was failing with Alva. The greatest failure for any man is to fail with a woman. No one will ever know how much . . . it hurt me to watch helplessly as she went away from me, to see her grieve for her children, her family, normality, security, her white world. (*The Quality of Hurt*, 323)

He became convinced that he must send her to her relatives in America, but he had no money. He resorted to desperate shifts, cashing two checks without funds (which he later repaid) (pp. 333–36, 341, 349, 350), and prepared himself for even more drastic gambits in his determination to help Alva, now truly a damsel in distress, and then, in the nick of time, a check arrived, a publisher's advance of one thousand dollars for *The Primitive* (p. 349), the novel he had written during the happy time when his love for Alva had still held bright promise, for both of them. He put Alva on the boat train from Paris, firmly and gently, like a father bidding farewell to a beloved child:

> We stood very close on the platform and she kept turning to hide her face from the strangers all about us because she was crying. When the conductors blew their whistles for all aboard I took Alva in my arms and kissed her and it seemed to open the floodgates for I had to lift her onto the train. She stood in the open coach door, dangerously, perilously, waving frantically, desperately, until the train had turned the bend way up the track and passed from sight, although I doubted if she could have seen me through her tears.
>
> I went across to a bar on rue Saint-Lazare and had a couple of Cognacs. Suddenly I found myself crying like a baby. Tears streamed down my cheeks. Frenchmen at the bar turned to stare at me. (*The Quality of Hurt*, 351)

The ending of this passionate account of a passionate affair is singularly satisfying, both esthetically and emotionally, a kind of ending that life, and autobiographies, seldom afford. But Himes had written of this love affair once before, in a strange little work that he had published, in French translation only, in 1963, a novella entitled *Une Affaire de viol* (*A Case of Rape*), which was in many ways a preliminary sketch for some of the smoothly factual narratives later incorporated into *The Quality of Hurt*. The love affair with Alva was, evidently, too perfect a subject for fiction not to have tempted Himes, at least once, to make a novel out of it. In *Une Affaire de viol*, however—in form, a detailed account of a criminal trial in France in 1956, cast in a flatly objective, pseudolegalistic style—the ending of the love affair was, by any criteria, extremely messy. The novella's central figure, Scott Hamilton, is a black American intellectual who resides in Paris. He is the husband of a celebrated black singer, from whom he is separated, and his only apparent vocation is the pursuit of his own dreams. In April 1953 on a French transatlantic steamer, bound for France for the first time, Scott had met an aristocratic white woman, Lisbeth Hancock, and they had fallen in love. She had left her sadistic European husband and her daughters to live with Scott in southern France, in London, and in Majorca. While Scott dreamed, Lisbeth wrote a novel. Her marriage had left her emotionally and spiritually damaged, and Scott, the fervent idealist, had been determined "to heal her spirit, to treat the wound in her soul," convinced that he had been "born to fill a role of this type."[6] The descriptions of this stage of the affair closely parallel the account of the Himes-Alva affair given in *The Quality of Hurt*. Financial insecurity ruins the relationship, and Scott raises the money to send Lisbeth back to America (*Une Affaire de viol*, 135). But he soon follows, taking up residence in New York, and the affair resumes, only to collapse again in the racist atmosphere of the United States. Scott returns to Paris. Lisbeth follows. But he finds her changed, no longer the fearful, gentle, and good woman for whom he had definitively abandoned a wife "who was neither gentle nor good, and who was afraid of nothing" (p. 127, my translation). Lisbeth has become a sensualist and Scott breaks with her in puritanical disgust. But then a secret enemy writes to the prospective publisher of Lisbeth's novel, suggesting that the work was ghostwritten by a black man, and the publisher no longer wants the book. Lisbeth turns to Scott for comfort in this moment of crisis, and he takes her to his hotel room, where he has an appointment with three other black American intellectuals who live in Paris, all highly educated men, from backgrounds of wealth and culture. He hopes that they will be able to convince Lisbeth that he, black as he is, is a person of value, and that their liaison need cause her no shame. The men's efforts to calm Lisbeth are earnest, and for a time successful, but she is strangely distraught, and passions soon run high in the little gathering, becoming twisted and dangerously intense. One of the men, yielding to a sudden vicious impulse of antiwhite feeling, passes some sherry to Lisbeth that contains a powerful aphrodisiac stimulant. She drinks it, experiences violent convulsions, and dies. The French police, who have come to investigate the noise, arrest the four black Americans. They are tried for murder and rape by a racist French jury that laughs at their attempts at a defense, and all four are sentenced to life imprisonment. Lisbeth had spent the night before her visit to Scott in marathon lovemaking with her perverted former husband, and it was principally the strain of

6. Chester Himes, *Une Affaire de viol* (*A Case of Rape*), p. 132 (my translation).

that ordeal that had killed her (and convinced the medical examiner that she had been raped many times). Scott knows about this incident but feels he cannot reveal it:

> Scott could not admit publicly that after having heard Mrs. Hancock confess what she had done the preceding night with her ex-husband, he had still felt it necessary to convince her of the dignity and integrity of his race by introducing her to his friends. Even nailed to the cross, he did not dare cry in the face of the world that the esteem of Mrs. Hancock had so great an importance for him—so great an importance simply because she was white, American, and upper-class. (*Une Affaire de viol*, 162, my translation)

Himes, incidentally, also made use of this novella—in the descriptions of Scott Hamilton's background—to present to the world a circumstantial account of the distinguished white ancestry of one black American (pp. 92–95), a "line of lords," similar to the genealogical account prepared by his mother that he had once been afraid to use in *The Third Generation*.[7] In *The Quality of Hurt*, however, in marked contrast to the account given in the novella, his mother's claims to illustrious ancestry are again given only the briefest of passing allusions (p. 5).

The man that Chester Himes came closest to in his lifetime, sharing a communion that was both personal and professional, was Richard Wright, another initiate into the special problems and burdens of the black American novelist. Wright is a figure second in importance only to Alva in *The Quality of Hurt*—and he was also the model for a major character in *Une Affaire de viol*, the autobiography's forerunner.

Wright's name occupies a privileged position in the surprisingly small list of some of the people Himes had actually liked that he gives in the autobiography: "I never had liked American blacks simply because we belonged to the same race; I had liked only the ones who had interested me—my wife, some racketeers around Cleveland, several fellow students at Ohio State University, several fellow convicts at the Ohio State Penitentiary, several fellow workers I had met here and there in my many occupations,

7. See p. 137, this volume.

and Richard Wright. I liked Dick" (*The Quality of Hurt*, 224). Further, Himes had a very solid—though not uncritical—admiration for Wright's abilities as a writer, and he stood ready to defend his opinion with violent gusto whenever Wright's work was attacked or disparaged in his presence, something that happened fairly frequently, as he records in *The Quality of Hurt*:

> A professor from Austria asked me point blank what I thought of Richard Wright. "He's a great man," I said. "We're speaking of him as a writer," the professor said. "He's a great writer," I said. The professor looked at me with indulgent condescension. . . .
> . . . I resented these people carping at Dick. Whatever his faults or deficiencies, Richard Wright was the first American black writer to break into the big time, and by so doing he had convinced the world that it was possible for the American black descendants of slaves to possess the talent and the intellectual capacity to contribute to the world's literature. (*The Quality of Hurt*, 210–11)

In his conversations with John A. Williams some time after the completion of *The Quality of Hurt*, Himes repeated his conviction that Wright had played a uniquely important role in opening up the publishing world to black writers, though at the same time he expressed substantial doubts as to the reality and extent of Wright's impact on the white reader: ". . . it didn't mean a damn thing to them."[8] The basis of the Himes-Wright relationship, as described with Himes's customary reckless frankness in *The Quality of Hurt*, was not admiration, however, so much as mutual sympathy and respect. "I respected Dick more than anyone else I knew" (p. 187), he remarks, in the midst of a detailed account of Wright's bizarre suspicions.

Their friendship was solid enough to tolerate the lively curiosity with which each one regarded the other's faults. Himes, a formidable egotist himself, felt only the mildest resentment, he

8. John A. Williams, "My Man Himes: An Interview with Chester Himes," p. 52; cf. Fuller, "Traveler Down that Long, Rough, Lonely Old Road: An Interview with Chester Himes," pp. 93–97. For a very early Himes comment on Wright, see Himes's contribution to the *New Masses*, "Pros and Cons," feature on *Native Son* (May 21, 1940): 23–24.

assures us, at Wright's fanatic egocentricity, his truly heroic selfishness: "From the time I had met him after the publication of *If He Hollers Let Him Go*, until his death, Dick and I had a somewhat secret understanding that I wouldn't ask him for any favor he did not want to do, and he wouldn't do it" (*The Quality of Hurt*, 116). He notes with affection Wright's tendency toward "such self-indulgent exaggeration that the buzzing of a blowfly could range like a typhoon in his imagination" (p. 177). In all of Richard Wright's fiction his protagonists suffer small mishaps that lead inexorably, as though the universe were governed by an insanely malignant God, to incredibly catastrophic consequences, a basic plot structure that sometimes served him well, and sometimes miscarried disastrously. At the time Himes first visited Wright in Paris, renewing the friendship begun in New York, Wright was completing *Savage Holiday*, one of the disasters, and Himes's ready tolerance for his friend's shortcomings evidently proved equal even to *Savage Holiday*: Dick told [me] that the plot for the story had come to him suddenly several months previously when he had been in bed with a high fever. . . . when he let me read the finished manuscript, I believed him (*The Quality of Hurt*, 190, 191).

Wright was the one really outstanding celebrity, the acknowledged "king" (p. 179), in the small community of black American expatriates living in the Latin Quarter at the time Himes arrived in Paris. Himes was amused by the air of "boisterous condescension" Wright assumed when he was holding court in the local bistros, but the savage determination, the brutality, even cruelty, with which Wright would sometimes assert his position came close to shocking him. Involved, almost as a kind of official "witness," at a "confrontation" between Wright and James Baldwin at the Deux Magots cafe, he found amusement impossible:

> I was somewhat surprised to find Baldwin a small, intense young man of great excitability. Dick sat down in lordly fashion and started right off needling Baldwin, who defended himself with such intensity that he stammered, his body trembled, and his face quivered. I sat and looked from one to the other, Dick playing the fat cat and forcing Baldwin into the role of the quivering mouse. It wasn't particularly

funny, but then Dick wasn't a funny man. I never found it
easy to laugh with Dick. (*The Quality of Hurt*, 200)

Just before Alva was due to arrive in Paris, to begin her new
life with Chester Himes, Wright enthusiastically joined in Himes's
search for better, and cheaper, hotel rooms, the two distinguished
black American novelists presenting a singular impression of
unity: "We made the rounds of the cheap hotels. . . . We both
wore belted trenchcoats and dark-green Polaroid sunglasses. Seeing the apprehensive expression of a woman who ran a cheap
residential hotel, I suddenly realized we must look like two North
African gangsters collecting tribute" (p. 216). But Wright's openly
antagonistic attitude toward Alva, after she arrived, severely
strained the friendship of these two gifted men. "He resented my
considering her something special" (p. 216), Himes notes, calmly
proceeding to analyze his famous friend's remarkably boorish
behavior:

> I had never seen Dick behave so badly toward anyone but I
> realized that I was at fault. I had praised Alva so highly
> as a lady, he felt self-conscious around her and was furious
> with himself for feeling so. This caused a resentment that
> might have taken a vicious turn had it not been for me. The
> only comparison that I can make to his behavior that night
> is the characterization Laurence Olivier has given to Shake-
> speare's Othello. Perhaps Olivier has the key. Black people
> do show their resentment toward whites by accentuating the
> characteristics for which the whites judge them inferior.
> (*The Quality of Hurt*, 220)

The friendship survived, however, as it would much later survive
the strains resulting from Himes's open lack of enthusiasm for
Wright's attempts to turn toward more "universal" themes in his
work,[9] though the two writers' good-byes, when Himes left Paris
with Alva, were definitely on the chilly side: "I got a note from
Dick . . . asking me to come by and get the money I had loaned
him. I went by that afternoon and found him in bed. He gave me
a pinned bundle of notes the way they came from the banks and
told me he was leaving the next day for Ghana. . . . I wished him

9. Williams, "My Man Himes," pp. 50, 89–91.

a good trip and left. I hadn't sat down" (*The Quality of Hurt*, 220–21). Himes's final word on the episode was his "I liked Dick," with the supplementary observation: "When I deliberately avoided him it was simply because I didn't want to have to hurt him" (p. 224). It was, above all, their common legacy of hurt, the special experiences of the brilliantly gifted black man that both had known, that bound them with as firm a friendship as two notably "difficult" men have ever known.

The account of the friendship in *The Quality of Hurt*, a carefully weighed and measured account published more than a decade after Wright's death, must, however, be balanced against the slightly acid portrait of Wright that Himes included in the 1963 novella *Une Affaire de viol*. After Scott Hamilton and his three friends (who are also acid portraits of black Americans Himes knew in Paris) are sentenced to life terms in French prisons, one of Scott's friends, Roger Garrison, the world's most famous black American writer, who is permanently residing in Paris, attempts to reopen the case of the rape and murder of Lisbeth Hancock, and he launches his own investigation. But Roger Garrison is so blinded by his own racist preconceptions, his obsessive belief in a worldwide white conspiracy against black men, responsible for his own recent literary setbacks as well as his friends' imprisonment, that his efforts finally come to nothing. Further, it is revealed that Garrison himself, who had hated Lisbeth Hancock for her whiteness and her aristocratic bearing, had himself been the author of the nasty letter to Lisbeth's publisher that had started the whole unfortunate chain of events (*Une Affaire de viol*, 149, 162, 163). The description given of Roger Garrison's insulting behavior toward Lisbeth is essentially the same as the descriptions of Wright's behavior toward Alva in *The Quality of Hurt* (*Une Affaire de viol*, 112, 113). Under the cover of the novella, Himes openly charged his friend with a lack of sensitivity, specifically the special sensitivity needed to understand a love affair of great depth and beauty: "Garrison had been content to assume, brutally, that Mrs. Hancock was like all other white American women, that is, that she desired black men sexually and that she had come to Paris, like so many others, only to satisfy that desire, abandoning husband and children for the sole purpose of sharing Scott Hamilton's bed" (p. 112, my translation). It is an impressive indication of the extent of Himes's real regard for Richard Wright, and Alva, that he later took the trouble to re-dress the balance, to retouch rather fundamentally the angry caricatures presented in this novella, with the longer and much more judicious accounts of *The Quality of Hurt*. *Une Affaire de viol* is not without virtues—it is skillfully managed and quite amusing, if one is in a mood to chuckle at four Parisian Scotsboro boys who bear passing resemblances to Ollie Harrington, William Gardner Smith, James Baldwin, and Chester Himes[10]—but its virtues do not include dispassionate objectivity. Himes's Paris is best visited in the pages of *The Quality of Hurt*.

Richard Wright and Alva are the only two "characters" in *The Quality of Hurt*, that very frankly novelistic autobiography, to be given more than the most perfunctory, passing treatment, with the notable exceptions of a great many cats and dogs, and two great writers, Ralph Ellison and Robert Graves, both of whom are the subjects of quick but vivid sketches (pp. 95, 299, 306, 317).

The attention given to individual cats and dogs is so extensive, however, as to suggest that *The Quality of Hurt* might have been aptly subtitled: *A Few People, and Many Animals, I Have Known and Liked*. There is Uncle Tom, "a little cunning black-and-white mongrel," who shared caretaker duties with Chester and Jean Himes on a New Jersey estate, and managed to complicate their lives to the breaking point, and even a bit beyond:

> Whenever Uncle Tom got mad with us he'd go out to his house and draw the curtain and sulk. During the winter, when the lake was frozen over, he used to slip across the ice to the kitchen of the roadhouse to beg, although we punished

10. As Michel Fabre, in a long article on *Une Affaire de viol*, noted, how-ever, these "resemblances" are extremely hard to pin down: "When one tries to construe it as a *roman à clef* one is immediately shunted back from actual events into the world of fiction." Fabre also noted, on the basis of in-formation received from Himes himself, that *Une Affaire de viol*, written in 1956–1957, had originally been intended only as a kind of preliminary "synopsis" for a very long work: "a long, Dostoievskian work, possibly consisting of several volumes. The alleged 'rape' was only to be considered the unifying episode." Michel Fabre, "A Case of Rape," *Black World* (March 1972): 40.

him when we caught him; and once, during a quick thaw, he broke through the rotten ice in the middle of the lake. . . . we were sent for. I grabbed up an extension ladder and roared down to the lake in the old Mack truck . . . a brave village youth crawled out on the ladder and dragged him from the water. We rushed him back to the house and wrapped him in warm blankets and spoon-fed him brandy eggnog. Two days later he was fawning on the white people and disagreeable toward us as ever. (*The Quality of Hurt*, 107)

Then there is Jeff, another caretaker companion, a miniature pure-bred shepherd, "one of the bravest dogs I have ever known" (p. 118). And there is the cat Monsieur Berdoulas, "a long lean ancient insolent tom" (p. 231), who shared Yves Malartic's villa in Arcachon with Himes and Alva:

I first saw him several days after our arrival. He was in the paved court in the shade of the small maple tree, calmly eating one of the glistening white sole filets we'd left in the kitchen for lunch. I rushed toward him angrily and yelled, "Hey!" He gave me a brief cynical glance and continued calmly eating. I gave him a sound hiding with a bamboo garden rake, but he escaped through the loft of the garage and took the filet with him. The next day he returned and stole some fresh sardines.

I developed a great respect for M. Berdoulas. He took whatever he found that was edible, and accepted his beatings philosophically. Doubtless he reasoned if I derived as much pleasure out of beating him as he did out of eating our delectables, that made us even. In time he grew fond of me also, and would rub his scabby sides against my leg and give me a toothless grin. (*The Quality of Hurt*, 232)

The autobiography of a man who lives each moment as intensely and observes the passing scene as closely as Chester Himes, would obviously require more than one volume. Toward the end of *The Quality of Hurt* Himes takes a moment to describe himself, as he was on July 29, 1954, his forty-fifth birthday, ending with the remarks: "I had an almost unlimited vitality. All in all, I was an attractive man" (p. 316). Echoing Himes's own reaction as he finished Richard Wright's *Savage Holiday*, the reader of *The Quality of Hurt* may well remark, "I believe him."

There are, of course, also an abundance of warts on this scrupulously objective self-portrait, and, unfortunately, more than a few exasperating gaps. Himes frankly discusses his irrational antipathy for Robert Graves—"Graves noticed immediately that I had become resentful and tried to draw me into the conversation by asking what musical instrument I played. That always makes me angrier than any other question a white person can ask me. I told him I played the radio" (*The Quality of Hurt*, 306)—but nothing at all is said of the stresses and strains in his relationship with Louis Bromfield that led him to present a savage caricature of that early benefactor in *Lonely Crusade*.[11] Bromfield, described by his own daughter in a singularly affectionate memoir as "a stubborn, willful, mood-ridden, raging tyrant,"[12] should not have been unduly disturbed by the bullying eccentricity of his fictional Himesian namesake, Louis Foster, but presenting the great apostle of individualistic agrarian reform in the guise of a power-grubbing industrialist was surely a low blow, suggestive of a depth of antipathy that called for at least a few words of clarification in Himes's autobiography.

II Tragedy and Allegory

In the latter part of *The Quality of Hurt* Himes records the fate of a proposed anthology of his short stories that had been prepared for publication in 1954:

> Then I received [in Majorca] the collection of short stories that Donald Friede, the editor at World, had selected from the batch I had submitted for a book of short stories. I had been paid an advance of eight hundred dollars for a book to be called *Black Boogie Woogie*. When I read the stories again . . . they all seemed wrong and there was scarcely one that I was proud of having written. And when I considered the fact

11. See pp. 30, 128–29, this volume.
12. Ellen Geld, *The Heritage, A Daughter's Memories of Louis Bromfield* (New York: Harper and Brothers, 1962), p. 70.

that World had rejected both *The End of a Primitive* and *The Golden Chalice* and wished to publish this trash, I hated the stories. I didn't want my name attached to such a collection. I wrapped them up one morning and took them down to the bay and threw them into the sea. (*The Quality of Hurt*, 329)

By 1971, when he wrote the foreword to *Black on Black*, the selective anthology of his shorter works published by Doubleday in 1973, he had become much more tolerant toward the shortcomings of his own earlier writing, fully confident at last of the solidity of the talent he had drawn on so abundantly for so many years. "I think my talent is sufficient," he affirmed, "to render these . . . writings interesting, or at least provoking."[13] All but three of the Doubleday anthology's selections dated from the earliest part of his career, the 1930s and the 1940s, and they have been discussed, along with some of the stories Himes cast to the waves, in an earlier section of this study.[14]

Baby Sister, the earliest and the longest of the more recent pieces in *Black on Black*, is a film scenario, written, "at the instigation of European producers who thought the American film *Raisin in the Sun* was a failure" (p. 7), while Himes was living in Antibes in 1961. "French critics who read the scenario," Himes noted with quiet pride in his introductory remarks, "termed it a 'Greek tragedy' " (p. 7).[15] He was attempting a radically new genre with *Baby Sister*, but, perhaps to offset the difficulties of the new form, in writing it he drew upon very familiar material. The setting is Harlem and all of the characters closely resemble characters and character types that appear regularly in the detective novellas Himes was writing during the same period. The protagonist, a seventeen-year-old black girl with the bizarre name of Baby Sister Louis, has the "bedroom eyes," "big hard breasts molded in a tight sweater" and "big cushion-soft red-painted lips" that are standard issue for the luscious black damsels that Coffin Ed and

13. Himes, *Black on Black*, p. 7.
14. See pp. 31–69, this volume.
15. In his interview with Hoyt Fuller, Himes said that several NAACP leaders, furious over allusions to themselves they had found in *Pinktoes*, blocked the proposed filming of *Baby Sister* in Harlem (Fuller, "An Interview with Chester Himes," pp. 88, 89).

Grave Digger spend so much time threatening and choking, and occasionally rescuing (p. 12). And she "exudes" the same "effluvium of sex urgency" (p. 12). The most important secondary character, Baby Sister's hulking big brother, an uncontrollably violent and murderous hoodlum who is named, rather startlingly, Susie Louis, is immediately recognizable as a younger version of the familiar Luther McGregor type: "twenty-two years old, broad shoulders stretching the seams of a blue serge suit, strong lumpy face looking rock-hard."[16] In point of fact, Susie had already appeared briefly under his own name, two years before, in *The Big Gold Dream*.[17] Baby Sister's secret lover, the white police detective Lt. Timme Fischer, is a dead ringer for Matt Walker, of *Run Man Run*, without the psychotic overtones: "handsome enough to be a movie actor . . . tall and slender with a lean face and a tiny flickering smile, blue eyes, dark brown eyebrows, light blond hair with a slight wave" (p. 20).[18] All of this overly familiar material, however, has been cast in an authentically new frame, fundamentally different from both the uncomplicated, popular "heroic" mold of the standard Grave Digger-Coffin Ed stories and the terrifyingly absurd universe of *Blind Man with a Pistol* and *Run Man Run*. In form and theme, *Baby Sister* is, indeed, quite close to Greek tragedy. It is, at least in part, an exercise in awe before the phenomenon of human greatness, the classic tragic formula. It offers a protagonist who is larger than life, heroically intense, crushed by forces that are inexorable and irrational but also predictable and consistent. It has the stark simplicity of myth and the precise symmetry of ritual.

The greatness of the protagonist, Baby Sister, is in the sheer intensity with which the life force burns within her. The things she wants, attractive clothes, the attention of handsome men, the ecstatic thrills of dancing to loud, fast music, and sex laced with romance, are ordinary enough, but she pursues them with a singleness of purpose and a limitless enthusiasm that are astonishingly pure. She is an extraordinary human being, and it is the recognition of her uniqueness, her natural and unchallengeable superi-

16. See pp. 47, 49, 123, 219, this volume.
17. Cf. *The Big Gold Dream*, pp. 22, 116, 120, 152, 153.
18. See p. 253, this volume.

ority, by all those around her—and the unbearable desires it kindles in them—that makes her the focus of equally extraordinary dangers. She and the other five members of her family live in a tiny tenement apartment in Harlem's worst slum section. Her every entrance into the rank, crumbling, and crowded building she lives in is a kind of battle:

> *BABY SISTER* hurries up the stairs, passing numerous people. Every man she passes accosts her, tries to proposition her or rubs against her. She fends them off, some angrily, some laughingly, some flirtingly. The women avoid contact with her as though she is contaminated. (*Black on Black*, 38)

When her mother bursts into a tirade of indignation against Baby Sister's free and easy ways, Buddy, the middle brother, impatiently interrupts: "What do you expect, Ma, the way she got to live. Sleeping on a cot in the dining room, ain't got no place to dress; can't do nothing without everybody seeing, can't even go to the crapper without having to climb over everybody in the family" (p. 41). On the very day her father is buried, after being stabbed to death trying to defend her from two hoodlums who had seized her in the street, Baby Sister has to fight off two determined attempts at rape, one by the minister of her church and another by a mysterious unknown assailant in the dark tenement hall. The film's narrator, in the opening sequence, compares her to a lamb beset by savage wolves:

> Only the *will* of the community can save her from the wolves. But the inhabitants of this community, restricted, exploited, prostituted, violated and violent, timid and vicious, living in their rat-ridden, hotbox, stinking flats, are either the hungry wolves themselves, or are struggling desperately to save themselves from the hungry wolves. (*Black on Black*, 11)

By contrast, the family depicted by Lorraine Hansberry in *Raisin in the Sun* was distinctly upper crust.

The action of *Baby Sister* is crammed into three busy days, each ending with an explosion of violence around the person of Baby Sister. On the first day, the day of her father's funeral, Baby Sister seems to be hemmed in, to the point of suffocation, by eager, but inept protectors. Her youngest brother, Pigmeat, fourteen years old, sees her talking to Slick Collins, a notorious pimp, and begins to throw rocks at Slick's car to save her from whatever Slick has in mind. But Slick takes out after little Pigmeat with a flashing knife, in "a killing rage" (p. 13) and Baby Sister has to dash into church, "her tight skirt drawn up to her garter belt, exposing long brown legs, running hard and fast in her high heels, her hard buttocks jiggling" (p. 13), to fetch Susie to save Pigmeat. After Susie, "his big hard body in the tight blue suit moving like a football player's, his face swollen in a brutal rage" (p. 17), has broken Slick's jaw and rescued Pigmeat, he turns on Baby Sister, slapping her to the sidewalk. Older Sister Lil, a successful blues singer with her own apartment, then backs off Susie with a drawn knife— all the characters in the story, including Baby Sister, carry concealed knives—and Lt. Timme Fischer takes Baby Sister for a ride in his shiny official car, buys her a yellow dress, apologizes for having made her pregnant—"It was an accident." "An accident! Is that all it means to you?"—and assures her he has made arrangements for an abortion. Back at the tenement, Susie, coming on strong as usual, rips the yellow dress from Baby Sister and pursues her down the stairs and out into the street, where some passing workmen decide to rescue her and beat Susie to a pulp: "Come on then, boy, and kick him in the things" (p. 41). Baby Sister, eager to escape Susie, is picked up by a young black man in a fancy car, who almost gets into a knife fight himself a little later in his efforts to defend her, and, after some wild nightclubbing, she makes her way back to her home territory. There she must fight off the two rape attempts, the last one with the assistance of most of her family, who come running when she screams, her younger brothers armed with a meat cleaver and a butcher knife and her mother with "a red-handled fireman's ax" (p. 55). On the second day, however, Baby Sister's protectors all develop conspicuous feet of clay, and she is able to burst through their snarelike defenses to total freedom. Pigmeat, whose assiduity in following Baby Sister and spying on her verges on the abnormal, begins to be a little suspicious himself of older brother Susie's insensate brutality toward their lovely sister. "He always beating her up, more like she's his girl than his sister," he tells middle brother Buddy. Buddy could care less: "He always slipping back to her bed at night. Why don't you watch 'em, you want to know so bad" (p. 61). A few scenes later, Susie and the sinister pimp Slick, sitting side by side in barber chairs, with the barbers listening and "smiling cynically . . . as though they'd heard this kind of talk all their lives" (p. 71), discuss just how much money Susie ought to get for selling his sister to an established pimp. Later in the day, Baby Sister's family, "all, except Mama, who looks bewildered, seem gripped in horror and repulsion" (p. 87), as they come to the realization that the unknown assailant who tried to rape Baby Sister in the hall the night before was Susie. Susie, shamefaced and sullen, will give no more orders at home, and Baby Sister sets out triumphantly, and openly, for a night on the town, though before the evening is over she will have to scream for Susie—who shadows her at night almost as assiduously as Pigmeat does during the day—to save her from a jealous black woman who has attacked her with a knife in a posh night-club's powder room. On the third day, Baby Sister, at Lil's urging, consolidates her new freedom by appearing in Harlem's Apollo Theater's amateur contest, an absolutely reliable avenue to well-paid singing and entertainment jobs, and she wins so overwhelmingly that she is an instant celebrity: "*BABY SISTER* gives out with the naughty, suggestive song 'In the Night,' in the whining, breathless voice that goes with sexual intercourse, taking her body through all the motions. Again the audience goes wild" (p. 110). "She can't come to no harm, she famous now" (p. 114), a family friend complacently notes at the victory party that evening. But the prospect of Baby Sister's imminent departure, her definitive escape, drives both her dubious protectors and the hovering wolves to acts of insane desperation. Susie contemplates suicide. Pigmeat, with a gun sneakily provided by Slick, his jaw still sore, shoots at Lieutenant Fischer and Baby Sister, thinking that she is leaving with him—"I know I ain't gonna let you run away with no white man" (p. 115)—and Lieutenant Fischer returns the fire, killing the lovelorn boy, but he is unable to bring down the enraged Susie, who hurtles through a rain of bullets to plunge his knife into Fischer's heart, just before he falls dead himself. In the epilogue, the funeral of the two strange brothers —at which the rape-inclined minister repeates the same capsule sermon he had used at the father's funeral on the opening day— Baby Sister, who had secretly determined to bear Timme Fischer's baby after all, sits in the church with the remnants of her family, "(*screaming hysterically*) I can't stand it! I can't stand it!" (p. 120) and Lil, kissing her "consolingly," pleads, "Don't cry, baby, don't cry! Life ain't worth it" (p. 121).

The elemental violence that explodes so constantly around Baby Sister, ripping her hopes to shreds almost as quickly as they are formed, soiling them with ultimate degradation, threats of incest and prostitution, do excite pity and fear, the emotions traditionally associated with tragedy. The characters are neither subtle nor complex, but they do have the solidity and intensity necessary for tragedy. The forces mustered against Baby Sister Louis, however, are not precisely those of classical tragedy. She is deprived, not of justice, nor of the wisdom required to adjust one's expectations to the unbreakable and unbending patterns of life, society, and the world—deprivations of universal scope, that touch commoners and kings alike—but rather, quite simply, she is deprived of physical safety, freedom from assault. And a complete lack of physical security is a very special, not a universal condition, in a civilized society, a society that can create and enjoy the spectacle of human greatness, revealed in adversity, that is classical tragedy. Tragedy, the most selective of literary genres, deals only with the universal, not with the particular or the exceptional. What happens to Baby Sister could only happen under the very special conditions of degradation that exist in a slum. Baby Sister herself is triumphantly healthy, and splendidly vital, but the motivations of everyone around her are tainted with sickness. She is a victim of peculiar social conditions, a sickness that is in society itself, and her story, though very much like tragedy, is, in the final analysis, more nearly protest. The average reader, not alerted to the piece's "tragic" dimensions by Himes's foreword, must be moved, primarily, to abhor the conditions that produce a Pigmeat, a Susie, a Slick, or a Lieutenant Fischer, and only secondarily to admire the gallant, wonderfully alive Baby

Sister. And, though admiration is the special goal of tragedy, indignation belongs to the realm of protest. Whether it is regarded as tragedy or protest, however, the scenario like Susie, "erupts into motion as though exploding" (p. 116). It is one of the most consistently exciting stories that Himes ever wrote.

Himes had apparently assumed, in writing the scenario, that a film director should have no trouble in duplicating the effects he achieved in his novels with metaphor, allusion, and suggestion, and he set his potential director such knotty problems—"The atmosphere is gay, loose, whorish and fascinating" (p. 102)—that no director who was not absolutely confident of his genius would attempt to film *Baby Sister* yet the scenario clearly holds the possibilities, if approached with due respect for its qualities of ritual, fantasy, and myth, of a truly remarkable film. Only a freely imaginative, frankly expressionistic treatment could possibly succeed, however; filmed in a determinedly "realistic" style, *Baby Sister* would emerge as little more than a sordid and brutal chronicle of the seamier side of slum life.

Like the scenario *Baby Sister*, the short stories "Tang" (1967) and "Prediction" (1969), the other recent pieces in *Black on Black* represent excursions into a highly specialized, and rather archaic genre: allegory. Allegory is essentially the presentation of an abstract concept, a very definite idea or set of ideas, in the form of a story. Its objects are persuasion, conversion, conviction. It is the most purely didactic of literary genres. The point of departure for the writer is always the abstract idea itself, and the story evolves from it, with the idea retaining its primacy at all times. Himes had used allegory before, in his days as a Civil Rights activist in the 1940s,[19] and the pivotal idea then had been that if all the black people in America stood together and spoke with a common voice to demand their rights the "big white God" would have to listen, and send Old Jim Crow to hell. This concept is essentially the one he had presented in his 1944 essay "Negro Martyrs are Needed,"[20] in which he called upon outstanding black individuals to take the first dangerous steps needed to make such a united stand. It was

19. See pp. 59ff., this volume.
20. See pp. 61–62, this volume.

the standard message of the Civil Rights leadership of the time, presented with total conviction. In the stories he wrote in 1967 and 1969, however, the basic idea was radically different.

In his conversations with John A. Williams, Himes stated that when he was ready to write the later volumes of his autobiography, covering the events of his career after 1954, the most important single development to be described would be the "change in my attitudes toward the entire American scene, and my change from pessimism to optimism."[21] He explained that he had become convinced that a violent uprising, a revolution, by the black people of America against the white establishment and power structure, could be successful. He had, in fact, begun to write a book, a visionary novel, "the bloodiest book that [he had] ever worked on,"[22] in which he intended to embody his conviction, in full detail, and the two *Black on Black* stories appear to be early results of that effort.

> Well, yes, because I can see what a black revolution would be like. Now, first of all, in order for a revolution to be effective, one of the things that it has to be, is violent, it has to be massively violent. . . . in any form of uprising, the major objective is to kill as many people as you can, by whatever means you can kill them, because the very fact of killing them and killing them in sufficient number is supposed to help you gain your objectives. . . .
>
> Now, when you have resorted to these means, this is the last resort. Well, then, all dialogue ceases, all forms of petitions and other goddamned things are finished. All you do then is you kill as many people as you can, the black people kill as many of the people of the white community as they can kill. . . .
>
> . . . So I am trying to show how this follows, how the violence would be if the blacks resorted to this. . . . What I'm trying to do is depict the violence that is necessary so that the white community will also give it a little thought, because you know, they're going around playing these games. They haven't given any thought to what would happen if the black people would *seriously* uprise.

21. Williams, "My Man Himes," p. 44.
22. Ibid., pp. 44–45.

... Because one thing is sure—I have said this and I keep on saying it over and over again—the black man can bring America down, he can destroy America. The black man can destroy the United States.[23]

The message spelled out this time, with the singular emphasis and clarity of allegory, would be the standard message of the black militants of the 1960s and 1970s, addressed less to the conscience of an entire nation than to the wellsprings of anger and hate in the hearts of its oppressed minority and to the deep fears of the oppressive majority.

"Tang" is a solemn warning to the black community, a warning about the traitors within. The story's two characters are a bedraggled black prostitute, Tang, and her equally bedraggled and hungry pimp, T-bone Smith. They represent the final result of all the pressures that have degraded the black American community through the centuries. They look very much alike but their characters are very different, because Tang has kept her heart, her soul, free of the degradation, and T-bone Smith has not. It is set sometime in the future, the eve of the black revolution, and a messenger delivers a very sophisticated automatic rifle to their "cold-water slum flat" in Harlem, with a note warning them of the need for absolute secrecy. T-bone immediately determines that he must inform the police. " 'Uprising?' He shied away from the thought as though it were a rattlesnake" (p. 136). Tang seizes the rifle, tries to intimidate T-bone with it. " 'You going to tell whitey?' she asked in surprise. 'You going run tell the man 'bout this secret that'll make us free?' " (p. 137). But T-bone, though he has a servile slave mentality, is a very dangerous man, and it is Tang who lies dead on the floor at the end of their confrontation. John Brown, more than a century before, had found that the militant abolitionist's call for insurrection could fall on unreceptive black

23. Ibid., pp. 45–46. In his interview with Hoyt Fuller, Himes suggested that a black revolution in America "would result in the death of three million people . . . most, or at least two-thirds . . . Black people themselves," a notable escalation from the figure of "125,000 dead Black men in America," the absolute maximum which "the American morality . . . could . . . sustain," that he had given in a 1945 *Chicago Defender* article (Fuller, "An Interview with Chester Himes," pp. 18, 92).

ears, and a latter-day, black John Brown must be prepared to find the paralyzing fears engendered by the unspeakable experience of slavery still deeply entrenched.

"Prediction" is a lesson in tactics, a demonstration of the impact that a single urban guerrilla, armed with an ultramodern automatic weapon, could have, if he picked the time and place of his attack with sufficient skill. It throws into high relief the extraordinary vulnerability of the modern American city to any such attack. In his preface to the 1969 novel *Blind Man with a Pistol*, Himes stated, "all unorganized violence is like a blind man with a pistol" (p. 5), and he spelled out that notion, in simple allegorical form, in the novel's culminating episode, in which a blind elderly black man tries to shoot a white man who has slapped him and only succeeds in killing another black man and one white police officer before he himself is gunned down by the white police (pp. 220–38). In "Prediction," however, the black guerrilla is launching a revolution with a one-man suicide attack, and represents premeditated, planned, organized violence, as against the unorganized blind-man variety, has picked his weapon, his defenses, and his targets with great care. He is crouched down, inside a large metropolitan cathedral, behind the poor-box slot in the cathedral's massive door, a slot that is impossible to see from even a short distance away. A parade of six thousand marching white police officers is passing on the avenue outside, and the sidestreets are densely packed with spectators. The black gunman's heart is pure, his resolve inflexible, "He would have to do it alone, without comfort or encouragement, consoled only by the hope that it would make life safer for the blacks in the future" (p. 282). His weapon is "a heavy-caliber blued steel automatic rifle of a foreign make" (p. 282). Before the police riot tank arrives to destroy him—and much of the cathedral as well, killing hordes of innocent bystanders in the process—the lone gunman has killed "seventy-three whites, forty-seven policemen and twenty-six men, women and children civilians, and . . . wounded an additional seventy-five" (p. 286). Himes spares the reader no detail of the carnage: "In a matter of seconds the streets were strewn with . . . nasty gray blobs of brains, hairy fragments of skull looking like sections of broken coconuts" (p. 284). The militant martyr's attack is a huge success: "In the wake of this bloody massacre the stock market crashed. The dollar fell on the world market. . . . Confidence in the capitalistic system had an almost fatal shock" (p. 287).

And Chester Himes had demonstrated that allegory, that moldy medieval relic of a genre, can have immense impact when it is addressed to contemporary problems, when it is used, for example, to give graphic form to the hellish dangers that confront modern man, "for his sins."

III Trading Punches: Himes and the Critics

"Yes, the Negro is deprived of his vote and sometimes of his life in many Southern states but where else in the world can a person yell as loud and long about it except in America?"[24] triumphantly demanded the staff writers who penned Ebony's "Thanksgiving" editorial in November 1947, pointedly addressing all those who sympathized with Chester Himes and his latest novel, Lonely Crusade, "an invidious, shocking, incendiary work," "a virulent, malicious book full of rancor and venom," a novel that "answers white hate with Negro hate, substitutes emotions for intelligence, dictates thinking with the skin rather than the brains." The Ebony piece was, of course, ostensibly an editorial rather than a book review, and it was therefore entirely proper that its opening remarks on Himes's Lonely Crusade should quickly lead into a detailed exposition of the writers' own views on what they assumed to be the broad general themes of Himes's novel. They even perfunctorily expressed gratitude to Chester Himes for his arduous labors in setting up the target they intended to belabor: "Himes is not exaggerating for today there are many Lee Gordons who in counteracting race discrimination have become guilty of every crime of which they accuse their enemies. . . . have indulged in hates and prejudices as rabid." The Ebony editors had come not to bury Chester but to shout the praises of the land of the Thanksgiving turkey:

24. "Ebony Photo Editorial: Time to Count Our Blessings," Ebony (November 1947): 44; cf. Ebony (February 1948): 7, for reader reaction to this editorial.

But with all that, is it so terrible to be a Negro in the United States?

Certainly not!

American Negroes live a more prosperous, more enjoyable, more creative life than at least 90 per cent of the world's population.

The *Ebony* piece is, nevertheless, remarkably typical of a large proportion of the reviews that Chester Himes's books have received in America. Reviewers have all too often felt called upon to answer the verbal violence of a Himes book with some choice verbal violence of their own. "Himes . . . writes in a jive style that lumps sex, 'race' and politics into a series of firecracker-strung words. I suspect he wants you to 'trade punches' with him," remarked Earl Conrad of the *Chicago Defender* in a 1945 interview-review piece on the author of *If He Hollers Let Him Go*.[25] Himes's books seemed to appeal directly to the hidden editorialist that lurks in most reviewers, and many responded eagerly to the implied challenge to "trade punches" with him.

Reviewers have been particularly prone to scold Himes for the attitudes toward race they found in his books. Earl Conrad delivered the blow in a personal conversation with Himes:

I couldn't help but notice the repeated use of the term "race consciousness," and I slipped the remark, "You know there's only one race, the human race."

It struck me that Himes jarred visibly, that possibly nobody had ever said quite the same thing to him.[26]

Almost thirty years later, in a *Saturday Review* article on *The Quality of Hurt*, Richard Gaines repeated the blow, in much the same form: "The racial tribalism implied in [Himes's] use of 'soul brother' also put me off, believing as I do that no race has a monopoly on soul and that all men are brothers."[27] Richard

25. Earl Conrad, "American Viewpoint: Blues School of Literature," *Chicago Defender* (December 22, 1945): 11. Conrad gave credit for the expression "trade punches," with reference to Himes, to Dr. L. D. Reddick, curator of the Schomburg Collection of the New York Public Library, in a private discussion of the book.

26. Ibid.

27. Richard Gaines, *Saturday Review* (April 15, 1972): 69.

Rhodes, in a singularly complacent review, and selective reading, of *Blind Man with a Pistol* in the New York *Times*, used an open accusation of racial intolerance (antiblack) as his "punch" line, "At the risk of seeming captious, I must assert from the evidence of 'Blind Man With a Pistol,' that Chester Himes is prejudiced."[28] Anthony Boucher, in a "Criminals at Large" piece in the *Times*, was content to hover on the brink of the same conclusion, in a distinctly unenthusiastic review of *Cotton Comes to Harlem·* "If a white writer created so many shiftless or vicious denizens of Harlem, he would be accused of using derogatory stereotypes. But since Himes is himself a Negro, it would appear that the enjoyment of these cruel and fantastic nightmares is *au fait* rather than ofay."[29] Edward Margolies, a critic who has written on Himes at some length[30] expressed, in an extended *Saturday Review* essay on *Blind Man with a Pistol*, very similar misgivings before the "derogatory stereotypes" of Himes's detective fiction, though, at the same time, recognizing their claim to literary validity: "On the one hand Himes' Harlemites are terribly sophisticated. . . . But there are other occasions when Himes images his blacks in such minstrel-like caricature . . . such Amos'n'Andy dialogue . . . that it sounds as if he were telling a 'nigger joke'. . . . the joke is on the whites as well—all caught up in the absurdity of racism, the meanness of violence that reduces their humanity to cartoon dimensions."[31]

Sex was, of course, another subject area in which sharp, critical raps on the knuckles were often judged necessary. Himes's taste in this area was called into question almost routinely, by critics concerned with displaying, as the case might be, either broadly urbane tolerance or the rigorous purity of their own standards, and, occasionally, both at the same time. The rather sedate *Library Journal*, for example, allowed *Cotton Comes to Harlem* to slip by—"It may shock some but the final thrust is hilarious"—

28. Richard Rhodes, *The New York Times Book Review* (February 23, 1969): 32.

29. Anthony Boucher, "Criminals at Large," *The New York Times Book Review* (February 7, 1965): 43.

30. See Selected Bibliography.

31. Edward Margolies, "America's Dark Pessimism," *Saturday Review* (March 22, 1969): 65.

but drew the line at *Pinktoes*: "Although Mr. Himes' purposiveness is evident, his between-the-sheets approach is too much. . . . it is . . . not for libraries."[32] Equally authoritative, W. R. Burnett in *Saturday Review* speedily lowered the boom on the Jimmy-Dido relationship in *Cast the First Stone*: "a feverish account of a love affair between two young men serving long sentences for armed robbery. Although the author—frank otherwise—insists on calling this business 'friendship,' it bears no resemblance whatsoever to any sort of friendship I've ever noted or experienced."[33] Sturdy unflappability, even a touch of boredom, in the face of the deliberately risqué, was, however, clearly the unkindest cut of all; "Mr. Himes tee-hees interminably over the devil beneath all skins," yawned one critic of *Pinktoes*.[34]

Some reviewers were less punchers and jabbers than pushers and shovers. Feeling that Himes was leading his readers in the wrong direction, sociologically, ethically, or spiritually, they elected to interpose themselves between the author and the reader, shouldering Himes aside to advance their own "corrective" interpretations of the characters and events of his novels. These are the kindest, and cruelest, of critics. Roy Wilkins, in the *Crisis* review of *If He Hollers Let Him Go*, while making it absolutely clear that no condemnation of Himes was intended—"Every book on the race problem does not have to offer a 'solution.' Some can be merely protest books. Such a one is 'If He Hollers Let Him Go' "—authoritatively noted that Bob Jones is "wrong and foolish,"—"Most Negroes will be puzzled by his lack of an objective and a plan for attaining it"—and that "Alice, his sweetheart, talks common sense to him."[35] Henry Winslow, continuing the tradition in his own *Crisis* reviews, pronounced Kriss and Jesse of *The Primitive* "two unworthy souls," Lillian of *The Third Generation* "foremostly a fool," and openly rejoiced at Dido's grisly suicide by hanging in *Cast the First Stone*: "Never was there a more justi-

32. *Library Journal*, February 1, 1965, and April 1, 1965.

33. W. R. Burnett, "Helpless Waiting," *Saturday Review* (January 17, 1953): 15.

34. Martin Levin, *The New York Times Book Review* (August 15, 1965): 30.

35. Roy Wilkins, "Blind Revolt," *The Crisis* (December 1945): 361–62.

fiable fate than that which comes to the pathetic creation that was Dido."[36]

The lowest blow of all, however, was the suggestion that Himes, as an aging expatriate, had lost touch with the current black scene, that he had come to lack the most vital commodity of all: up-to-dateness. "Expatriates do sometimes suffer a kind of arrested development; their native land and their countrymen remain always as they left them," noted Nathan Huggins in his review of *The Quality of Hurt*, "This book, then, is perhaps directed to American readers of the early 1950's."[37] "Sometimes the tale is reminiscent of Harlem in the 1920's, rather than of the present time in which it is set," observed Richard Shepard, in his review of *Run Man Run*.[38] David Llorens, also reviewing *Run Man Run*, for *Negro Digest*, found in Himes's "sociology," "no apparent defects for having lived a number of years outside of this country," and then proceeded to cavil at length over Himes's use of the strange term "mother-raper," though largely in a spirit of pure fun: "*Run Man Run*, I think, is not his best yarn, but Chester Himes is, to be sure, a writing mother-what-have-you."[39]

But the game of trading punches with critics, in fun or in earnest, was not at all to the taste of Chester Himes. He expected from critics, if not exactly the kind of "adulation" Jimmy Monroe had received from the convicts in the cripple company before his affair with Dido, at least a full measure of sympathetic support. He did not understand, or refused to understand, how easily his books could goad readers into assuming a fighting, or hypercritical stance, and every unfavorable review he read kindled in him a strong urge to retaliate, which he usually managed to resist, but

36. Henry Winslow, *The Crisis* (April 1953): 246, 247; (April 1954): 247, 248; (November 1956): 571, 572.

37. Nathan Huggins, *The New York Times Book Review* (March 12, 1972): 32.

38. Richard Shepard, *New York Times* (November 12, 1966): 27.

39. David Llorens, *Negro Digest* (July 1967): 78, 79. Brooks Johnson, reviewing *The Heat's On* in *Negro Digest* (March 1966): 96, hit the basic point even harder: "The reader is left with the feeling that Mr. Himes would have been better off to have returned to Harlem to restudy some of the patterns and vernacular that now are in vogue, rather than depending on his memory for things about Harlem that were true before he left there for residence in Paris."

not always. Early in 1946, in an article in *Saturday Review* aimed at the critical establishment in general, he concluded with a point-by-point refutation of the more important criticisms directed at *If He Hollers Let Him Go* by defiantly, and imperiously, defining borders beyond which future critics must not venture: "I have decided it is my small, self-appointed task to write the truth as I see it. . . . and the only thing critics may say that will ever influence me is to correct my technique."[40] Two years later, Himes replied to Milton Klonsky's review of *Lonely Crusade* in *Commentary*—an awesomely lofty exercise in intellectual snobbism in which the whole of "American mob culture," typified both by *Lonely Crusade* and "the grafitti in the men's rooms," is roundly damned—with an angry open letter to the magazine's editors, pitching at Klonsky retorts and innuendos as viciously and inexcusably personal as those that the *Ebony* editors had recently aimed at him: "Reactions as expressed in Mr. Klonsky's comments come only from subconscious disturbances within the individual. *Lonely Crusade* has touched upon such a disturbance in Mr. Klonsky's personality to bring forth this geyser of vituperation."[41] Himes gleefully treasured several conspicuously ornate phrases from John Brooks's faintly condescending review of *The Third Generation* in the New York *Times*—"Mr. Himes seems to have set out to grip the reader in a vise of despair," "the whole seems at times to lack a certain necessary measure of animal fun"—and he later worked them into the pompous pronouncements of Mr. Pope in *The Primitive*.[42] He "settled" with the *Ebony* editors in much the same fashion in the same novel.[43] As the years passed, however, Himes did acquire some degree of tolerance for the frailties of critics. In 1972 Nathan Huggins virulently denounced *The Quality of Hurt* in his New York *Times* review as "a vacuous and unimportant autobiography" that had failed to provide "a single clue to what Himes has stood for or

40. Chester Himes, "*If He Hollers Let Him Go*," *Saturday Review* (February 16, 1946): 12; see pp. 73, 202, this volume.

41. Milton Klonsky, "The Writing on the Wall," *Commentary* (February 1948): 189–90; Chester Himes, *Commentary* (May 1948): 474.

42. John Brooks, "Tragedy in Sepia," *The New York Times Book Review* (January 10, 1954): 29. See p. 7, this volume.

43. See p. 200, this volume.

on, except perhaps for the pleasure of his personal pain," that had also utterly failed in its obligation, incumbent on all black writing, to be "direct, straightforward, honest, self-critical, socially critical, and proud."[44] Huggins's review drew a direct, angry reply from the black writer Julius Lester, a devoted fan of Himes, "To me [Huggins's] comment was . . . so unkind and cruel in tone that I couldn't help feeling he was not reviewing a book but settling an old score."[45] In an interview with *Publishers Weekly*, however, Himes refuted Huggins's implied thesis that all black writers must be spokesmen for the race in the very mildest of tones: "They aren't looking for any 'spokesmen.' They can speak for themselves. The best a black writer can do is to deal with subjects which are personal; so he can tell how it was for him."[46]

Himes did tend, however, to see the hostility, or condescension, implied in reviews in highly exaggerated terms. Even *Lonely Crusade*, despite Himes's insistence to the contrary,[47] did not receive uniformly hostile reviews. *Negro Digest* ran the novel's third chapter as a "book digest," prefaced by Carl Van Vechten's glowing tribute, "This novel boasts such power of expression and such subtlety of treatment, that I, for one, am not afraid to call this book GREAT."[48] Arthur Burke's review of the novel in *The Crisis* was almost unreservedly laudatory from beginning to end (though he did off-handedly refer to Lee Gordon as "a plain rat," suggest that Lee's maturation was "needlessly melodramatic at times," and lament the "coarseness of a few passages").[49] Eric McKitrick in *Saturday Review*, was also full of praise for the book, and he took the trouble to squeeze all of his reservations, which are mild enough, into a single sentence: "Chester Himes has given us a psychologically unstable protagonist; to stay with him often requires that the reader's sympathies work

44. Huggins, *The New York Times Book Review* (March 12, 1972): 5, 32.
45. Julius Lester, *The New York Times Book Review* (April 30, 1972): 39.
46. Michael Mok, "Chester Himes," *Publishers Weekly* (April 3, 1972): 20.
47. See p. 133, this volume.
48. "Lonely Crusade," *Negro Digest* (December 1947): 83–96.
49. Arthur Burke, "The Pathology of Race," *The Crisis* (January 1948): 27.

overtime, and the events in the story run a dizzy race with credibility."[50] Nash K. Burger, in the New York *Times*, though with similar reservations about the novel's "psychopathic protagonist," nevertheless wholeheartedly endorsed the book: "Lee Gordon operates in a tough, jungle world, and Mr. Himes presents it like it is."[51] Stoyan Christowe, in the *Atlantic Monthly*, complained of *Lonely Crusade*'s poor organization, its "long generalizations and oversimplifications," mournfully noted, "Hatred reeks through [Himes's] pages like yellow bile," but he pronounced the book "a brave and courageous probing into the Negro psyche."[52] Arna Bontemps, in the New York *Herald Tribune*, had some definite reservations—"This is not exactly the mood in which to work for any kind of progress, and those who look to *Lonely Crusade* for a chart are likely to turn away sour"—but he had strong words of praise as well: "Chester Himes' talent, apparent to many in *If He Hollers Let Him Go*, has produced an even more provocative book this time."[53] Even James Baldwin, who, in his *New Leader* review, hit the book harder than almost any other reviewer—"the most uninteresting and awkward prose I have read in recent years," "the resolution—the holding aloft of the union banner—leaves one with that same embarrassed rage produced by a reading of *Invictus*"—found more than a few hard truths about the black experience effectively spelled out in the book, and his few grudging words of praise have the ring of unmistakable sincerity: "The book, nevertheless, has flashes of power and insight," "[Himes's] integrity has actually the cumulative effect of making him seem far wiser and more skillful than he is."[54]

50. Eric McKitrick, "Through Many Eyes," *Saturday Review* (October 25, 1947): 25.

51. Nash K. Burger, "Fear in Our Midst," *The New York Times Book Review* (September 14, 1947): 20.

52. Stoyan Christowe, *The Atlantic Monthly* (October 1947): 138.

53. Arna Bontemps, *New York Herald Tribune Weekly Book Review* (September 7, 1947): 8. This review is one of those discussed in some detail in Carl Milton Hughes's *The Negro Novelist*, pp. 210, 211.

54. James Baldwin, "History as Nightmare," *The New Leader* (October 25, 1947): 11, 15.

Himes, it seems clear, did not consciously choose to be controversial—he wanted to be popular, even extremely popular—but, he was in fact controversial. His books spurred readers to think about and react to subjects that invariably inspire anger. Something deep within himself—Baldwin's use of the word *integrity* seems an apt choice—had chosen for him the roughest road available, and he could hardly blame the critics for that. But, as a novelist, a man in the business of making verbal scale models of the world as he has known it, felt it, and lived it, as a constructor of elaborate extended metaphors designed to guide readers into his own unique and private realm of experience, Chester Himes did, fairly often, have legitimate grounds for complaint against critics who refused to accord him his full share of artistic license, refused to respect fully his need to write subjectively in one of the most highly subjective of literary genres.

IV   The Not-impossible Himes, and the Real Himes

What would Chester Himes's career have been like had he not been exposed to racist pressures? In the case of a black writer such a question is not as futile as what-might-have-been speculations generally are, because so many of the results of the limitations imposed on black Americans are easily identifiable. Himes's failure to obtain a university education, for example, was a direct result of the policies of racial segregation that were tolerated by the university authorities in Columbus. His dismissal from his brief try-out position as a script writer in Hollywood was caused by the racist policies of the studio management. His failure to hold down a decent job during the war boom in California and build up the savings he needed to keep his first marriage afloat was another direct result of the rampant racism of that time. And the effects on his literary career are equally obvious. His early choice of genres was limited by what the public would then accept as serious writing from a black man: realistic "protest" fiction.

A Himes free from racist limitations might have sought a career in the theater and developed into an outstanding innovator of new forms in that plastic medium, entirely free from what he has called "the whole nightmare of the novel form."[55] Had he remained a novelist, he would certainly have given a freer rein to his flair for fantasy and his taste for structural and stylistic experiments. Of course, there never could have been a tactful or a nonabrasive Himes, and whatever his choice of themes and media might have been, a great many critics would have found his treatment of them violently and deliberately offensive.

The visible effects of racism on its victims, however, are like the peak of the proverbial iceberg. The psychological effects, for example, of spending an hour a day just hating the white folks, the fate of the black man in Himes's classic parody protest sketch (*The Primitive*, 44),[56] are rather difficult to measure. This involuntary effusion of hate, that has become a part of yourself, as regular and inescapable as breathing, is not really very much like hating the people who laughed at you the last time you made a fool of yourself. Oppression injures the mind, the soul, in dark and mysterious ways.

Racism, the hurts it inflicts, and all the tangled hates, is the dominant subject of the literary works that Chester Himes actually did produce. He did not choose the subject. It was thrust upon him. He did not at first even choose the literary forms that he used. But he drove deeper into the subject than anyone ever had before. He recorded what happens to a man when his humanity is questioned, the rage that explodes within him, the doubts that follow, and the fears, and the awful temptation to yield, to embrace degradation. If you lock up a first-rate literary talent for a lifetime in a small box, it will give you a complete statement of how it feels to be locked up in that particular box. It is a simple situation, but a complex experience. And being caught in a trap, boxed-in, in one way or another, is perhaps the essence of the modern experience. Himes has had the advantage —dubious but real—of a highly visible trap. Racism was Chester Himes's box, and he has produced, in the form of a long series

55. Fuller, "An Interview with Chester Himes," p. 15.
56. See p. 216, this volume.

of novels, both heavy and light, what was, arguably, the most complete and perfect statement of the nature of native American racism to be found in American literature, and one of the most profound statements about the nature of social oppression, and the rage and fear it generates in individuals, in all of modern literature.

Selected Bibliography

Primary Sources

There are no standard editions of the works of Chester Himes. Many of his works are not readily available in any edition. The editions listed below are those I found the most readily available. Additional information concerning editions is provided in the text and footnotes.

Himes, Chester. *Une Affaire de viol* (*A Case of Rape*). Translated by André Mathieu. Paris: Les Yeux Ouverts, 1963.

————. *All Shot Up*. New York: Berkley Publishing Corporation, 1960. Published by The Hearst Corp., Avon Books, 1960. Translated into French by J. Fillion as *Imbroglio negro* (*Negro Imbroglio*). Série Noire 601. Paris: Gallimard, 1960. Originally titled *Don't Play with Death*.

————. *The Big Gold Dream*. New York: The Hearst Corp., Avon Books, 1960. Translated into French by Yves Malartic as *Tout pour plaire* (*Everything to Please*). Série Noire. Paris: Gallimard, 1959.

————. *Black on Black*. New York: Doubleday & Co., Inc., 1973.

————. *Cast the First Stone*. New York: The Times Mirror Co., New American Library, Inc., A Signet Novel, 1972.

————. *Cotton Comes to Harlem*. New York: Dell Publishing Co., Inc., 1970. Published by G. P. Putnam's Sons, 1965. Translated into French by Pierre Sergent as *Retour en Afrique* (*Back to Africa*). Paris: Plon, 1964. Basis of the 1970 film *Cotton Comes to Harlem*.

————. *The Crazy Kill*. New York: Berkley Publishing Corporation, 1966. Published by The Hearst Corp., Avon Books, 1959. Translated into French by J. Hérisson and Henri Robillot as *Couché dans le pain* (*Stretched Out on Bread*). Série Noire 522. Paris: Gallimard, 1959. Originally titled *A Jealous Man Can't Win*.

————. *The Heat's On*. New York: Berkley Publishing Corporation, 1972. Translated into French by J. Fillion as *Ne nous énervons pas* (*Be Calm*). Série Noire 640. Paris: Gallimard, 1961. Basis of the 1972 film *Come Back Charleston Blue*.

————. *Hot Day, Hot Night*. New York: Dell Publishing Co., Inc., 1970. Published as *Blind Man with a Pistol* by William Morrow and Company, Inc., 1969. Translated into French by Henri Robillot as *L'Aveugle au pistolet*. Paris: Gallimard, 1970.

————. *If He Hollers Let Him Go*. New York: The Times Mirror Co., New American Library, Inc., A Signet Novel, 1971.

————. *Lonely Crusade*. New York: Alfred A. Knopf, Inc., 1947.

————. *For Love of Imabelle*. New York: Dell Publishing Co., Inc., 1971. Published by Fawcett World Library, Gold Medal Books, 1957 (chapter divisions altered in later editions). Published as *A Rage in Harlem* by Avon and Panther Books of London, 1965. Translated into French by Minnie Danzas as *La Reine des pommes*. Série Noire 419. Paris: Gallimard, 1958. Originally titled *The Five-Cornered Square*.

————. *Pinktoes*. New York: Dell Publishing Co., Inc., 1966. Published in Paris by Olympia Press, 1961. Translated into French by Henri Collard as *Mamie Mason, ou un exercice de la bonne volonté*. Paris: Plon, 1962 (does not contain many of the more ribald passages of the English version).

————. *The Primitive*. New York: The Times Mirror Co., New American Library, Inc., A Signet Novel, 1955.

————. *The Quality of Hurt: The Autobiography of Chester Himes, Volume I*. New York: Doubleday & Co., Inc., 1972.

————. *The Real Cool Killers*. New York: Berkley Publishing Corporation, 1966. Published by The Hearst Corp., Avon Books, 1959. Translated into French by Chantal Wourgaft as *Il pleut des coups durs* (*It's Raining Hard Knocks*). Série Noire 446. Paris: Gallimard, 1958. Originally titled *If Trouble Was Money*.

————. *Run Man Run*. New York: Dell Publishing Co., Inc., 1969. Published by G. P. Putnam's Sons, 1966. Translation of an early draft into French by Pierre Verrier as *Dare-dare* (*Double-quick Time*). Série Noire 492. Paris: Gallimard, 1959.

————. *The Third Generation*. New York: The Times Mirror Co., New American Library, Inc., A Signet Novel, 1956.

Secondary Sources

Bone, Richard. "The Protest Novel," in *The Negro Novel in America*, pp. 173–76. New Haven, Conn.: Yale University Press, 1958.

Fabre, Michel. "*A Case of Rape*." *Black World* 21:5 (March 1972): 39–48. A French view of Himes's novella and its "often scathing evocation of the prejudices encountered by Black exiles in Paris."

————. "Ecrire, une tentative pour révéler l'absurdité de la vie," and "Un redoutable argot." *Le Monde des livres* (November 13, 1970): 20–21.

————. "A Tentative Check List, A Selected Bibliography of Chester Himes," *Black World* 21:5 (March 1972), 76–78. Useful bibliography.

Fuller, Hoyt W. "Traveler on the Long, Rough, Lonely Old Road: An Interview with Chester Himes." *Black World* 21:5 (March 1972), 4–22, 87–98. A freewheeling interview with Himes.

Hughes, Carl Milton. *The Negro Novelist*. New York: Citadel Press, Inc., 1953. Perceptive readings of *If He Hollers Let Him Go* and *Lonely Crusade*, with useful summaries of magazine reviews (pp. 68–76, 206–12).

Margolies, Edward. "Race and Sex: The Novels of Chester Himes," in *Native Sons: A Critical Study of Twentieth-Century Negro American Authors*, pp. 87–101. Philadelphia and New York: J. B. Lippincott Company, 1968. Brief but cogent (though generally negative) analyses of five of Himes's major works (*If He Hollers Let Him Go, Lonely Crusade, The Third Generation, The Primitive, Pinktoes*), suggesting several unifying themes: America's "dehumanized culture" symptomized by its racism, and "the emasculating effects of racism" on black intellectuals.

————. "The Thrillers of Chester Himes." *Studies in Black Literature* (June 1970), 1–11.

————. "America's Dark Pessimism, *Blind Man with a Pistol* by Chester Himes." *Saturday Review* (March 22, 1969): 59, 64–65. Critiques less negative in tone, despite the "pop-campy dime-detective format" of Himes's thrillers, than those devoted to the earlier works in *Native Sons*.

Micha, René. "Les Paroissiens de Chester Himes." *Les Temps modernes* (February 1965), 1507–23. Finds Himes's detective novels—in which free rein is given to the ecstatic delight he feels before the inexhaustible kaleidoscope of Harlem and the Harlemites, and to his own bounteous sense of fun and fantasy —clearly superior in interest to the early "major" works, burdened by too-visible theses and a decidedly nineteenth-century concept of the novel form.

Nelson, Raymond. "Domestic Harlem: The Detective Fiction of Chester Himes." *The Virginia Quarterly Review* 48 (Spring 1972): 260–76. Traces a firm line of development into—and then out of—the traditional forms of the genre; finds sociological importance in Himes's studies of Harlem's criminal "institutions," "explained in minute detail, often through portraits of the individual personalities they have helped to shape."

Reed, Ishmael. "The Author and his Works, Chester Himes: Writer." *Black World* 21:5 (March 1972), 24–38. A brilliant young black writer's personal perceptions of some of Himes's major work.

Williams, John A. "My Man Himes: An Interview with Chester Himes," in *Amistad I*, pp. 25–95, eds. John A. Williams and Charles F. Harris. New York: Random House, Inc., Vintage Books, 1970. As useful to the student of Himes as *The Quality of Hurt* itself; a beautifully structured interview, accompanied by a useful bibliography.